YOUNG MUSLIMS, PEDAGOGY AND ISLAM

Contexts and Concepts

M.G. Khan

First published in Great Britain in 2013 by

The Policy Press
University of Bristol
Fourth Floor
Beacon House
Queen's Road
Bristol BS8 1QU
UK
t: +44 (0)117 331 4054
f: +44 (0)117 331 4093
tpp-info@bristol.ac.uk
www.policypress.co.uk

North America office:
The Policy Press
c/o The University of Chicago Press
1427 East 60th Street
Chicago, IL 60637, USA
t: +1 773 702 7700
f: +1 773-702-9756
sales@press.uchicago.edu
www.press.uchicago.edu

British Library Cataloguing in Publication Data
A catalogue record for this book is available from the British Library.

Library of Congress Cataloging-in-Publication Data
A catalog record for this book has been requested.

ISBN 978 1 84742 877 6 paperback
ISBN 978 1 84742 878 3 hardcover

Cover design by The Policy Press
Front cover (and on page 101): image kindly supplied by the Muslim Youthwork Foundation. 'Skratch Punk' font created by Nik Coley.
Printed and bound in Great Britain by Hobbs, Southampton
The Policy Press uses environmentally responsible print partners

FSC
www.fsc.org
MIX
Paper from
responsible sources
FSC® C020438

In memory of my father
Hajji Muhammad Abdul Khan
and my wife
Sevda Inik-Khan

**My existence is from you
And your appearance is through me
Yet if I had not existed
You would not have been.**

Ibn Arabi (1165–1240)

Contents

List of tables and figures

Tables

Figures

Acknowledgements

This book has taken some time to get around to writing, and I am grateful to the individuals who have been there along the way. Colleagues new: Bal Gill and Steph Green for the support and insight they provided (I think you read more drafts than I did), and colleagues old: Gill Cressey and Wayne Richards, who gave of time and thought.

There are individuals who have inspired, read, commented and 'cussed' who are not just a part of this book but also a part of my life: Mehdi and Ingrid Razvi, Charlie Husband, Tom Wylie, Mohammed Shafique, Abdoolkarim Vakil, George and Teresa Smith, Taniya Hussain, Sheikha Halima Krausen (who inspired the relationships model used in this book), Man Yee Lee, Taz Bashir, Zahoor Iqbal and my smuggler of rare and precious texts, Carola Nielinger Vakil, and others who I have missed out, probably because I am rushing to meet a deadline, and who are now breathing a sigh of relief.

This book is dedicated to youth workers such as Phil Hamilton who has been an inspiration in many young people's lives, mine included, and youth workers such as Adil Hadi, not forgetting the Nibbler … and there are many others.

I am very grateful to the students at Ruskin College for putting up with me – you are special people and in being a part of your learning journeys I have learnt much about mine.

I am indebted to the patience and support of my family and friends – life is short and there is an opportunity cost for everything one does.

Last, but not least, I would like thank The Policy Press – Karen Bowler, Laura Vickers, Laura Greaves and Susannah Emery, and others whom I have not come across as yet – who have been nothing but patient and supportive and who have made this book possible.

Places we look for ...

Welcome to the ruins

Welcome to the ruins

Don't get fooled by the exterior

Don't get put off by the cold

There is no need for veils

You can leave your guilt at the threshold

All is visible to the keeper

Nothing of shame to behold

Gone will be the inhibitions that trap you

Gone will be the desire to present

It is not shamelessness that meets you

Gestures and pretence don't frequent

Truth has laid bare the decorations

There is no lean to for the world

No table to put the cup on

Or *qibla*[1] to look towards

Are you tired of looking through the keyhole

Have you the strength to break down the door

Don't be blinded by the light that greets you

Let it embrace you

Like you were once embraced before.

M.G. Khan

---

[1] Direction to Mecca.

... and places we find

Fuck it all

Fuck it all

Your preaching

Your answers

As if

You've been where I'm going

Seen all I've seen

Your obvious metaphors

Your crappy analogies

And fuck you

Your pretentious piety

And your sly interpretations

To suit your fetishes

Your uniform of sobriety

Over eyes that leave nothing untouched

Well fuck you

As I have time for everything

But you.

M.G. Khan

ONE

Return to sentiment

If God became an infant in your
Arms
Then you
Would have to nurse all
Creation.

Hafiz (1320–1389);
translated by Daniel Ladinsky (1999)

Idries Shah (1978) explains that the danger of sentiment is that once it is expressed, it becomes worn out, turns into truisms, things repeated without thought or feeling, its speech becomes a mechanical act, devoid or disconnected to the reality that it seeks to articulate. Sentiments are propagated and used for their 'sign' value rather than their 'use' value. Notions around equality particularly come to mind, such as, 'we live in an equal society' or 'equality of opportunity'. Does sentiment reflect reality? Does it mask it? Is there an absence of a profound reality that underpins it? Or does it have no relationship to reality at all? Baudrillard (1994) coined this last stage the 'desert of the real', a space where the world of film, television and the virtual world is more real and intense to us than our 'real' lives.

If sentiments are also truisms, undoubted or self-evident truth, they are difficult to oppose because all of us, to a degree, believe in them enough not to reject them outright; but they are something that we instinctively think that somebody else is going to do – that they apply to a community, to a collective rather than an individual. Shah explains the impact of sentiments with the following example:

> Nobody will oppose the principle "peace for all the world".
> Believing that they believe in this, they have to do nothing
> about it. Oh, yes they may talk about it; keep the matter in
> the headlines. But they do not apply the central character
> of the peace to themselves as individuals. They think that
> peace is something that applies to groups not the individuals.
> That is why there can be no real peace just the absence of
> actual fighting. (Shah, 1978, p 131)

Daniel Dorling (2011) extends this notion further in the context of contemporary society by claiming an emboldened elite whose real beliefs are that elitism is efficient, exclusion is necessary, greed is good, prejudice is natural and that despair in many cases is inevitable, all of which suggests that statements about equality and justice are mere platitudes by those in positions of privilege and power.

Public policy that seeks to deliver public services on the basis of sentiment is nothing new in the UK, as the history of the voluntary sector (and included within this, the faith-based voluntary sector) demonstrates. The championing of the 'Big Society' is a return to the politics of sentiment, an extension of New Labour's poorly handled agenda on devolved services where far too much was presumed of people being asked to step into jobs that others had studied and trained for – noble intentions alone do not support, equip and keep safe the volunteers required for such an agenda. Now, the Big Society volunteer is expected to run the youth centre, the library, the school, the hospital, the parish or ward council, the neighborhood watch, as well as any housing association they may be connected to. We can all picture it, happily looking forward to spending our evenings choosing types of speed bumps, colour of bins and or reading a long headteacher's report – saving your questions until the end, of course. But how many Big Society volunteers will come back to a youth club when they have been told, in no uncertain terms, to 'fuck off' the week before by a young person? The thought that 'I have better things to do with my time' may cross their mind. The idea of the volunteer has been sentimentalised, something for somebody else to do, as hard-up families try to make ends meet – and, in the context of the Big Society, it has placed volunteering as an act of politics rather than of service.

The impact of the 'invisible collective' described by Shah is further developed by Renata Salecl (2011) in her book *The tyranny of choice*, in which she makes the argument that the crucial thing for the maintenance of inequities and powerlessness and with it privilege – the status quo is for people not to express their disbelief in what is happening, 'for them to abide by the majority opinion all that matters is that they believe it to be true that most of the people around them believe' (Salecl, 2011, p 10), and this same process is true in terms of 'choice' – we may not have much choice in our lives, but people seem to believe that somehow this choice exists, as public opinion, and the media, suggests, so it must be something that 'I am doing wrong' and this silences us. Therefore Salecl states:

> For the ideology of choice to hold power in post-industrial
> society, all that is needed is for people to keep their disbelief
> to themselves. (Salecl, 2011, p 11)

The return to sentiment could be seen as a return to the historical motivations of social action determined by fear, faith, service or politics in relation to youth services, and in this history the voluntary sector is significant, as chronicled by Bernard Davies in his history of youth work trilogy (1999a, 1999b).

Déjà vu

Two related circles have been completed in the youth work story. The first is about its defining purpose and ideas that informed periods in its history. This movement is demonstrated in a broad brush way given

Figure 1.1: The youth work story

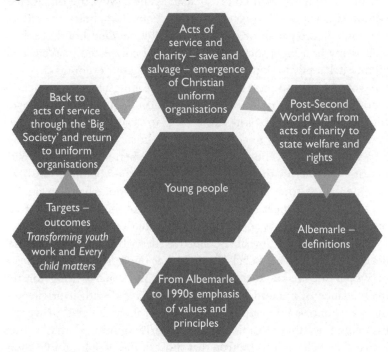

the limitations of such diagrams, but essentially it aims to convey a return to the past (see Figure 1.1).

The second is of the approaches or strategies adopted or imposed on youth workers or youth services in working with Black young people historically, and how they are being made visible or revealed in their application to Muslim young people today (see Figure 1.2). Historical reference is necessary to understand how these approaches emerged and to better recognise their influence and presence today. History seems to be something that most Black academics and practitioners writing about youth work with Black young people have felt the need to visit when writing about this subject, and the work of John (1981), Sallah and Howson (2007) and Shukra (2008) are helpful to read, providing evidence of this instinctive resort to history to make sense of the present. To understand this history is a political need and a pedagogical necessity if we apply Dewey's (1997) notions of continuity and interaction, of how our past shapes our present and by impact, our future. While Dewey develops these concepts to understand what informs student learning experiences, the same can, metaphorically at least, be applied to collectivities (communities or organisations), of how the past finds its way to inform the present. It is a political necessity to be able to

Figure 1.2: Youth work approaches

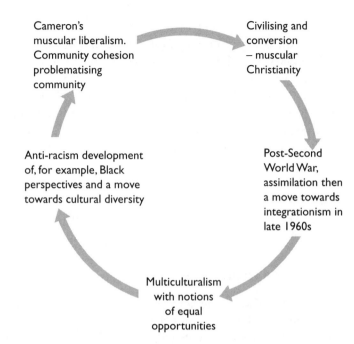

Cameron's muscular liberalism. Community cohesion problematising community

Civilising and conversion – muscular Christianity

Anti-racism development of, for example, Black perspectives and a move towards cultural diversity

Post-Second World War, assimilation then a move towards integrationism in late 1960s

Multiculturalism with notions of equal opportunities

analyse the narratives and politics that inform the youth work landscape today, and to make sense of the experience of participation within this field for new participants. It helps us to understand the strength and rootedness of narratives, organisations and approaches to work with children and young people, that is, in the case of statutory youth work, which is being fundamentally challenged and dismantled by the Conservative-Liberal Democrat coalition in England. While statutory sector youth services have taken the brunt of coalition 'austerity measures' that have fundamentally challenged the social contract between the state and the individual (Giroux, 2009), the voluntary sector has also been affected, with local authority cuts in grant aid. This is not to say that parts of the voluntary sector have not, at times, been looked on as the possible preferred locale to maintain this activity through commissioning models, localism and the Big Society agenda being pushed by the coalition government.

By looking at the diagrams presented here, it seems that none of these approaches disappear, but appear and re-appear, depending on the awareness of those working with young people and the political motivations of the context. The timelines of what appeared when can be drawn from work by Shukra (2008) and Chauhan (1989), among others already mentioned and are rough indicators merely to indicate stages /cycle.

These circles have been completed because of the assertion being made here that the policy motivations, impact and interpretation of the Community Cohesion and Prevent strategies, and the variety of other measures that have sought to respond to the 'radicalisation' of Muslims, have generated a civilising agenda that has reified Huntington's (1998) clash of civilisations discourse and reframed a civilising agenda reminiscent of the intentions of youth services a century ago. Giroux's (1999) nexus of power, reframing the relationship between the state and the individual, that is, the nexus between right-wing think-tanks, military interests and corporate power, is probably more applicable in making sense of what he describes as the 'war on youth', which many young Muslims interpret or experience as a war against them and against Islam.

The committed mainstream

Youth work as we know it today is a historic exercise influenced by understandings and relationships that go back over a significant period of time. The struggles within have been made visible by the history that generated them. It is a locale like many other professional locales within the broader heading of education that I would suggest is committed in ways that leave little, if any, room for alternative narratives or participants. This, it could be argued, is due to the historic underfunding of this work, and its peripheral presence in local authority or state services, being further exacerbated with £200 million of cuts made by April 2012, according to Unison (2011). Yet its local authority portfolio peripherality (as it is not a service established by statute) belies the importance it holds in communities because of the relational nature of its work in neighbourhoods. It is, I contend, a service that has been committed:

- ideologically
- relationally
- in terms of curricula and narrative
- in terms of information – who gets it and who does not
- in terms of resource allocation or use, that is, the historic use of resources despite changing demographics.

These are the *fronts* in which this engagement has taken place, and yet they are all interrelated – if one access point is unavailable, then it is more than likely that others will also be difficult to negotiate.

The 'committed mainstream' has always felt too committed and principled to respond on the basis of 'race' or faith, seeing its principles as the necessary foundations that would 'equalise' their approach, decisions and actions. It has regarded itself as 'race'-less and faithless, normal and fair, and therefore rational and equally accessible to all. The phrase *regardless of* is often included in statements to describe this value, for example that 'I/we work with young people *regardless of* religion, "race", sexuality etc', often having little clue of what is denied to the young person, or what the young person is forced to leave at the doorstep of this relationship or of the youth service or provision.

It is possible that Nicholls (2012) captures the basis of this approach, which appears to be formed by the perspective that the most valid position from which to interrogate status and experience is that of class:

> The fascination with difference and the replacement of a notion of class exploitation with notions of multiple 'oppressions' encourages the insidious cult of the victim. This gives a shrunken and introverted focus of attention. Depicting ourselves as defeated victims of terrible forces divides and demoralises, and it was a demeanor taken up within youth work for many years. (Nicholls 2012, p 93)

It is an approach that has been intensely experienced by victims of racism, sexism, homophobia and Islamaphobia, a position that runs contrary to the Freirian necessity to 'name' your reality in order to transform it. There is nothing 'victim' about being a victim, but it does marginalise and discourage its naming because when victims raise these issues they are made to feel that they are being divisive, overly sensitive, rocking a steady boat, and ultimately it is a position that reinforces the constituents of the committed mainstream. It is not a 'fascination', as Nicholls describes it, but a need; the notion of oppression does not emerge from an abstract theoretical claim but from an experience in which class is but one dynamic. Stephen Lawrence was killed primarily not because of his class but because of his colour – his 'race'. Homosexuals are victimised not because of their class, primarily, but because of their sexuality. Muslim women wearing the *hijab* are harassed and abused not because of their class but because of their Islamic faith. It appears that only victims of class survive the confinement of victimhood. Recent history suggests that revolutions/

struggles based on class rarely privilege the women even when they have been at the forefront of the struggle, as the French Revolution demonstrated. Nicholls (2012) questions the ability of unions to give parity/recognise any other oppression than the one of class and therefore questions their ability to effectively represent their members.

There are constant calls for innovative practice and for 'diversity'. The irony is that the more innovative you get, the less likely you are to be recognised in straight transactions of ideas outside the realms of trust relationships that allow risk to be taken. Where policy has arisen it has been as a result of events rather than the day-to-day lives of young people – Hunt (Youth Service Development Council, 1967), Scarman (Home Office, 1985) and Macpherson et al (1999) being examples of key reports that have emerged out of such events concerning young people. These seem unable to be weaved into the meta narrative of the mainstream. This responding to events rather than the details of lives was also noted by Chauhan (1989) in his astute analysis of youth services, and Black young people noting how moral panics over Black young people led to provision being dedicated for their use.

In the context of this committed mainstream, Muslim young people have been and are part of both discourses of 'race' and faith that influence youth work practice and policy, and which have an impact on the life chances of young Muslims growing up in Britain. British young Muslims are subjected to a 'new racism' based on moral incompatibility, ethical differences and notions of Islam that have led to a reinvented modern form of racist discourse – *Islamophobia* (Barker, 1981). This is particularly intense as it does not replace earlier racist discourses based on biological, cultural, scientific theories of superior and inferior 'races'; rather, it adds to them (Modood, 1997). Howson (2007) quotes Sivanandan's assertion that the state is acting on two trajectories, the 'War on Terror' and the 'War on Asylum', that have:

> … converged to produce a racism which cannot tell settler from an immigrant, an immigrant from an asylum seeker, an asylum seeker from a Muslim, a Muslim from a terrorist.

To simplify all this into simple notions of 'race' and prejudice constrains not only the way that prejudice can be perceived, but also the manner in which it can be resisted (Thompson and Betts, 2003). Everyday experiences are seldom recognised; more often they are resigned to silence by their intensely subjective and perceptual nature.

Figure 1.3 demonstrates the visible and invisible in youth work. The activity of youth work does not takes place in a vacuum but is informed and supported by university training programmes, national bodies, local services and organisations, publications including journals and magazines, unions, academic critique, political support and faith-based organisations as well as ministerial briefs. Work with Muslim young people relies on this infrastructure being able to inform those working with young people, politicians and policy makers. The development of Muslim youth work is about identifying an authentic narrative that informs practice with young Muslims and the development of an infrastructure that can enable and support it.

Figure 1.3: The visible and the invisible in youth work

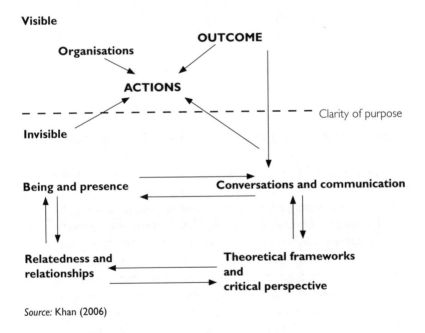

Source: Khan (2006)

One of the experiences of the Muslim Youthwork Foundation, soon after its founding in 2006, was responding to the well-intentioned interest from Christian organisations in wanting to work with Muslim young people and to offer support through sharing of models but also, by association, offering political recognition. The story that I developed to make sense of my resistance to these offers was as follows:

First imagine a forest, and you are trying to get to the clearing in the centre of this forest. There are paths already cut out, but whilst some young people take this path, either out of choice, habit, opportunity or necessity, others do not (you could say that in the youth work context the paths cut out have been by the different religious and secular youth work traditions). I would then have to work on the premise that these paths have issues for those who choose not to take them and therefore would need to cut another path. And this work is challenging, progress is slow as each step takes effort because there are obstacles and issues, but each step also reveals something of what the journey is about and what is similar or different to the other paths in the forest. This may be perceived as a rejection of existing paths or perceived as isolationist and separatist, however, people already are used to lots of different paths so why the fear of this new path, especially if it is heading in a similar direction and is attracting young people who otherwise may not entertain this journey.

Acts of service and the moralising of the deviant

Those working with young people have always been either vulnerable to or attracted by the civilising instincts of politicians responding to the moral panics that are generated about young people on a regular basis.

This discourse around young people had a profound impact on the historic curricula of 'services to young people' – discipline, fitness and safety being key concerns, being informed and informing a muscular Christianity, given form by leading figures with often strong Christian ideals who founded institutions operating on the basis of charity, for example, Benjamin Waugh (Society for the Prevention of Cruelty to Children, later the NSPCC) and Robert Baden-Powell (the Scout Movement). Knight describes them as follows:

> They were slightly wayward entrepreneurs, pitting themselves against enormous odds, and setting themselves against an unsympathetic establishment whose harsh glare they disregarded. They were brave and abundant personalities, willing to take risks. Almost all of them had a deep Christian commitment. Their activities were avowedly

political ... and saw themselves campaigning against evil.
(Knight, 1993, p 12)

This panic about young people and self-discipline has appeared, disappeared and re-appeared, its latest appearance in the comments and analysis of the summer riots of 2011, with the accumulated headlines picturing 'English rioters being poorer, younger and less educated' (BBC News, 24 October 2011) and, according to the National Centre for Social Research (NatCen) (Morrell et al, 2011) study commissioned by the Cabinet Office, in its summary, listing the causes of these young people rioting as something to do, the opportunity to 'get free stuff' and a chance to 'get back at' the police.

Davies' (1999a) historical analysis of the motivations of the early pioneers in youth work as driven by a need to rescue and re-moralise the working classes, often motivated by a need for the preservation of the existing order, is useful for an analysis of the responses to the riots as they emerge, but this lens can also be applied to understanding public policy interventions in the lives of young Muslims over the last 10 years at least. This moralising agenda that informed at least some of youth work history has bequeathed a legacy that has entailed a tension between the educational drivers for youth work and its 'salvage and save' agenda driven by political necessities and the faith-based motivations of many of the pioneers of youth and children's work that are now part of the mission statements of some of the key organisations that they established. Although the role of the church in delivering youth services is perceived as normative and part of the youth work landscape, religion and youth work are seen as much more problematic in Britain, at least where Islam is concerned. It is a similar discourse to the one that connects Islam to democratic incompatibility and the fear of the Islamification of the Arab world as result of the Arab Spring.

The history of the church in the development of youth work has meant that historical relationships between the state, local authorities and the church have normalised a presence, relationships, and often a confessional agenda. By default Christian approaches to youth work or work with young people have provided the frame by which other faith-based approaches are recognised, acknowledged or judged. The irony is that youth work from other faith perspectives is only recognised when it is at its most 'Christian' in the models that it adopts, an issue that I encountered particularly in the early days of establishing the Muslim Youthwork Foundation. It is often unclear whether negative reactions are because of any further religious intrusion in the democratic vision of youth work, previous relationships or experiences with Christianity or Christian youth work, or with Muslim approaches taking shape and being put forward and their impact on generating a place for 'Islam' in the public space.

Historically, as Davies (1999a) notes, the relationship between the White working class and British Empire was often mediated through such youth organisations as the Scouts and later the Boys' Brigade that intrinsically supported the nation, faith and empire as connected entities, the protection of one being the preservation of the other. The objectives and curricula of these organisations prepared young people with an understanding of their role in this enterprise, and the synthesis of faith and 'race' gave an 'ordained' sense to this relationship. The 'salvage and save' agenda was an exercise of self-preservation in a climate where the 'ruling classes' and the upper middle class were fixated with the fear of the working class, and the maintenance of Empire. For leading figures such as Baden-Powell there was a need to incorporate and pacify an increasingly aware and militant working class that was threatening national cohesiveness by juxtaposing national unity and the defence of the British Empire and patriotism against class and socialism. Organisations such as the Boys' Brigade, Church Lads' and Church Girls' Brigade, Girl Guides Association, Girls Friendly Society, Girls' Guildry, National Association of Boys Clubs (this also included the Association of Jewish Youth), Girls' Life Brigade, National Association of Girls Clubs, Welsh League of Youth, Young Men's Christian Association (YMCA), National Federation of Young Farmers' Clubs, the Scouts and others not only lay the foundation of services to young people that later became known loosely as youth services but, just as importantly, some mediated a relationship between Britain and the Empire and by connection, with 'race' and other faiths for young people in Britain.

These organisations have become part of the cultural landscape of Britain; while some have retained their original name, others have rebranded themselves, for example, the National Association of Girls Clubs are known today as UK Youth and the National Association of Boys Clubs are now known as Clubs for Young People.

Most are now international as well as national organisations, claiming significant participation from young people; the Boys' Brigade claims to work with over 60,000 young people in over 1,500 companies in the UK and Ireland, while Girlguiding UK (formerly the Girl Guides Association) has half a million members.

Of particular interest is the continued role of religion in the defining purpose and identity of these organisations. The statements below, from the Boys' Brigade and the Church Lads' and Church Girls' Brigade, are taken straight from their respective websites (2011):

The Object of the Boys' Brigade is:

'The advancement of Christ's kingdom among Boys and the habits of Obedience, Reverence, Discipline, Self-respect and all that tends towards a true Christian manliness.'

'The Church Lads' and Church Girls' Brigade (CLCGB), often referred to as "The Brigade", is The Anglican Churches' own uniformed youth organisation: welcoming children and young people of all faiths and none. This organisation has a lot of history and, for over 100 years, The Brigade has been fulfilling its object to extend the kingdom of Christ among lads and girls.'

On its website, the YMCA introduces itself as the largest and oldest youth charity in the world: 'We believe that all young people deserve to have a safe place to live and the opportunity to reach their full potential. The YMCA's vision is of an inclusive Christian Movement, transforming communities so that all young people truly belong, contribute and thrive.'

The Welsh League of Youth, referred to as Urdd Gobraith Cymru (Figure 1.4), captures the essence of its identity through the triangle logo consisting of three colours: green at the bottom of the triangle symbolising Wales, red in the middle symbolising the 'fellowman' and the white at the top of the triangle symbolising Christ. Today it is an organisation that aims to work with young people of all religions (and with those who do not claim a religious belief).

Religion is clearly a defining feature of these organisations, not just in terms of their emergence but also their current identity and ethos. Christian organisations are able to differentiate between the faith that informs their organisational presence and motivations and their actual activity through terms such as 'faith-based organisations' – religion informs their history and motivations but this does not mean that they are proselytising. This is a differentiating ability that is not as easily accepted as possible from Muslim organisations. While there is much resistance to Islam in the 'public space', there continues to be explicit presence and investment in Christian youth organisations through government; for example, the Boys' Brigade has or has had posts supported by the government's Department for Children, Schools and Families, while Clubs for Young People is one of the strategic partners in the Catch22 National Citizen Service (NCS) Partnership, one of 12 pilot groups delivering the NCS on behalf of the Conservative-Liberal Democrat coalition government. The development of the YMCA's youth work has been pump-primed by the award of £30 million plus from *myplace*, a government programme, funding the largest investment in youth centres for young people since Albemarle.

Figure 1.4: Welsh League of Youth/Urdd Gobraith Cymru logo

urdd.org
Urdd Gobaith Cymru

© Welsh League of Youth/Urdd Gobraith Cymru 2013

Consider the £10 million of funding announced by Eric Pickles, Minister for Communities and Local Government, to support the development of volunteering to be managed by an organisation initiated by the Prince of Wales and supported by the Prince of Wales's Charitable Foundation, Youth United. Member organisations include The Scout Association, Girlguiding UK, St John Ambulance, Army Cadet Force, Sea Cadets, Boys' Brigade, Girls' Brigade, Volunteer Police Cadets and Air Training Corps. According to Children & Young People Now (*News*, 1 February 2012),[1] the aim is to recruit and train up 2,700 new adult volunteers between 2012 and 2015 to run 400 new youth groups so that 10,000 additional young people would be able to join a pack or troop with the areas identified being Birmingham, Bradford, Knowsley, Hackney, Haringey, Manchester, Middlesbrough, Newham, Redbridge, Rochdale and Tower Hamlets.

It is hard to ignore historic comparisons and the symbolism in this meeting of largely Christian uniformed organisations, or 'military lite', with young people from cities with significant Muslim and Black and minority ethnic (BME) communities. The above organisations are facilitated by Youth United, an organisation whose chair was a recent Deputy Assistant Police Commissioner for the Metropolitan Police Service – Rod Jarman – whose consultancy company, Rod Jarman Associates Ltd, seems to suggest the ability to speak community languages as a key company competency, a service normally provided for people who are sick by care providers, and for those who find themselves in police custody.

> We are a young diverse organisation with associates from a range of backgrounds and with a number of skills. We have

---

[1] www.cypnow.co.uk/cyp/news/1071672/10m-boost-youth-volunteer-training

associates who speak languages from English to Punjabi to Swahili and who come together because we believe that we can make a difference to improve leadership, increase safety and engage communities.[2]

The return of the cycle to service is accompanied by a return to the past, with limited statutory youth work provision, populated by established uniformed organisations or large bodies, accompanied by a call to a muscularism, reinvented today as muscular liberalism, epitomised by Prime Minister Cameron's call for muscular liberalism in Munich 2010 against the corrosive effects of multiculturalism on British values. The following is an excerpt from Cameron's speech in Munich:

> Under the doctrine of state multiculturalism, we have encouraged different cultures to live separate lives, apart from each other and apart from the mainstream. We've failed to provide a vision of society to which they feel they want to belong. We've even tolerated these segregated communities behaving in ways that run completely counter to our values.[3]

The notion of divided communities from the Cantle Report (2001), and value incompatibility, according to David Cameron, as well as long established notions such as 'culture clash', are manifestations of a historic process that puts in place a notion of 'othering', which trains the societal lens focus firmly on individuals, families and communities rather than policy and institutions. Rarely has this lens shifted to institutions except in the Macpherson Inquiry, following the murder of Stephen Lawrence and the campaign by his family against institutional racism (see Macpherson et al, 1999). The invisibility of the structural analysis is captured by Colley's (2001) insightful analysis of New Labour's Bridging the Gap programme, which was aimed at tackling social exclusion, that, despite stating a concern for social exclusion, located its causes in the arena of individual agency while deep-seated structural inequalities continue to be left invisible.

There is a contemporary resonance to Bernard Davies' analysis of the historic motivations of the early pioneers expressed in the form of a re-moralising of the 'lower orders', particularly at a time of imperialistic interest being fanned by a version of history that 'idealised and glamorised' (Fryer, 1988) Britain's role in the world in general, and

[2] www.rodjarman.co.uk/Policing-Services.html

[3] www.number10.gov.uk/news/pms-speech-at-munich-security-conference/

the Empire in particular. Davies (1999a), in charting the role of youth organisations, identifies the patriotic fervour that bred a pre-occupation with physical prowess to defend their country and in fulfilling the 'white man's burden, that is, transmitting its self-evidently superior values to the Heathen and uncivilised peoples of the world' (1999a, p 10). However, this struggle over the ownership or honest stewardship of these values has continued to find itself in professions where values and principles play a defining part and are therefore particularly prone to internalising this struggle.

bell hooks (2003) identifies educators as one of the most reluctant groups in acknowledging racist thinking and how it informs small details of everyday life and culture. She experienced the effort and energy that went into just dealing with denials of racism from both White and Black educators, leaving aside the anger of this supposition or what we can do about it.

Profoundly influenced by Paolo Freire, hooks applied his notion of 'naming the world'. For Freire, this naming of the world, that hooks refers to as 'imperialist, white supremacist, capitalist patriarchy' (2003), cannot be an act of arrogance or hate, or a feeling that one belongs to an elite; for Freire this naming is a necessary act in the process of creation and re-creation. To name your oppression is an act of courage, where often the language used has been pushed outside the borders of common courtesy, political acceptability and generalisable truth and into the realm of delegitimised subjectivity, where personal, political and theoretical marginality are outcomes. And I, writing this, feel a significant resistance to using terms such as those employed by hooks, in case this language 'pisses people off' – it is an example of how I have internalised this resistance to 'naming the world', a world in which 'race', faith, class, gender, sexuality and age can so powerfully inform how the world responds to you.

Gus John, *In the service of black youth* (1981), comments on Stuart Hall's assertion that 'race' was always abstracted out, as something that was imposed on British society, and this provided some rationale in keeping 'race' connected with issues of immigration, and what Hesse and Sayyid (2006) today call the 'immigrant imaginary', with issues of immigration continuing to be associated as a perceived assault on 'British culture and identity' and a danger to the already threatened British homogeneity (Beckett and Macey, 2001).

There is much to consider in the supposition that funding priorities determine the dialogue taking place and whose needs are met, as was obvious to Hartley in the early 1980s:

That the youth service is in a dilemma as to whether its goal is to promote integration or to meet the needs of coloured young teenagers, because the two do not necessarily coincide. (Hartley, quoted in John, 1981, p 2)

I am not sure this was a dilemma for youth organisations then and now, as a dilemma suggests a level of anxiety, critical self-appraisal and also some uncertainty. The context required a response from youth services, but it was not clear that it was a dilemma or more of a problem or issue that had to be managed in most cases. But what is accurate is that these priorities were pulling in different directions for young people.

This fault line, mentioned by Hartley, is present today where there is a tension between supporting and empowering young people to be who they want to be, that is, their identity, and supporting them to be or aspects of society may want them to be or behave as – their role identity, Castells (1996) terms this as the struggle between role and meaning, the investment in roles being an economic exercise and in meaning one of belonging – one requiring skilling, the other a process of individuation. Henry Giroux (1999) is much more direct in naming it 'a war' that both commodifies youth and if necessary, criminalises youth – the only identity nurtured is one of the consumer where market sovereignty has taken precedence over state sovereignty.

It is often difficult to reconcile the Freirian pedagogy that often motivates those working with young people and in youth work and the definitions that have operationalised it. Colley and Hodkinson's (2001) damning analysis of New Labour's Bridging the Gap programme captures the disconnect between the individual and institutional as to which is problematised – structure or agency – in addressing social exclusion.

Colley and Hodkinson's (2001) point is that it is often the proximal cause that is problematised rather than the distal cause (the underlying, the structural) (see Table 1.1), and services and organisations can internalise this analysis and express it through lack of empathy and willingness to listen or understand 'the other'. Already disenfranchised

Table 1.1: Who is the problem?

	Proximal cause	**Distal cause**
Individual	Family Friends and peers Neighbourhood Unemployment Poverty	Corporate world State institutions Foreign policy Media – marketing

communities are particularly prone to the stigmatisation produced by this form of analysis.

The incremental impact of reports such as *Transforming youth work* (DFES, 2002) highlighted the comparatively poorer performance of statutory youth services compared to the voluntary sector, and the possible influence of Leon Feinstein's work on *Aiming high for young people: A ten year strategy for positive activities* (DCSF, 2007). New Labour's last statements of purpose for young people and youth work, compounded by the historic suspicion of youth work, has led youth work, and particularly statutory youth work, to being perceived as a proximal cause offering provision with no measurable benefit, according to Feinstein's analysis, while the voluntary sector has re-emerged again due to the marginalisation set in motion by New Labour and accelerated by the Conservative-Liberal Democrat coalition of the statutory youth sector, which itself was set in motion by the Education Act 1944 and resourced by the Albemarle Report as part of the postwar social contract between the state and the citizen (not the customer) (Ministry of Education, 1960).

The return to 'services of sentiment' is the political context and background noise that those working with Muslim young people themselves are seeking to understand; it is a return to a 'services for youth' that historians of youth work will find familiar and many will find alarming. Government statements of intent, as expressed through the Positive for Youth Strategy (2011) and the Localism Act 2011, make no bold statement of ensuring outcomes as *Every child matters* did through its five outcomes, although three at least seem to have survived and have been reframed – health, unemployment and the youth voice, through funding to the British Youth Council. Nevertheless these and other aspirations provide the mood music for the local target setting advocated by the coalition government.

The ability of the 'local' to accommodate the established and the new with substantially reduced resources is to be seen, but the messages being sent out as to the key organisations that government will 'do business with' and the historical, symbolic and the visual narratives they wish to privilege, is very clear.

TWO

Youth work, pedagogy and Islam

**Power is safest in the poet's hands,
Thus for an artist
God will
Pose.**

Hafiz (1320–1389);
translated by Daniel Ladinsky (1999)

Maxine Green (2006), in *A journey of discovery: Spirituality and spiritual development in youth work*, refers to the opportunity youth work has in drawing concepts and articulations from different cultures and traditions as an activity that seldom happens, and this missed opportunity is captured by her use of Chandu Christian's observation that:

> Youth work has yet to absorb and use the multi-faith or multi-cultural concepts that are now available to it. For example the concept of Guru-shishya as relationship, Islam as submission, the Tao as the way, Zen as a method of self-actualisation without complicated rituals, the Shabad (word) as a revelation – these and many other concepts are now part of our multi-cultural legacy. Youth work can apply them for both personal and spiritual development of young people as well as to create a tolerant and understanding society. (*Youth & Policy*, Autumn 1999, p 25)

This is due to what can be termed 'the committed mainstream', with its history, its heroes and its stories, despite a societal context in which notions of wellness, mind, body, spirit and wholeness rarely allow borders, whether religious, ethnic or national, to censor their movement or knowledge. However, the strength of notions such as 'wellness' in Europe are finding their way into children and young people's discourse in Britain (Nairn, 2011).

Green's (2006) book captures the repeated invocation throughout youth work history for the need for the spiritual development of young people and the role of the youth worker or educator to facilitate this exploration. The relationship between Christianity and youth services in Britain is closely intertwined, and events, practice dilemmas and challenges of context and issue have built a body of knowledge that tries to make sense of what Christian youth work is supposed to be about, alongside a Christian youth work sector that has developed the infrastructure over a period of time to be able to make and refine models and design programmes to train youth workers or leaders. The amorphous nature of the term 'spirituality' enables it to be owned across different traditions, whether based in a belief in God or not, as the case may be. Green points out that spiritual experiences are not limited to religion or experiences only religions can bring forth.

In terms of understanding organisational types and locations, and also in skills sets required and defining features, the Jewish experience is particularly interesting when considering the development of Muslim models. And it is a useful comparison in revealing the different standards of belonging applied to different communities in Britain. Israel has a role in the imagination of a Jewish or Israeli identity for young people who are seen as British but whose loyalty to Britain is rarely questioned or seen as compromising, despite the core aims of many of these organisations in establishing a relationship with primarily Israel rather than the UK. They can find meaning from either one, two or all of the following aims – religious (Jewish), race based (chosen people – distinctive community experience) or political (Zionist) – and there will also be a position that all these are interconnected or that they are not. The role of mother tongue languages so often seen as compromising integration is not applied to the Jewish community, nor is the communities' focus on it questioned as something that excludes belonging to Britain. For Jewish informal educators this linguistic identity and survival is important on a number of levels, and especially in the use of concepts within Jewish tradition to inform and give resonance to its aims and activities. Key values such as equality are given a Jewish identity (*shivyon*), but also, in drawing from its tradition, educators are able to provide a nuanced understanding and a distinctive approach through, for example, *kvod ha-adam* (human dignity). These concepts not only give ownership to these values through an authentic identity, they also provide gateways to explore Jewish history, religion, art, politics and so on, and make visible what is lost in translation. Chazan's (2003) definition of Jewish informal education makes reference to the need to experience Jewish moments emerging from a curriculum based on Jewish values and experiences, led by 'Jewishly literate' educators. The role of the Jewish educator appears to be similar to that within the Christian youth work traditions as somebody who sincerely attempts to model their beliefs – a youth leader rather than a youth worker.

In coming to propose a Muslim theoretical framework it is necessary to revisit how youth work practice has been defined. The Muslim Youthwork Foundation defined Muslim youth work as:

> Creating safe spaces for Muslim young people to explore
> personal, social, spiritual and political choices. (Khan, 2006,
> p 16)

This definition is not too dissimilar to one adopted by Sapin (2009, p 12):

> To work with young people to facilitate their personal,
> social and educational development and enable them to
> gain a voice, influence and place in society….

Here, I have to stop this quote as the next element of this definition provides room for exploration 'In a period of their transition from dependence to independence' – for me, this need to stop and question is due to the theoretical frame being presented and the cross fire that young people get caught between in belonging to communities that have differing perceptions of this dependence/independence paradigm. Instead, one needs to consider this as a possible expression of the 'us and them' that binary notions cultivate and which find themselves in the case of youth work as professional orthodoxy which then extricates it from the value base that informs it and represents it as an ethical position, a pedagogical approach, a necessary rite of passage, an act of agency that is part of a being and becoming (Imam, 1995). Simply put it can be perceived as naming individual maturation and becoming as an act of separation rather than belonging.

Bernard Davies (2010) describes youth work through a series of principles, namely:

- starting where young people are at (person-centred)
- developing trusting relationships
- tipping balances of power in favour of young people
- promoting equality of opportunity and diversity in areas of responsibility.

Tony Jeffs and Mark Smith (2010) take the same approach, listing five essential components:

- voluntary participation
- acts of education and welfare
- that it is about young people, so it is age-specific
- association, relationship and community
- being friendly, accessible and responsive while acting with integrity.

The theoretical frame for Muslim youth work focuses particularly on the notion and role of relationships, covered in the above principles. Jeffs and Smith describe relationships as a fundamental source of learning and happiness, while Blacker (2010) describes relationships as the fabric of our existence, as a means of exchange, of an ability that is at the heart of the youth work process and also that relationships are influenced by their purpose and expectations of roles in society.

Sapin also defines youth work as 'based on building relationships with young people that recognise the reality of their lives' (2009, p 55). The importance of youth work relationships being something that is entered into voluntarily is a foundational principle, something that is outside the realm of negotiation (Batsleer and Davies, 2008, 2010; Sapin, 2009). The establishment of relationships with young people are the means through which meaningful dialogue and learning takes place.

The Muslim youth work conferences in December 2005 and March 2006, supported by the National Youth Agency at the time, in particular by Tom Wylie and Viv McKee, led on both defining Muslim youth work and also in establishing a series of principles that could inform youth work with young Muslims for Muslim organisations and those who work with young Muslims. They brought to the surface the idea that there is or should be something called 'Muslim youth work' for the following reasons:

- *Universal values*: the principles that emerged out of the ministerial conferences (Ministerial Conferences Steering Committee, 1990) are also values that should inform this pedagogy. The cultural nature, the expression of the universal claim, must be broadened. The principles are universal but the narrative that makes sense of them is not; it is selective and situated in Judean, Christian or Hellenistic thought.
- *Because young people need to make sense of what they do and who they are*: as Kerry Young states so powerfully (1999), youth work is about identity – for Muslim young people the private nature of this maturation is constantly challenged by the public nature of the interest in Islam and Muslims, and the public drawing out of what they think or feel about what can be best described by 'headline Islam'. This is above and beyond the questions that young people are normally asking of themselves … this is a powerful, and, for youth workers and researchers, an attractive point of engagement with young people.
- *It allows people to place and critique aims, objectives and outcomes*: for those working with young people and communities, the need for guiding principles and models that have resonance is critical when asked to implement or challenge public policy, whether Community Cohesion, Every Child Matters or latterly, the Big Society.
- *For people to approach youth work with some authenticity*: as a former area youth officer and previously involved in policy and management, when receiving interest from Muslim organisations for funding or

support, there was often, but not always, a feeling of them coming across as disingenuous which emerged because of a difficulty to make the case 'on their terms professionally' (in terms of youth work values, ethics and practice); they had to do it on somebody else's terms.

- *Youth work is about process and not just about product, and we want to establish the nature of the process:* Brenda Crowe's (2008) notion 'that people do not grow by being measured' is an apt metaphor for the culture of the quantitative measuring of young people through examination and accreditation that has informed the formal and informal education sector, but how does the notion of 'process' sit in the learning act in Islam? How can it be given value, authenticity and importance within Muslim organisations often informed by a pedagogy of emulation and a learning approach that could best be described as a classic banking model of learning and teaching?

- *There needs to be ownership and participation:* participation is based on a sense of ownership of spaces and ideas; without this you are either a beneficiary or a subject and therefore peripheral to the professional field.

- *To give space to thinkers and reflective practitioners as well as representatives:* the 'professional' space is important to challenge the representational needs and agendas that emerge from the establishment and that are responded to by Muslim communities. This demand for leaders or bodies that the government can talk to is a political necessity, but it is also the meeting of two versions of patriarchy – class and tribal. The professional space is important for identities informed by youth, disability, gender and sexuality that are often excluded from these systems but whose experiences, reflections and actions inform new platforms that speak the detail of experience.

- *Because the nature of the issues that face young people if not in their type, in their depth, may change. Every era or generation is faced with new challenges:* for youth work and informal education this means the need for core values to take on new inflections, to accept new stories that often convey the same message. In an age where people's reaction to things is 'What am I supposed to…?' rather than 'What should I…?' coming from a secure and reflexive 'What am I?' grows ever wider, it seems that the need to reconnect with the 'Who am I?' grows ever more urgent. During our work at the Muslim Youthwork Foundation, Bernard Davies suggested the following frame to name the same, to explore the distinctive, the absent, and to identify the 'new':
  - Muslim youth work is the same as all other youth work
  - Muslim youth is the same as some other youth work
  - Muslim youth work is like no other youth work.

- *To be able to critique new locations and environments for youth work:* the idea of the youth club is part of the cultural landscape of Britain, something familiar, grudgingly accepted for the purpose its serves, but valued for the impact that it can have despite the picture posed by Leo Feinstein's (2005) influential study that seemed to say that young people who attend youth clubs derive no benefit from them. The strength of this romantic ideal is both helpful and unhelpful. It is helpful because it maintains an imaginary that is on the whole positive; it is unhelpful because the kind of hard issues that emerge in youth work practice go unrecognised and unacknowledged. The strength of this ideal maintains the idea of its existence despite the decimation wrought on the statutory sector by the politics of the Conservative-Liberal Democrat coalition government and the policy marginalisation and challenge under New Labour.

There is a danger of Muslim youth work being defined by place or gender rather than by values and principles. The preoccupation with 'place', especially confessional locales, leaves those who are actively engaging with young Muslims on the basis of principles and values comparatively invisible, often because they are deemed to be politically irrelevant.

The response to the idea of working with young Muslims is often formulated along the following lines, by playing on the term 'Muslim youth work':

- *Muslim + youth = Muslim youth work*   In this formula, if you are working with young Muslims, then that is Muslim youth work. It is essentially an activity defined by the presence of a worker and Muslim young people.
- *Youth + work = youth work*   'Muslim' is not really relevant and has no bearing on approach because everyone is treated equally, and all young people are the same, imposing an identity of invisibility in this act of 'normalising' young Muslims. This is the formula that has often been employed by the larger voluntary and statutory sector services, but the Muslim identity has been made relevant by the Prevent strategy.

In response to working out what 'Muslim youth work' is, the following principles emerged at a post-conference workshop in 2006. The workshop included representatives from a number of Muslim organisations, Muslim youth workers, Muslim young people and youth work academics. Although these were initially established to work out a principles-based identity for the Muslim Youthwork Foundation, I have adapted them here for Muslim organisations seeking to develop youth work. The third principle was initially worded to challenge the way policy towards Muslim young people was an act emerging out of events rather than the details of their lives – thus the principle that Muslim youth work aims to focus on the details of young people's lives rather than events. Looking back, this was a sentiment of its time to aspirationally generate a cognitive kick towards a political need to do something about the threat to national security emerging from Muslim young people. The years since have revealed the innocent idealism and the political naivety of the intention of this reflexive kick.

The seven principles of Muslim youth work

1. Muslim youth work is for all young people who self-define themselves as Muslim.
2. Muslim youth work is non-sectarian and committed to fairness and inclusion.
3. Muslim youth work aims to focus on the details of young people's lives *and* the political imperatives emerging out of events.
4. Young people are integral to the leadership and development of youth work.
5. Muslim youth work is led by realities and issues, not dogma.
6. In Muslim youth work knowledge is inseparable from practice – it is experiential.
7. Empowerment is the ability to contribute to a community. It is this that gives momentum for learning and belonging.

The principles locate individuals and organisations developing services for young Muslims – including youth work – outside issues of judgement as to who is a Muslim and what is Muslim or Islam for that matter, 'being Muslim' being an act of self-definition.

In his chapter on mapping Muslim youth work, Hamid (2011) lists dimensions of Muslim youth work, and suggests a distinction between Islamic youth work and Muslim youth work. This list, dividing youth work conceptually, methodologically and in terms of delivery, is helpful, recognising Muslim youth work as being, for example, values-based, recognising the spiritual dimensions of young people, youth-focused, tapping into Islamic tradition, and that it is empowering and educative. It also provides an opening to explore sentiments that have been used in relation to work with young Muslims but which I am not sure should be defined within the notion of Muslim youth work. The idea of Muslim youth work being 'faith sensitive' carries the caution of the outsider, not the confidence of the insider – an approach that was historically 'done to' Muslim communities, which stifled risk and with it, creativity. Hamid also describes Muslim youth work as solution-focused – it can be described as process-led or as a journey, but the idea that it is solution-focused seems to contradict the idea that it is person-centred and process-led, both key principles. The model proposed here questions Hamid's proposed distinction between Islamic youth work and Muslim youth work. Hamid makes a valid point that the naming of it as Muslim needs a Muslim reality. This does not automatically mean that the Muslim journey needs to be a confessional one – 'inculcation or teaching' is not part of the Muslim youth work pedagogy being developed. It has a place within the work of services *for* young people, whether weekend schools, *madrasahs* (religious schools) or even movements, which will be touched upon in the chapters on Muslim organisations.

A conclusion that I came to on reflecting on what is Muslim youth work (Khan, 2006) was that it was not a confessional exercise, it was not an exercise in cultivating belief, nor was it an exercise of mission – but what, then, makes it Muslim? I even described it as essentially a 'secular' exercise because of the constant invocation to use reason, as so often stated in the Qur'an, but this locating of 'reason' in the secular is a powerful example of the associations that have been developed in the discourses around religion in Europe and then been applied across other traditions around the world. The need and ability to reason is a necessary act in the knowing of God through reaching understandings of the Qur'an, that Sardar so accurately describes:

> The Qur'an does not yield its meaning without a struggle with its text. To see the significance of an allegory or metaphor, to separate the truth from the simile, the external from the transient, the universal from the local, one has to struggle with words and concepts, contexts and interconnections, and the structure and style of the Qur'an. This is not a quick and easy task. It requires effort and patience. (Sardar, 2011, p 11)

For me this struggle is captured over meanings of concepts, and one key locale of this struggle is whether the Qur'an uses the term 'Muslim' to describe an individual with a particular state of being, described as the accumulation of the meanings below, or an external identity label. Secular/confessional and reason/faith binaries are limited in conceptualising a Muslim perspective. It is the relationship between the two that makes it Muslim. Here I do not use the term 'Muslim' in terms of identity, but in terms of its etymological roots which, according to Halima Krausen,[1] can mean all of the following:

- *Salima:* to be safe, whole, complete
- *Salam:* safety security, freedom from harm
- *Salim:* safe, secure, free, complete
- *Taslim:* acquiescence, assent, consent, acceptance, submission
- *Islam:* reconciliation, surrender
- *Muslim:* a person who surrenders/is at peace (to God).

It seems the above meanings are not necessarily about an external identity but about an internal 'being', of how one feels about oneself and how one feels about oneself in relation to what one has faith in.

In Islamic thought these stages of being or faith have traditionally been described as *Islam, Iman* and *Ihsan,* but what they describe is not actually faith or belief per se. Jacques (2010) seems to suggest that the use of the terms 'surrender', 'faith' and 'belief' to describe these three stages has been an cumulative achievement of limited translations. They are conceptual terms whose meanings become evident through an etymological journey. The following key dimensions from Halima Krausen's reflection on *What is Islam?*[2] aim to reveal what they cumulatively may mean as an act of being (Table 2.1).

Table 2.1: Dimensions of being: *Iman* **and** *Ihsan*

Iman	Ihsan
Amuna: to be faithful, trustworthy, to be convinced, to have faith *Aman:* certainty, protection, safety, peace *Amin:* reliable, trustworthy, loyal, honest *Amana:* entrusted object, reliability, faithfulness *Mu'min:* believing, trusting, convinced, reliable	*Hasuna:* to be good, beautiful, adequate *Husn:* goodness, beauty, perfection *Hasan:* good, beautiful, pleasant *Istihsan:* agreement, consent, finding the best and most practical

The three stages suggest a movement from Islam as an act of acceptance, to an act of trust which then, as *Ihsan,* 'beautifies' one's actions and behaviour. They are more succinctly described by Buchman (1998, p xi) as 'doing, knowing and being: or practice, doctrine and realisation'.

---

[1] www.halimakrausen.com

[2] www.halimakrausen.com

They are more attributes to be cultivated than a simple invocation to believe, and lead to the idea that discernment is not something done to young people but something that can only emerge from the development of self-consciousness, that is, *taqwa* – how principles such as empowerment find resonance and expression in Islam.

Muslim youth work has often been 'understood' as the management or the gendering of space, that by separating young men from young women an inference is drawn that this is Muslim youth work or a Muslim social pedagogy. It is work with young Muslims but this does not mean that it is youth work or Muslim youth work. Tom Wylie's (House of Commons Education Committee, 2012) model is one means of differentiating between different types of organisations and their association or work with young people (see Figure 2.1).

Figure 2.1: Wylie's young people, organisations and youth work model

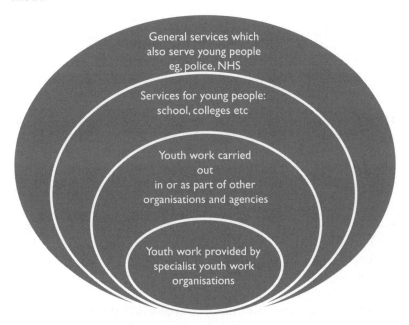

General services which also serve young people eg, police, NHS

Services for young people: school, colleges etc

Youth work carried out in or as part of other organisations and agencies

Youth work provided by specialist youth work organisations

Source: House of Commons Education Committee (2012)

Spence (2006) cites a number of motives that have informed work with girls and young women including character building, challenging gender inequality legitimised by legislation (see, for example, the Sex Discrimination Act 1970) and a space away from the 'male gaze', as well as challenging a masculine professional landscape that leaves little scope for the needs of young women in mixed gender contexts. Cressey (2007) titled her book *The ultimate separatist cage?* to challenge the way gendered work with Muslim young women was being perceived as an extension of the veil in public spaces, offering examples of practice from a variety of organisations from England and Wales. Perversely, the strength of Muslim stereotype makes it difficult to see where gendered space can empower and support critically.

Freire and the pedagogical space

A seminal figure in the world of radical pedagogy, Paolo Freire divides the worlds of learning uncompromisingly between the formal educational world characterised by the powerlessness of the student and the powerfulness of the teacher and the institution, and the informal world which challenges this powerlessness, presenting a dialogical approach to learning based on an equal relationship between the students and teacher. He identifies five conditions for a meaningful dialogue, and by extension, a meaningful learning relationship (Freire, 1970):

> love   hope   faith   humility   trust   critical thinking

These conditions not only say something about the relationship but also about the informal educator, their character, critical awareness of the context and also the student. For Freire these conditions for a dialogical approach to learning were not followed by a section on professional boundaries or ethical conduct, which is very much part of the professionalisation of services for young people today, including youth work. His writing captures the intensity of the relationship needed and the transformational nature of this for the learner and the teacher. Carl Rogers, in his earlier writings (1961), formulated core conditions that include the need for unconditional positive regard towards the client and the genuineness of the therapist in what should be a relationship, yet towards the end of his life, he emphasised the importance of 'presence' in his book *A way of being* (Rogers, 1980). Professions with established ethical conduct guidelines such as medicine and law are often about a contractual understanding, with the boundaries acting more in the interest of the doctor and lawyer then the client or patient, and this boundary space is one that informal educators are constantly questioning and negotiating, seen both as a strength in times of societal crisis or panic, and suspicious or unprofessional during 'peace time'.

Freire's message is not just about realising the self but also the world in which we live; for him, education that is liberatory encourages learners to challenge and change the world, not merely uncritically adapt themselves to it through what he refers to as magical consciousness where people adapt themselves passively to a superior force. Freire's content and purpose of liberatory education is the collective responsibility of learners, teachers and the community alike who, through dialogue, seek political, as well as economic and personal empowerment. Clearly influenced by Freire, bell hooks (2003) saw education for critical consciousness as important to develop and sustain contexts for Black empowerment and self-esteem and critical in emancipatory struggles, whether on 'race', gender or sexuality (the struggles of prominent activists such as Malcolm X and Steve Biko are examples of this), and the life and death implications of this critical consciousness is clear to both Freire and hooks.

The theoretical framework that I propose here for Muslim youth work is essentially about relationships, and in part it is a reaction to the way that the idea of relationships has often been treated by youth workers as a means to an end rather than an end in itself. The advocacy of the voluntary nature of relationships that characterises the relationship between the youth worker and the young person is so deeply ingrained that it can become a mantra, as something beyond question, and thus no longer a conscious act. This ability to establish relationships and to build trust can make informal educators extremely influential people in the lives of young people, and knowledgeable about the experiences and outlooks of young people. This explains why funding work with young people has often taken a meandering route through such agendas as reducing teenage pregnancy, preventing violent extremism, drugs awareness and community cohesion, and then 'sub-contracted', in the case of statutory sector, to youth work projects rather than youth services directly, despite the fact that these workers may have been employed by them. This can mean that these relationships become necessary for the continued policy relevance of the youth worker rather than the need of the young person. The principle of the voluntary relationship has made the move from an idea of ethical action to a foundational belief that can make informal educators extremely sensitive to any charges that challenge how they may work.

The following differentiation between types of knowledge helps in further visualising types of youth work or informal education approaches, and perhaps helps tease out the differences between Freire's pedagogy and the limits of what has often been possible or allowed, in the British context at least. McLaren (2003, p 73) models three locales of knowledge posited by Habermas:

- *Technical knowledge:* about knowledge that can be measured and quantified. It is a form of knowledge that McLaren states is used to sort, regulate and control learners. It has often involved youth workers in first-step vocational programmes that have often been linked to receipt of benefits or allowances. It is also what governments have sought to do to youth services through the targets set by New Labour's *Transforming youth work* agenda.
- *Practical knowledge:* the ability of the learner to describe and analyse social situations. It is a form of knowledge that aims to help people understand what is going on in events and situations.
- *Emancipatory knowledge:* aims to 'reveal' how social relations are distorted and manipulated by relationships of 'power and privilege'. This is the locale and role of the critical educator. This awareness reaches into the distal or underlying, structural causes, and as Freire says, 'names' them.

Butters and Newell (1978) suggested that, historically, there are three main perspectives in youth work.

- Character building for the mature serving citizen.
- What they term as the 'social education repertoire'. The first is one of cultural adjustment to create healthy young adults, the second is the need to generate involvement in community and the third is informing institutional reform through mobilising young people and groups.
- Self-emancipation through collective struggle directed towards institutions and ideologies that oppress them.

Contemporary youth work, as we have come to see it, often appears to sit in the first two of these categories; this includes voluntary sector youth work, which as it has become increasingly state aligned has often found it difficult to embrace sitting in the latter, in Freirean pedagogy. This pedagogy is not a politically neutral or purely educational exercise; it is an exercise in political awakening, asking for engagement, not passivity, to one's condition and context. Couss et al (2010) describe it as an oscilation, a tension between the role of the worker as a liberator as part of some social movement or as someone domesticating young people. Neil Thompson's (2006) PCS model seems to have become the standard model to understand how oppression works.

It identifies oppression working in three spheres: personal, cultural and structural. Freire, through his key notions of conscientisation or critical consciousness and 'naming the world', does not shy away from challenging oppression in any of these worlds, but this is a particularly precarious task for young Muslims where an analysis or challenge to the 'system' has been 're-translated' into the language of extremism and fundamentalism rather than of political radicalism (political awareness) – it has, in effect, become a denial of politics.

Spence (2006) acknowledges the attraction and adoption of this radical pedagogy within the social education traditions in youth work (Davies and Gibson, 1967), but goes on to observe how this social education paradigm has failed, as yet, to materialise into the kind of radical paradigm that Freire models. Where Freire names the oppression in mainstream learning pedagogies, hooks names her oppression as a Black American woman as White, supremacist, patriarch capitalism; it seems that what youth work has done over the years is name principles based within a person-centred approach that have shied away from structural issues. This does not mean that young people were not naming their oppression, whether it was young Black people who named their oppressor as Babylon in the 1980s or young Muslims who have named theirs as the *kuffar*.

Knowledge, knowing and consciousness

The ideas central to youth work and informal education have a powerful history and tradition in Islam. Seyyed Hossein Nasr (2010), in the introduction to his chapter on 'Islamic education, philosophy and science', states that:

> As far as Islamic education and science are concerned, they both cover such a vast expanse of intellectual space and historical time that it is hardly possible to do justice to them. (Nasr, 2010, p 129)

In Islam, knowledge, according to Nasr (2010), was never divorced from the sacred; it was the means to the sacred, as this verse from the Qur'an expresses:

> O my Lord! Make me perfect in knowledge and conduct and include me among those whom You have rewarded with Your nearness. (26:83)

The human ability to acquire knowledge is by itself sacred. The notion of 'wholesness' is closely related to the ideas of holiness in which education is meant to encompass the whole being. Nasr points out that the transmission of knowledge (*ta'lim*) cannot be divorced from the process of training the whole person (*tarbiyyah*) – the student; he captures this idea in the following story which seems particularly apt and applicable when applied to the banking crisis that has recently engulfed the world:

> The Persian poet Sanai calls a person who possesses knowledge without moral and spiritual character is a virtual thief more dangerous than an ordinary robber: 'if a thief comes with a lamp, he can steal more than precious goods.' (Nasr, 2010, p 131)

For Imam al-Ghazali (1058-1111), the purpose of knowledge 'is to come to understand the article of belief rather than accepting them on faith' (Bakhtiar, 1994, p 11). The process of coming to this understanding is essentially Socratic in method as this understanding is already innate; the purpose of the educator is to bring this forth. The Qur'an refers to the recognition of signs (*ayat*) as an impulse of this bringing innate qualities to the surface and intuitive sense or knowledge of the self and the world:

> And among his signs is the creation of the heavens and the earth, and the variations in your languages and your colours; verily in that are signs for those who know. (*Surah*, 30:22)

> We shall show them Our signs upon the horizons and within themselves until it is clear to view that it is the Real. (41:53)

The idea of signs is a key theme or invocation that appears on a regular basis in the Qur'an (288 times) (Murata, 1992); it is the means by which God is asking to be seen and recognised. Murata lists the human responses to God's signs as 'remembering, understanding, seeing, reflecting, gratitude, the use of the intellect...' (1992, p 24). An *ayat* represents something beyond its surface meaning and function; the repeated invocation and reminder of signs is a repeated call for humans to be critically conscious or aware of the world in which they live because 'things tell us something beyond themselves'. Signs are the connection between the visible and invisible, natural phenomenon and divine revelation. They ask a movement from the habitual to the cognitive, from the unconscious to the conscious, from mindlessness to mindfulness. This signalling to something within is captured by the Islamic equivalent to the notion of spirituality, *ruhaniyyah*, which, when rendered in English, means spirit or souls, and *ma'nawiyyah*, meaning pointing to something inward in contrast to something external (Nasr, 2010).

This cognition of signs also frames time. El Guindi (2008) divides times and space between ordinary time and space and sacred time and space, with the experience of the signs generating the movement between the two for individuals. It is in this movement that the spiritual and the transcendental are experienced.

The 'knowing' of the signs is possible from the individual due to the notion of *fitra*, which Kahteran describes as follows:

> The linguistic and religious meaning of *fitra* is the immutable, natural predisposition to the good. Innate in every being from birth, or even from the pre-existent state in which, as Islamic doctrine teaches, the human soul enters into a covenant with God. (Kahteran, 2006, p 211)

The concept of original sin is found in the New Testament teaching of the Apostle – Romans 5:12-21 and 1 Corinthians 15:22 do not exist in Islamic theology. The notion of *fitra* suggests a predilection to the 'good' rather than the 'evil' as inherent at birth.

The importance of experiential learning and the process of individuation so central to youth work pedagogy has a powerful tradition in Sufi teaching methods. Idries Shah captures the importance of experience and process to an individual's ability to value knowledge or to at least know its value through the following saying in his book, *Learning how to learn*:

> The wise know because they have paid for their wisdom. You do not accept their counsel because it is offered for so much less than they have paid for it. (1978, p 283)

The idea of learning how to learn is central to Shah's work, and his use of stories such as those of Mulla Nasruddin is an example of what he describes as 'conduct teaching', where the lessons are drawn from the conduct of the protagonists in the story. The story often reveals the importance of looking beyond the surface or simple cause-and-effect explanations for people's conditions or circumstances. Shah provides a fascinating and empowering definition of a learner 'as someone who learns, not someone who thinks he is a student' (1978, p 282). This seems to reveal a similar idea to that of Freire's 'banking' metaphor of schooling, but his language takes us out of the teacher–student paradigm. Within this tradition reading does not equate to knowledge or wisdom; it is not automatic that schooling is education or that education is wisdom or knowledge, or that it will make you less oppressive or humble – the opposite can be the case. This difference between the two can be useful to explore when considering the first exchange between the Archangel Gabriel and the Prophet Muhammad (pbuh, peace be upon Him) in which Gabriel commands the Prophet to 'Read in the name of thy Lord who creates', to which the Prophet replied that 'I am not a reader'. He does not say he has no knowledge or is not educated, simply that 'I am not a reader'. A messenger of God who cannot read is an interesting idea to explore with young people. It seems to separate knowledge which is defined by experiential learning and that of education or schooling which is often defined by reading and writing or what was traditionally termed as the 'three r's' (reading, writing and arithmetic), treating the later as an acquired skill rather than an innate gnosis (knowledge).

Imam al-Ghazali is one of the most significant figures in Muslim history after the Prophet Muhammad (pbuh). In his book *Letters to a disciple*, probably written towards the end of his life, he illustrates the importance of action to knowledge, giving the following advice to his students (Mayer, 2005):

- Disciple, knowledge without action is madness and action without knowledge is void. (Mayer, 2005, p 16)
- Disciple, be neither destitute of good deeds nor devoid of spiritual state, for you can be sure that mere knowledge will not help. (p 16)
- If a man studied a hundred thousand intellectual issues and understood them but did not act on the strength of them, they would not be of use to him except by taking action. (p 8)

The above are three examples from this text among many; the relationship to action and within this to experience and *dhawq* (taste), is both pedagogical and political. Within this personal 'contract' in the acquisition of knowledge is the commitment to act, and the commitment to act seems to be central to the ideas of knowing and becoming for learning.

For Nasr (2010) it seems it is Mulla Sadra (1571-1640) who captures the transformative purpose of knowledge, 'for knowledge transforms the being of the knower' (2010, p 159), and this is the purpose of education. Jalaluddin Rumi captures this constant transmutation in his famous poem from the 'Mathnavi':

> I died as a mineral and became a plant,
> I died as plant and rose to animal,
> I died as animal and I was Man.
> Why should I fear? When was I less by dying?

Relationships, experience and action are intertwined and co-dependent concepts within a Muslim pedagogy, and in their centre are the acquisition and use of knowledge as a personal transformative agent; a societal transformative agent and the role of the 'guide' is captured and described by Hafiz in his poem 'Elegance' (translated by Daniel Ladinsky, 1999):

> It is not easy
> To stop thinking ill of others
> Usually one must enter into a relationship
> With a person
> Who has accomplished that great feat himself
> Then
> Something might rub off on you
> Of that
> True
> Elegance.

Putting forward a Muslim youth work theory

A theory for Muslim youth work is conceptualised as an ideal type to frame youth work practice and critique perspectives. The principles, motivations and values that have shaped youth work over the last hundred years have become part of normative theory, practice and language that has created a paradigm that shapes youth and community work. These paradigms are assumed to apply to all groups while resisting the presence, relevance and compatibility of alternative paradigms that give resonance to key principles in a new story:

> The prevailing paradigm is quite simply taken for granted within the contemporary scientific ethos. Any challenges

that are mounted tend, at the start at least, to be dismissed out of hand. Normal science, Kuhn says, often suppresses fundamental novelties because they are necessarily subversive of its basic commitments. (Crotty, 1998, p 35)

The force confronted in putting forward alternative paradigms brings to focus Apple's (1990) assertion that education institutions do not just process people, they also process knowledge, 'acting as agents of cultural and ideological hegemony, selecting both tradition and means of cultural incorporation' (p 6). Presenting alternatives involves a price to pay for the presenter as I, too, often experienced in my youth work practice. The effort in presenting and making a case for the alternative is often been met with queries, questions and problems that are taken for granted in 'normal youth work'. Too often when the case is made and 'won' you are left too exhausted to give it the energy required to enact.

Analytical tools are needed to understand the opportunities young people have, how they are 'constructed' culturally, historically, spiritually and ethnically as Muslims, and their confidence and sensitivity as participants in the public sphere (Brah, 1996). In Bronfenbrenner's (1979) social ecology model, the young person is presented in the centre of a series of circles.

Each layer represents the range of influences informing and having an impact on the young person. This is by and large a one-way process. Each layer demands a particular kind of relationship often associated with ideas of compliance and affiliation, and this relationship is named through the notion of being someone's son/daughter, a student, a citizen, a believer, a member or employee, and not forgetting the consumer; all entail a sense of belonging to somebody or something. The development of a sense of agency in a world of imposing structures for the young person is a key function of the informal educator or youth worker, and this role is informed by the principles named by Davies and Batsleer et al.

However, as Christian (1999) states, youth work thinking and practice has done little to consider or integrate the concepts that are made available in a diverse multicultural and multireligious society and that could be employed for the spiritual development of young people.

It is in this context that I now discuss a proposed theoretical framework for Muslim youth work. I have deliberately used the term 'Muslim' as for me it captures the diversity of culture and understandings that make up the Muslim world. Both Islam and youth work have in common an importance for process. After all, the Qur'an was revealed over 23 years, during which time it was reflected, meditated and deliberated on rather than in one act, of revelation. When you make a cursory study of the first four *Khalifas* (meaning successor or representative), it quickly becomes obvious that they were four quite distinct individuals who spent 23 years experiencing the same revelation with the Prophet Muhammad (pbuh), each experiencing and reflecting this revelation in their attributes and spiritual being.

The journey to this text began approximately 12 years ago (in 2000) with the aim of identifying a Muslim youth work curriculum. I did not begin the 'Muslim youth work journey' to develop a theoretical model, but it became increasingly clear that what was required was a theoretical framework to which a variety of curricula could be applied and understood. This meant that existing operational curricula could not be made redundant because they did not have the badge 'Islamic' next to them, whether this was environmental youth work, or a drop-in youth club. To me, curricula mean a type of activity or a 'vehicle' for learning. What the theoretic framework enables is a Muslim connection, purpose or meaning. It addresses the purpose of youth work, articulated by Young as:

> ... an exercise in moral philosophy in the sense that it enables and supports young people to ask and answer the central questions of self – 'what sort of person am I', 'what kind of relationships do I want with myself and others' and 'what kind of society do I want live in?' Integral to this process is the issue of identity, 'who am I?' – a concept which refers not only to a person's self-image – their description of self, or knowledge of membership of a social group – but also to their self-esteem, an individual's evaluation of their self-worth. (Young, 1999, p 2)

Young (1999) demands that values and virtue be core principles of youth work as these are key components that determine individual world views and relationships. For Young, it is what they believe, their sense of right and wrong, good and bad, that makes young people who they are and that contributes to their sense of self-worth. In my experience, it is relationships that enable this process of individual reflection and action for young people in the context of youth work. For Young, the purpose and nature of youth work is 'identity'; this is its defining philosophy. She views identity not as a problem but as a key feature of 'youth'. Therefore the ability to support and enable young people to form, critique, express and translate their own identity is critical for any individual or organisation working with young people.

The means to form and shape this identity is by means of relationships, and it is relationships that engage them in a learning process in which they:

> ... are supported to create and re-create themselves, take charge of their relationships (with self and others), actively engage in their community and contribute to the world. (Young, 1999, p 63)

The importance of 'relationships' has already been mentioned as a key principle. Its importance in defining a Muslim theoretical perspective is absolutely central, as will be discussed.

Yavuz (2004) captures this importance of identity, seeing Islam empowering people to cope with the three major dimensions of globalisation: social justice, identity and the ethics of engagement and morality. The relationship between the forces of globalisation and individual identity is, as stated earlier, captured by Castells' assertion (1996) that the struggle taking place in the global context is not the struggle between Islam and the 'West', but the struggle between global capitalism which requires people to have roles or roles that are changeable, which governments accommodate through 'a trained workforce', and the opportunity for workers to respond to the need of changing skills sets. Castells sets this in contrast to the individual need for meaning, identity and belonging. Abdoolkareem Soroush (2000) touches on this through his interpretation of the Kantian notion of essence and form, the inward essence or state and the outward symbolic or form.

The importance of Islam to young Muslims was particularly evident in a role-play exercise that I carried out with groups of young Muslims that asked a simple question, 'What would you give up to fit it in?'

You are decision makers of a small country at war with a much bigger and much more powerful neighbour. You neighbour has offered peace in exchange for you giving up the following. Your task is to decide at first individually and then collectively what you are prepared to give up for peace. The following is what is being asked to be given up:

Your language	Cultural food	Your neighbourhood	Your community
National dress	National flag	Your family	Your religion
National anthem	Your political beliefs		

In virtually every occasion when this exercise was carried out with groups of young Muslims they would choose religion as the last thing they would give up, if at all. The ages varied from 14 to 17, but the feedback would always be the same. What this scenario brings out is that there is always something that could not be given up, whether it is language, political beliefs or the national flag, and this scenario has been presented to people of many backgrounds, values and beliefs.

The Qur'an as source

Any responses in terms of ideas, application or interpretation gain legitimacy in the Muslim world if they find their roots in the Qur'an. It is here that they gain their moral authority, as the Qur'an is viewed as the book for guidance:

> This is the Book. In it is guidance, sure, without doubt. To those who fear Allah. (2:2)

Muslims have rarely argued the nature of the Qur'an as God's word, but have differed in terms of its meaning and role in society (Esack, 1997, Sells, 1999; Sardar 2011). This difference is reflected in the struggles of meaning; you only have to look at different translations of the Qur'an, as Sardar does, to see the divergent meanings attributed to verses within it, and his scathing analysis of Saudi-inspired translations in particular. Over recent times an attitude has been cultivated that has generated a cognitive predilection to caution and conservatism, a sense that the narrower the path you travel or the interpretation you choose, the purer your Islam. The limitation of translation to capture meanings of concepts and the politics of vested interests in what a concept means is played out by notions such as *taqwa*. Yusuf Ali, in the verse above (2:2), translates *taqwa* as fear, as do many other translations. Esack (1997) and Sells (1999) describe it as 'to guard against' mindfulness, 'heeding the voice of one's conscience in the awareness that one is accountable' (Esack, 1997, p 87). The difference between the two meanings affect one's approach to the Qur'an in terms of the level of deference to authority, the type of relationship to God and the importance attached to fear rather than self-reflection and critique. Esack (2005) lists the different approaches taken to the Qur'an or relationships that are made. Each can be a determinant of the interpretation and understanding derived:

- *Ordinary Muslim*, which he calls the 'uncritical lover' who is astounded by the doubt others express in what they find as perfect. S/he enjoys the relationship without asking too many questions about it.
- *Confessional Muslim scholar*, whom Esack refers to as the 'scholarly lover' who wants to explain to everyone the attributes of what s/he finds so perfect.
- The *critical Muslim scholar*, who he calls the 'critical lover', who will understand questions with regard to the object as something that will enable her/him to understand the object even more.
- The *revisionist*, one who is disinterested and whom Esack calls a 'voyeur', someone disinterested in the relationship of the lover and the beloved and views her/himelf as an impartial observer, matching sources with contexts to come to an understanding of Islam and the Qur'an. S/he views her/himself as value-free in approaching this subject.
- The *polemicist*, who is more interested in the virtues of another and wishes nothing more but to disparage the Qur'an.

For Nasr (2010), the Qur'an contains the roots of all knowledge, but not necessarily all its details. The word 'Qur'an' comes from the Arabic *al-Qur'an*, meaning the recitation, and Nasr also lists the following attributes or qualities – *Al-Furqan* (the discernment), *Umm Al-Kitab* (the mother of all books), as well as *Al-Huda* (the guidance), and the *Al-Hidayah* (the guidance that educates the whole human being).

The Qur'an is viewed and experienced as the most 'independent' non-partisan space that Muslims can go to; it is the book to which falseness has no access; it is a place that cultivates the internal grace to cope with external trauma. Muhammad Iqbal (1877-1938), also known as Allama Iqbal, a philosopher, poet and a political activist in British India who is widely regarded to have inspired the creation of Pakistan and is considered one of the most important figures in Urdu literature, emphasises this individual relationship:

> Until the Qur'an is revealed to your own heart, Neither Razi nor the author of the Kashaf will unite its knots for you. (Mir, 2006, p 3)

By referring to two immense figures in the history of Islamic thought, Imam Abu Hamid al-Ghazali and Fakhr al-Din al-Razi (1149–1209), Iqbal seeks to impress the need for a direct relationship and not one mediated by a third party. However, the fear of inculcation by mediators and translators and the institutionalising of meaning by religious bodies can deny the subjective and the personal, leaving the Qur'an as something to be followed rather than engaged with or understood.

Ziauddin Sardar (2011), in *Reading the Qur'an*, talks about the Qur'an as an emotional relationship with different encounters, evoking different experiences and emotional connections – his mother's unconditional love and reverence as well as respect and humility towards the Qur'an shaping his formative encounters and informing his relationship to the Qur'an; but there is also the fear that is invoked by his memory of the *imam* at the *madrasah*. Sardar achieves something distinctive (much as Esack earlier) through this book, and that is in bringing a private relationship to the Qur'an into a public space. The oft-repeated saying that there is no public and private in Islam is one that rather than empower the individual can be oppressive, disempowering and silencing. The public space is often claimed by privilege and consensus and the realpolitik of the public space is that it does not welcome dissenting perspectives or relationships. It is the space of the objective, the truth rather than the subjective, and the personal, as these cannot be deemed either objective or truthful. bell hooks (2003) suggests that claims of objectivity lead to claims of truth, and claims of truth lead people to want to bring others to their truth. Sardar, in bringing the personal into the public, challenges this, and gives legitimacy to this relationship and its expression publicly, whereas this would normally have been the preserve of the *ulama*, the Muslim clergy.

Sardar expresses the trepidation that I feel in writing of the Qur'an in this book. There is often a fear instilled towards the Qur'an, particularly by *imams* and *madrasahs* and family for that matter, that damages an individual's confidence to grasp ideas and concepts in the Qur'an and that creates a need for a third party mediator in the relationship. Fear that evokes caution is one thing, and a fear that disables has enormous implications for individuals and society, but what it definitely achieves is the need for mediators and the cultivation of deference that, according to Abou El Fadl (2003), allows an individual to surrender their private judgement in favour of special knowledge or authority. Yet the Qur'an does not address humanity through mediators; it speaks directly and powerfully to the person reading it.

The metaphor of the currents of a river is used by Elif Safak (2010) to describe the Qur'an – from a distance you can only see one current, but if you dive in you will experience that there may be a number of currents invisible from a distance. The person looking from a distance describes what they see, that is, the surface; the person diving in describes a sudden connection, a new relationship and appreciation, an experience and a realisation that there are a number of currents running that are invisible to the person looking at the surface.

This has been merely an introductory exploration of the power of notions of informal education and radical pedagogy found in Muslim history through the examples of key figures, the thoughts of polymaths and the inspiration of poets. However they might choose to describe their vocation and identity, social pedagogues, youth workers and informal educators will find a powerful tradition which can inform and enrich practice and approach.

THREE

The relationships model: a theoretical framework for Muslim youth work[1]

Since no one really knows anything about God
Those who think they do
are just
Trouble makers.

Rabia al-Basra (717–801);
translated by Daniel Ladinsky (2002)

---

[1] This model has been inspired by the work of Halima Krausen.

The importance of the development of theoretical frameworks has become increasingly necessary for a number of reasons:

- to analyse the configuration of individual relationships;
- to analyse the relationships prioritised by organisations and their subsequent investment;
- to identify relational deficits and priorities;
- to identify the purpose and outcome of an activity;
- that existing curriculum and thinking is not dismissed simply because it does not have the badge of Islam on it.

The proposed understanding of Muslim youth work as a relational exercise that integrates key principles of youth work practice and process is difficult to present due to the manner in which it may be understood as part of a cultural or confessional paradigm, and the manner in which Islam and Muslims have become involved in a struggle of symbols of identity that have been moved from acts of individual faith or piety to that of political and personal identity. Soroush's (2000) configuration of identity as consisting of form and essence (form being the 'clothing' of faith, its visible presence, and essence of values and principles) is useful in this working out.

The theoretical framework presented in this chapter acts as a means of identity analysis through actual relationships constructed. It has the potential to understand types of identity that are being created – consumer, believer, worker and so on – by identifying types of relationships that are being invested in and who they are being invested in by. It has an ability to make sense of questions that challenge Muslim constructions of the private and the public and to delve into the smokescreen that can be provided by commonly used or cited mantras of Islam being 'one', whole, all-encompassing, which does not differentiate the private or the public. It can draw out powerful theological questions as to the role of 'organised religion' in the relationships it seeks to connect individuals to – is it to a community of believers, to the *ulama* (clergy), to a better understanding of oneself? What is the type of relation to God that is being cultivated? And given that the notion of *ayats* (signs) discussed earlier is so powerful, then what is the relationship to creation or environment that has developed?

The 'relationships model' set out here is based, as stated earlier, on the concept of relationships as the pedagogic space and the outcome, using the Islamic concept of *jahiliyyah* and that of *salah* in terms of its basic literal meaning, which is connection, although the word is more powerfully associated with prayer – it captures the locales of where young people can sit in their relationships to themselves, community, God or belief and creation or environment. Therefore the relational trajectory runs from the concept *jahiliyyah* that I connect to distance and alienation, to a series of meaningful interconnected relationships. Together they frame an ideal type theoretical framework for Muslim youth work which I refer to here as the relationships model, or as a 'theoretical framework for Muslim youth work' (see Figure 3.1).

Figure 3.1: Disconnection and connection

Jahilyyah --- *Salah* (connections)

Jahiliyyah

Hitti (1970) rendered the term *jahiliyyah* to mean a time of ignorance or barbarism which in Islamic discourse often means the period in which Arabia had no dispensation, no inspired Prophet or revealed book. The context, according to Lapidus (1988), was that only Mecca stood out against the trend of political and social fragmentation and provided the one major focus of social and economic order. This period at the dawn of Islam in Arabia has been described as the *jahiliyyah* and as a time of economic advancement (Lapidus, 1988), but not necessarily spiritual or social enlightenment; it is associated with practices such as infanticide and idol worship. The image created alludes to a culture that is barbarous, without law and order, purpose or scruples. People's morality and ethics played a secondary role to their business needs and tribal status. A simple analysis of this period, however, shows that the people had access to food, shelter, transport and trade for other needs. They hosted large gatherings of pilgrims as the 'guardians' of the house of Abraham charged with the welfare of the pilgrims. They were international business people, proud of their ancestry, very much as today. Therefore the reality of this situation at the dawn of Islam is more complex than the image that is manufactured and sold to provide a clear break between now and then, as now we supposedly have law, order, meaning, scruples, a message and a Messenger (Watt, 1953; Hitti, 1970). The reality was that it was a sophisticated society, a city-state, whose leaders had grown proud of their success based on their mercantile skills and ancestry. The question this description leaves us with is, what has changed?

Jahiliyyah is not a state that can be crudely or simply defined as one that was without a message or a book, or a society that had forgotten the teachings of its ancestors when there was such unbending loyalty to ancestral tradition. It is not a state of affairs that should be fixed in time, but it has became useful in providing a 'revelatory' cut, a before and after. The behaviour that defined the *jahiliyyah* is human behaviour and as such can be repeated. Therefore the definition of *jahiliyyah* must be one that can illuminate this state at any time in history. It has particular resonance with the present time. Unlike the Prophet Jesus (pbuh) who represented a challenge to an empire and possibly an accommodation with power, and the Prophet Moses (pbuh) who challenged an emperor, the Prophet Muhammad (pbuh) challenged a recognisable 'city-state'. Mecca was a city rather than an empire. It was ruled via representatives of the various tribes (parties) that operated a form of consensus, as demonstrated by the decision to assassinate the Prophet Muhammad (pbuh) early on in his prophecy (Haykal, 1976; Lings, 1983).

It may be useful to come to understandings of *jahiliyyah* through the notion and process of 'alienation', a term associated with Marxist philosophy. Marxists and Muslims make interesting 'bed fellows' in relation to alienation. For Marx, the history of humanity is of the increasing control of humans over nature and at the same time increasing alienation. Alienation was understood by Marx (1964) to be a condition in which humans are confronted and dominated by forces of their own creation in capitalist society, such as religion, the state and political economy. Whereas Muslim understanding of *jahiliyyah* shares in the caution of material greed, it parts company for some people with the idea that religion is alienating. However, the Qur'an itself does recognise that empty ritualistic religious practices, with inappropriate and unclear intentions, can be alienating. It is interesting that Marx identified control over nature as historically linked with alienation; the Muslim understanding of *jahiliyyah* is also concerned with humanity's relationship with nature, but with the sharp distinction that nature is regarded as God's creation. According to Berger (1967, p 85), alienation is:

> ... the process whereby the dialectical relationship between the individual and his world is lost to consciousness. The individual 'forgets' that this world was and continues to be co-produced by him.

Yet the potential to reconnect is something innate in human beings, as *Surah At-Tin* says:

We have indeed created man in the best of moulds. (95:4)

Marx proposed that alienation in the domain of work alienated the individual from the object s/he produced, from the process of production, from her/himself and from the community of their fellows. The confusions that this may cause are commented on by the Qur'an, 'But leave them in their confused ignorance for a time' (23:54).

The notion and experience of alienation inform the ideal type theory for Muslim youth work. This proposes that there are four key relational domains, all interconnected to lead to *tawhid* (unity), an imbalance in one creating an imbalance in all layers of society, individual, family, communal, societal and environmental. The relationship to the self is prioritised as the key or central relationship as it understands and enacts all the other relationships. God is neither better nor worse if you do or do not have this relationship, but seeking relationships, without a deep awareness of self, can prove destructive in a variety of ways when the sacred is used to reaffirm beliefs and behaviours about the self and others (see Figure 3.2).

In this theoretical model relationships are seen as the outcome rather than a youth work method or as a means to an end. The relationship between, for example, an individual and God, is mediated through a series of relationships, each signposting and revealing something of

Figure 3.2: Relationships model

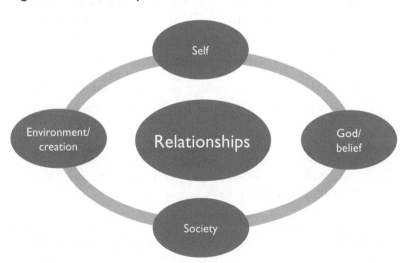

themselves and something of God. According to this reading of the Qur'an, the aim of Muslim lifestyle choices should be about bringing these relationships into balance. The Islamic term *deen* means to set things straight or to get things back into a just proportion, therefore the term *Yawm ad-deen*, the 'Day of Judgement', although today, *deen* is colloquially used to denote religion or faith. The relationships model could describe the spirit that underpins the legal principles of *shari'ah* (Islamic law) based on the concept of justice as expressed in the terms *adl* (justice in the sense of balance) and *qist* (justice in the sense of restoring the balance). Examples of these terms in use can be found in the Qur'an:

> O ye who believe! Stand out firmly for justice, as witnesses to Allah, even as against yourselves, or your parents, or your kin and whether it be (against) rich or poor. (4:135)

and:

> O ye who believe! Stand out firmly for Allah, as witnesses to fair dealing, and let not the hatred of others make you swerve to wrong and part from justice. Be just: that is next to piety: and fear Allah. For Allah is well acquainted with all that ye do. (5:8)

(In the above, Surah's *taqwa*, meaning God-conscious, is again translated and interpreted as fear.)

Alienation is referred to as 'those who lost their own souls'. This is particularly mentioned in relation to the Day of Judgement when this is a sign of those who have not 'believed', and the judgement alludes to the damage that this has caused in one's life in relation to the self and to God:

> Say: 'Travel through the earth and see what was the end of those who rejected truth.' Say: 'to whom belongeth all that is in the heavens and on earth.' Say: 'To Allah. He hath inscribed for Himself mercy. That he will gather you together for the Day of Judgement, there is no doubt whatever, it is they who have lost their own souls that will not believe.' (*Surah*, 6:11-12)

One aspect mentioned in 3:112 is 'the tie with God and the tie with people' (Yusuf Ali's translation is 'a covenant from Allah and from men').

This can be observed in every religious act, for example, the five pillars of Islam. Alienation from these pillars is also then seen as a weakness of these ties. Much of the ritual and rites of Muslim life are communal. To pray at the same time, to go through the same ablution rituals, to face the same direction in prayer, to come together at the same time for the same purpose on pilgrimage, to fast and begin your fast at the same time, to study the same book, to be conscious of your surroundings and of those in need to give *zakat* (alms) – these all connect, in varying degrees, time, place and location.

A conceptual Muslim youth work theory encompasses the dynamic that moves individuals from *jahiliyyah* towards balanced relationships. If Islam was and is the point of departure from *jahiliyyah*, the areas of alienation need to be considered as locations of intervention. The means of moving on from alienation is based on the principle of re-establishing and then having balanced relationships. In youth work discourse, relationship work is a key foundational principle; for example, all relationships between the youth worker and the young person have to be of choice and without compulsion. The relationship between the youth worker and the young person can be a space in which relationships are discussed, tested out and relational skills and attributes discussed, challenged and developed – for this, youth clubs are extremely important to facilitate a person-centred approach that can allow such relationships to be developed. Ideally, through this relationship and the work undertaken, either one-to-one or as a group, on specific issues and concerns, it often becomes clear that relationships matter to young people. To reiterate, within a theory of Muslim youth work the following would be the key overarching relationships:

- relationship with self
- relationship with God or from wherever one derives one's beliefs
- relationship with community (subdivided into immediate family, extended family, community, society)
- relationship with creation or environment.

Each of these elements needs further elaboration to understand or recognise the existence or absence of these elements in youth work practice. Each ideally involves communication, choice, responsibility, opportunity, respect, mutuality, enquiry, challenge and understanding. In the movement 'from alienation to relationship', a range of interventions or curriculum emerges, and its role and effect can be used selectively with the type of relationship one seeks to establish.

Relationship with self

According to Imam al-Ghazali (1058-1111), the establishment of any relationship begins with gaining knowledge of oneself (Bakhtiar, 1994); alongside this a recognition the starting point in understanding love, according Imam Ghazali, was love of self, a love we all can recognise (Al-Ghazali translated by Ormsby, 2011, p XXV). This knowledge of self is particularly important in the relationship to God. The self here encompasses the physical and what often is referred to as the soul. Bakhtiar (1994) calls the self the soul in human form.

Various terms are used to describe the self: heart (*qalb*), soul (*nafs*), spirit (*ruh*) and intellect (*aql*); although different in meaning, the spiritual sense of each of these terms refers to the same entity, the self (Bakhtiar, 1994).

In the book of the marvels of the heart, Imam al-Ghazali writes:

> The heart it is which, if a man knows it, he indeed knows himself, he indeed knows his Lord: it is also the heart which, if a man does not know it, he indeed knows not himself: and if he knows not himself, he indeed knows not his Lord – and one who knows not himself is even more ignorant of other things. (Al-Ghazali, 1992)

Imam al-Ghazali, in this discussion, seems to prioritise this relationship above all others – if this relationship is not established, then a person is in ignorance in other relationships. The Arabic terms for ignorance, *jahiliyyah*, has much more profound connotations in Islam; it not only defines a time, as in pre-Islam Arabia, but it also defines a spiritual state and the physical emerging from it through character and actions.

Attributes of God are used for spiritual development, to have an impact on one's self-esteem, character, morality and worldly outlook. The Qur'an refers to itself as a cure for the hearts of men and women:

> We send down (stage by stage) in the Qur'an that which is a healing and a mercy to those who believe. To the unjust it causes nothing but loss after loss. (*Surah*, 17:82)

This verse implies a process to this development, and talks about injustice as an illness of the self. In terms of youth work, these are important principles that are talked about in a clear and direct way. The addressing of injustice often dressed in the clothes of societal action is mentioned here as an individual illness that stifles individual growth for which justice and a 'process' are key principles. The awareness of injustice and an inability to respond is seen to be damaging in this relationship to the self. The ability to challenge injustice is an individual spiritual action as much as it is action for the betterment of society. It can be viewed as an act of 'witnessing'. The virtue of justice is further elaborated as a key component of establishing proportion and balance, another way at looking at professional boundaries:

> In order that ye may not transgress (due) balance. So establish weight with justice and fall not short in the balance. (*Surah*, 55:8-9)

These notions are extremely important in theoretically embedding anti-oppressive youth work practice in a Muslim youth work theory and practice, and connecting them to a relationship that is essentially about the self. The Qur'an often addresses itself to those 'who know', implying some form of self-actualisation or awareness that can draw one to Maslow's (1982) hierarchy of needs, but the hierarchical nature of Maslow's model is not without its criticisms (Batsleer, cited by Green, 2006), and the relationship to the self is exercised at every level with dignity and respect – it is an act of actualisation of what is often referred to as the becoming of an *insan-e-kamil* (the completed human being). Samsudin suggests that:

> There should be two types of motives: (1) biological motives, and (2) psychological motives. Biological or primary motives may include hunger, thirst, and sex. Psychological motives such as achievement, affiliation, manipulation and control, and exploration and curiosity can be grouped as psychological or secondary motives. And, from the Islamic perspective, religious motive should also be included as one of the psychological motives. (Samsudin, 2005, p 2)

Samsudin goes on to suggest that, 'the focus on the human soul is the single most important difference between the Islamic concept of motivation and contemporary Western concept of motivation' (2005, p 2).

Clarity in this relationship to the self provides clarity to external relationships; according to Sells (1999, p 18), the Qur'an is 'well aware that humans tend to hide from others and from themselves, what they are really', but that God sees into each being and there will be a moment of truth where each person is revealed inside and out, as expressed in this verse:

> And that which is (locked up) in (human) breasts is made manifest. (100:10)

This reference to the heart as a place of concelament is developed by Hamza Yusuf in his book, *Purification of the heart*:

> Everything we see happening outside of us is in reality coming from the unseen world within. It is from the unseen world that that phenomenal world emerges, and it is from the unseen realm of our hearts that all actions spring. (Yusuf, 2004, p 8)

For Iqbal, the concept of *insaan-e-kamil* is encompassed by his notion of *khudi* (selfhood), and the question 'Who am I?' defines his journey in his texts the Javid Nama (1932) and the Asrar-Khudi (1915, *Mysteries of the self*).

Islam exercises a powerful relationship to the body, whether through the physicality of prayer, and the physical and psychological tests posed by the *hajj* (Islamic pilgrimage to Mecca) and the month of Ramadan (the month of fasting), or cleansing rituals associated with all of the above. This relationship extends into what can or cannot be eaten.

Sultan (2004) describes three Qur'anic views of the self based on three interconnected components: *nafs* (ego), *ruh* (the spiritual self) and *qalb*, (the spiritual heart). These three can lead the development of three types of self:

> *Nafs al-Ammarah Bis-sou.* A soul that inclines towards evil and heads towards a spiritually and morally downward state. *Nafs al-Lawawamah*. A soul that struggles against the lower self, recognizing evil and wishing to submit to God alone. This is the most sensitive state because of the constant struggle. *Nafs al-Mutma'innah*. Best of all souls, which reaches a state of peace and satisfaction with constant remembrance of God. (Sultan, 2004, p 193)

In youth work this relationship with the self, the ability to be autonomous and to make reasoned choices, is an important outcome (Jeffs and Smith, 2005). It is a core requisite for young people and informal educators to express and challenge contrary opinion. This ability to challenge civic authority in particular is an important principle, for example, in Shi'a theology in which seeking justice in the face of tyranny is a constant theme (Shah-Kazemi 2011).

Another Islamic idea of the self has also been described as a composite consisting of the following seven elements as described by Sheikha Halima Krausen:[2] the *nur* or spark of divine light that makes each human alive and created by God, the *ruh* or breath, the *aql* or intellect, the *qalb* meaning the heart, that inclines us towards or away from God, the *nafs* or ego, the *batin* or interior/hidden in which interaction between body and emotions happens such as psychosomatic symptoms, and finally, the body or *jism*. We can be alienated from any of these aspects of the self through neglect.

Alienation from the self can be through becoming lost in the pursuit of material goals:

> Truly man is to his lord ungrateful and to that he bears witness and violent is he in his love of wealth. (*Surah al-Adiyat*, 100:6)

Thus following our lusts, 'selfishness' or 'egocentric behaviour' can alienate us not only from God but from ourselves and also from society, as this 'love can be a violent love' as the verse above suggests. At its roots in the contemporary context is an approach to the individual or young person as a consumer, something adopted in the attempted implementation of opportunity cards from the Youth Matters agenda by New Labour. Notions of selfishness, envy, are often referred to as dispositions, and when a disposition becomes embedded in a person, it becomes a character trait. The belief in 'being born in sin' does not exist in Islam – all are born 'pure' or with a 'clean slate', and the development of traits, according to Bakhtiar (1994), is informed through the relationship with one's environment. Leaman captures what this relationship with the environment is capable of intellectually for the individual:

> The words *tafakkar* (to think), *tafaqquh* (to understand), *tadabbur* (to contemplate), 'aql* (using reason) ... *'ilm* (knowledge), *'ulama* (those who have knowledge) *ulu'l ilm* (those with knowledge), *ulu'l absar* (those who have vision) (24:44). (Leaman, 2006, p 452)

---

[2] www.halimakrausen.com

And those who do not use the intellect are equated to beasts in God's sight:

> For the worst of beasts in the sight of God are the deaf and dumb, those who understand not. (8:22)

This verse questions the status of the *shahadah* (declaration of faith) as a permanent identity signifier; it may be externally useful, but its internal reality is one that is not fixed. It also questions the use of these terms (deaf and dumb) when describing individuals who cannot hear or speak, when in this verse it seems that they are applied to humanity at large and the levels of self-awareness in individuals.

The ability to provide from the pursuit of material wealth is differentiated on the basis of function and purpose. The search for greater material wealth can eventually become spiritually unrewarding. Today the highest suicide rates are experienced by the most sophisticated and materially wealthy societies. Depression, hopelessness and a sense of being forsaken are contextualised as events with a particular power to isolate, alienate and hurt. They are also seen as openings for a relationship, as alluded to in the following verse:

> By the glorious morning light, and the night when it is still – thy Guardian-Lord hath not forsaken thee, nor is He displeased. And verity the hereafter will be better for thee than the present. And soon will thy Guardian-Lord give thee (that wherewith) thou shall be well pleased. Did he not find thee wandering, and he gave thee guidance. And he found thee in need, and made thee independent. Therefore treat not the orphan with harshness nor repulse the petitioner. And the bounty of thy Lord proclaim. (*Surah ad-Duha*, 93.1)

A further verse states:

> Truly no-one despairs of God's mercy except those who have no faith. (*Surah ad-Duha*, 12.87)

One of the questions this asks is what counts as *kufr* (rejection of faith), and what counts as alienation? Can those who know about God but reject and cover it up intentionally be considered *kafir* while those who fall into a lack of consciousness about their relationships in life be considered alienated? The distinction is far from clear, as everyday Muslim rhetoric may imply, and can only be posed here as a question.

Personal change and development can be understood as emanating out of our relationship with ourselves. It involves our overall health, balance and wellbeing, our sense of identity and self-worth. It is also connected with activities that are both individual and communal, such as prayer and fasting, both multifaceted spiritual and self-educational practices. Reflection is built into activities such as the *hajj* as an opportunity for 'an interim' balance of one's life, like a rehearsal for the final day of reckoning, but also about new beginnings borne out of a physical and cognitive struggle.

The role of art in this relationship is important but little invested in; this is not art in terms of the object; it is secondary to the activity itself that encompasses longing, a desire to express and create. It is a means of what Freire would call 'naming the world' and it is in its naming that the potential to transform becomes possible.

Relationship with God

The proclamation of the *shahadah*, understood as the first pillar of Islam, is the establishment of this witnessing, the 'feeling' of a relationship that is then sustained by a covenant that is prior to creation when God asks humankind, 'Am I not your *Rab*?'. The word *Rab* is normally translated as Lord, but actually its meaning is closer to the idea of the teacher, suggesting that the first relationship established between God and humankind is that of the teacher and learner, not of the Lord and servant or believer, or the Lord and the sinner.

This relationship is expressed in a powerful way in the Qur'an by the idea that the spirit of God is blown into each and every person; this spirit is sought to be retained by God's remembrance, which is not just about prayer but also about *taqwa* (God consciousness):

> But He fashioned him in due proportion, and breathed into
> him something of His spirit. (*Surah*, 32:9)

The relationship with God exists at a number of levels. The importance of the Qur'an as part of the relationship with God needs to be borne in mind as it is the word of God and therefore it is God addressing us through text.

A relationship with God is also established through reflection on God's attributes that are expressed as the 99 names, as discussed by Imam al-Ghazali (translated by Burrell and Daher, 1992). These names are often used in reflection in Sufi groups for the spiritual development of the self and proximity to God as part of an individual's spiritual development and balance.

These are not just names of God but also name a potential. In discussions of Ibn Arabi's (1165-1240) discourse on individual potential, Chittick captures the importance of the divine names for Ibn Arabi and their importance for individuals to realise their capacity or potential as people. Chittick quotes a saying of the Prophet Muhammad (pbuh) where he replies to the question 'Which part of faith is most excellent?' to which he replies 'A beautiful character'. Chittick goes on to discuss the relationship between divine attributes and individual traits or character (*khuluq*).

> Many moral traits are also divine attributes, such as repentance (corresponding to the name *al-tawwab*), faith (*al-mu'min*), generosity (*al-karim*), justice (*al'adl, al-Muqsit*), forgiveness (*al-Ghaffar*), *al-Ghafur*), pardon (*al-afu*) patience (*al-Sabur*), gratitude (*al-Shakur*), forbearance (*al-Halim*), love ((*al-Wadud*), dutifulness (*al-Barr*) and clemency (*al- Rauf*). (Chittick, 2000, p 22)

This is by no means an exhaustive list, but the number of attributes that are about overcoming negative feelings about people and oneself gives credence to the idea of a relational God. According to Chittick, the divine names are the connecting thread in the Qur'an, each name revealing a new potentiality, a new kind of relationship to God and to oneself. For Husain and Ashraf (1979), God has bestowed among all living things this ability of humanity to 'recognise, understand, and emulate the attributes of God and realise them in practice in this life' (1979, p 10). bell hooks seems to reach a similar understanding of attributes and their function by differentiating religion from spirituality in suggesting the following inspired by the Dalai Lama:

> Religion – consists of notions of salvation, afterlife, acceptance of some form of supernatural reality, prayer, dogma.

> Spirituality associated with the qualities of the human spirit – such as love compassion, patience, tolerance, forgiveness, contentment and sense of harmony.

As a Muslim informal educator it is the latter qualities that God describes as attributes through which we realise our selves and our understanding of our relationship with God, and yet it is the former that Islam is the most strongly associated with.

Ibn Arabi distinguishes between these being called 'names' or 'relationships', and the following is a means to view the difference that Ibn Arabi posits:

- Name: used as a descriptive distant or legal act.
- Attribute: as aspirational statement.
- Relationship: when an individual's state or faculties are able to establish this connection.

It is a proposition of a relational God who we can come to have knowledge or experience of. This 'experiential relationship' is not activated by external, objective knowledge alone but by the experience of 'tasting' (*dhawq*), which, according to Ibn Arabi, cannot be described but must be experienced, and this experience is not something that is lightly attained but comes about through exertion (Chittick, 2000).

This exertion is both about the disclosure of the self and the self-disclosure of God, and its potential is realised by the concept of *jihad*, meaning to strive or struggle as a necessary part of the process of deriving meaning. The literal root *j h d* (to struggle), from which the word *jihad* emerges, is helpful to understand as an act of individuation that informs understanding, action and identity:

- I *j* t i *h* a *d*: the personal struggle to derive meaning of something
- M u *j* t a *h* i *d*: the one who makes this struggle (the inward identity)
- M u *j* a *h* i *d*: the name ascribed (the outward identity)
- *J* i *h* a *d*: to strive or struggle (the action)

In the construction of the above process it is *ijtihad* that transcends all the above layers, and which is central to *jihad*. The root of all four terms *j h d* (struggle) implies that action should emerge out of meanings derived through struggle and reflection which requires a close scrutiny of one's own intentions and inclinations and their implications. This is the relationship that is asked of the individual towards text, self and the world. This challenges the over-use of the idea of *taqlid* (emulation) that is so invested in by *madrasahs* and *masjids* (mosques) and for that matter state schooling systems that are also essentially about emulation, a regurgitation of implanted information and disposition that is powerfully managed by the state..

The value of process is demonstrated in another important root, *h l q*:

- K*halq*: creation
- K*huluq*: character
- Tak*halluq*: character traits assumed

Although a central concept in character development, the meanings, prejudices and feelings that the term *jihad* evokes in common discourse make it almost impossible to disassociate it from terrorism and fundamentalism; it means that it cannot be overtly used or applied as a learning tool, yet it is a powerful concept in this relational enterprise. You can imagine newspaper headlines if you developed a module on a youth work programme on *jihad*, of 'universities training *jihadi's*'.

The notion of accountability to God (*Surah*, 17:13-14) is also rooted in the Qur'an, and although it has an impact in the relationship with society, there is a clear reminder of the responsibility that goes with the power of choice and the eventual accountability being borne by the individual:

> Who receiveth guidance, receiveth it for his own benefit: who goeth astray, doth so for his own loss. No bearer of burdens can bear the burden of another. (*Surah*, 17:15)

This emphasis on the individual is often lost under the notion of the *ummah* taking on the shape of God's presence of the message. Ultimately, accountability on the Day of Judgement lies with the individual. Relationships of people with God can include a wide spectrum of emotions and experiences, but this relationship can be impeded by a discourse that suggests that God is an unbending condemner of human behaviour, set to punish people for insubordination, challenge or disobedience. For many Muslim young people the idea of obedience to God has been used or abused by teachers and parents to control their behaviour:

> Kill not your children for fear of want: we shall provide sustenance for them as well as for you. Verily, the killing of them is a great sin. (*Surah al-Isra*, 17:31)

The root of the Arabic word translated here as kill (*q t l*) means a lot more – it can also mean defeating, denying legitimate opportunities, suppressing. In this way great care needs to be taken not to 'kill' young people in the sense of 'defeating', controlling or condemning lifestyle choices and stifling with fear so that any relationship borne out of intellectual enquiry is disabled as it compromises authority applied to young people using scripture or ideas of right and wrong. Just as *halal* (permitted or allowed, usually applied to food) has become a market label under which the unhealthiest of foods are sold, so *haram* (forbidden) is used to limit curiosity and enquiry. This can alienate young people from God by creating an image of God as a tyrant. It limits the types of relationship that one can have with God, but can also have an impact on the types of relationships that can be constructed with society or with the environment. Tajfel's (1982) social identity theory is helpful in understanding the way religion cultivates the 'us and them' through notions of good and evil, of a human struggle between two invitations from God and the *Shaitan* (Devil), that is explored by Safak (2010) in the following dialogue between two protaganists in her book *The forty rules of love*:

> 'Since you claim that I am the devil's servant, could you kindly tell us what exactly your notion of Sheitan (devil) is?' asked Shems.

> 'Certainly,' Sheikh Yassin said…. 'Our religion, which is the last and best of Abrahamic religions, tells us it was Sheitan who caused Adam and Eve to be expelled from heaven. As the children of fallen parents, we all need to be alert, because Sheitan comes in many forms. Sometimes he comes in the form of a gambler, sometimes a beautiful young woman who tries to seduce us…. Sheitan can come in the least expected forms, like that of a wandering dervish.'

> As if expecting this remark, Shems smiled knowingly. 'I see what you mean. It must be a huge relief, and an easy way out, to think that the devil is always outside us…. If Sheitan is as wicked and indomitable as you are saying he is, then we human beings have no reason to blame ourselves for our wrongdoings. Whatever good happens we'll attribute to God, and all the bad things in life we'll simply attribute to Sheitan. In either case we'll be exempt from all criticism and self-examination. How easy that is!' (Safak, 2010, pp 256-7)

This is not to say that there is an inherent inclination to evil, but there is sense of a cultivation of the notion that the world is a place of potential damage or temptation rather than beauty that Shems challenges, and its effect on the psychology of an individual and then of a community in the way that they see the world. Rarely is Sheitan presented as a man who is the seducer; it is invariably always the woman who is presented as leading astray.

These binary notions of good and bad are also played out in the form *haram* and *halal* and buy into a theology where 'an inclination to be bad' is in the creation dna, the dominant factor that informs are relationship to it. Satan fulfils a useful function in projecting and identifying issues onto an external body, but it can leave the self unexplored, as Safak eloquently draws out in the conversation above.

The Arabic word *salah* (as used for ritual prayer) literally means 'connection', describing the link between the individual and God, and the individual and other human beings as expressed in the practice of congregational prayer. The dynamics between the relationship of the individual and God and the individual and society is of particular interest. The relationship between the individual and God can be about love, respect, fear, inspiration and acceptance, but it can also be about anger, doubt and a rejection that does not necessarily deny God's existence. These relationships can exist in the private realm but can and do challenge the content of the oft-quoted Muslim mantra that 'There is no public and private in Islam'. This may be so in the sight of God under the idea of *taqwa* (God consciousness); however, between individuals and society it can be difficult. Art, for example, is a means of expression of these relationships, but how doubt, anger and rejection are expressed can be extremely challenging in the public space. For these types of relationships the public space can be difficult for at least two reasons: the possible conservatism of the Muslim community in Britain for whom 'the public, private', 'all is one' limits 'unhelpful expressions'; and a hostile broader context that politically requires conformity and unity and is reluctant to facilitate the diversity of the Muslim world view, using 'relationships of', for example, doubt and anger, as evidence of the oppressive nature of Islam.

Poetry and music have acted as one of the key bridges in bringing the private relationship or experience of God into the public space, often extending the relationship beyond the boundaries of devotion into the realm of very personal experiences of love, ecstasy, illumination, challenge and doubt, and with it testing the boundaries of the possibilities of the private in the public space. This boundary is tested by the power that was in the directness of the poetry of the famous Pakistani Qawwal Aziz Mian (1942-2000), and as demonstrated below in the following lines found in some of his most well known work:

> O Kaaba, come and do *tawaf* [circumambulation] of me
> As the Prophet lives in my heart

Has God got himself lost that you go searching for him everywhere? ('Aashiqi Dillagi Nahin Hoti')

Trust me, the angels will ask the pious on judgement day: 'Why didn't you sin? Didn't you trust in God's mercy?' ('Milegi Sheikh Ko Jannat')

Or the poetry of Mansur al-Hallaj (858-922):

I saw my Lord with my heart's eye
And I said to him 'Who art thou' and He said 'Thou.'

Written in Urdu and Arabic respectively, many centuries apart, their popularity as pieces of poetry and music remains undimmed. The work of poets such as Rumi and Iqbal can be found in the music of the famous Qawwali singer, Nusrat Fateh Ali Khan, and many musicians today, and testifies to its continuing appeal to people despite a powerful discourse emerging from Saudi-inspired theology that challenges the Islamic authenticity of both.

Relationship with community and society

Verily! Allah will not change the good condition of a people as long as they do not change their state of goodness themselves. (Qur'an, 13:11)

Muhammad Iqbal, in *Rumuz i Bikhudi* (*Mysteries of selflessness*, written in 1918), explores the role and function of the individual. In it he proposes that an individual can only realise his or her true potential when they contribute to the larger objectives of community. This need for community is expressed as a counter-weight to the excesses of what he terms *khudi*, discussed earlier. The concept of *khudi* or selfhood has been described as a key theme present in all Iqbal's work and particularly in his poetry. His assertion of *khudi* or the self was influenced both by the colonial context in which Indians only seemed to be defined by religion, caste and tradition, and a mystical Islam that called on the annihilation of the self or the ego to realise God, and in effect compromised the individual's engagement with the world.

Iqbal both asserts this individuality in a context of forced collectivism and warns of the danger of *khudi* or the self becoming a law unto itself, and that there is therefore a need of others to find space between the worst excesses of the self, that is, selfishness and selflessness. This can be only realised in a community. The notion of dependence, interdependence and independence in Sapin's earlier quoted definition of youth work finds some sympathy with Iqbal, where Majeed (2009) cites Iqbal's premise that among the factors that compromise selfhood is dependence on others and an outlook that negates life and generates inertia and inaction. Annemarie Schimmel (1994) captures this tension between the spiritual needs of the self and the need to engage with the community through the example of the Prophet Muhammad (pbuh) for whom the need for the self was met by the need for seclusion (*khalwa*) and the need to engage with the world as a Messenger of God and all this entailed for him.

Huzun is a Turkish word meaning melancholy that has its roots in Arabic, meaning the same thing, *huzn*. According to Orhan Pamuk (2006), as a cultural concept it has come to convey worldly failure and spiritual suffering that had, in Turkey at least, inspired a state of mind. Muslim philosophers such as Al-Kindi interpreted it as at odds with the community, communal purpose and that it required healing. This alienation is seen as a spiritual state in the relationship between the individual and the community and as part of the balance discussed earlier. It is part of the continuing struggle between our individualistic and communal aspects. At the time of the *jahiliyyah*, a sophisticated mercantile society with rules and regulation was deemed as ignorant. A reason for this could be that a tribal society was exploiting the weak for its business and lifestyle purposes. There are several Islamic notions of community, all of which are included as responses to alienation, such as *ummah* and *qawm*.

It is clear that each 'community' has received a message and messenger and the means to stand for justice:

> We sent afore time Our messengers with clear signs and sent
> down with them the Book and the Balance, that men may
> stand forth in justice; and We sent down Iron, in which there
> is awesome power, as well as many benefits for mankind,
> that Allah may test who it is that will help, Unseen, Him
> and His Messengers: for Allah is Full of Strength, Exalted
> in Might. (*Surah al-Hadid*, 57:25)

According to Yusuf Ali's commentary (2000) in his translation of the Qur'an, 'the Book' stands for revelation, 'the Balance' for faculty to judge right and wrong and 'Iron' for resources, strength, power and discipline.

The so-called 'five pillars of Islam' each provide a different means of connecting to a community. In the testimony of faith (*shahada*), a relationship with God is established, but also a connection with the 'community of believers' mentioned earlier. *Zakat* (tax) should not just be a disconnected act of giving but based on a social awareness, starting with an awareness of the needs of your neighbour, but the act itself needs to be understood as part of the relationship with God rather than as an act of charity done to another. *Hajj* is an encounter with the origin and with fellow members of the community, both in space and across time. The benefits of Ramadan include that of sharing an 'experience' and expectation that binds you with the community, while testing you physically, emotionally and economically. Allied to the idea of relationship with community are concepts such as participation, rights, duties and citizenship. People's sense of belonging to collectivities is an essential aspect of the relationships they have with communities, including families, neighbourhood networks, school and workplace communities, as well as local religious affiliations and memberships.

The Qur'an does not believe in the idea of a 'chosen people':

> O mankind we created you from a single (pair) of a male and female, and made you into nations and tribes, that you may know each other. Verily the most honoured of you in the sight of Allah is the most righteous of you. And Allah has full knowledge and is well acquainted. (*Surah*, 49:13)

And again, the phrase 'those who know' implies that an awareness of this diversity is a sign of self-actualisation:

> And among his signs is the creation of the heavens and the earth, and the variations in your languages and your colours; verily in that are signs for those who know. (*Surah*, 30:22)

Status in society is a matter of 'virtue' rather than class or lineage. However, danger of arrogance and therefore ignorance can also exist where virtue and morality slip into an arrogance and elitism that denies others their rights.

It may be useful here to make a distinction between society and community and the tensions generated by the loyalty or affiliation that both demand. Alija Ali Izetbegovic (1993), the first Prime Minister of Bosnia Herzegovina, differentiates between the two by suggesting that society is composed of 'an external group of individuals gathered on the basis of interest' while community consists of people with a shared sense of belonging. While relationships in the community are internal, connected to personal events, relations with society are external, indirect and anonymous, the ascendency of the latter carrying the potential to destroy the former. For Muslim young people the tension between the two is manifested through questions of affiliation, loyalty and belonging, with the attack on community and neighbourhood delivered through accusations of closed impermeable communities that are made possible, among other things, due to the persistence with not learning English, a resistance to engage with anyone not Muslim and not within the community. These may be established communities but they are not exclusive communities. This focus on Muslim self-exclusion is useful to compare to the self-exclusion of the elite that remains uncontested. According to Dorling (2011), this self-exclusion includes exclusion from societal norms and values imposed or expected of others to follow, such as 'elitism is efficient', 'prejudice is natural', 'greed is good' and 'despair is inevitable'. The charge levelled against Muslim communities is as much of over-cohesion as it is of self-exclusion.

The relationship between the self and the community is determined by character traits and the impact on one's outlook informed by an opportunity to be of service:

> O possessors of faith, expend of the good things you have earned, and of that we have produced for you from the earth…. Satan promises you poverty and commands you unto indecency. But God promises you his pardon and mercy. (2:267-68)

This verse challenges miserliness, but also, by promising mercy and pardon in the context of this verse, it suggests an expectation of making mistakes in developing a outward positive outlook on the world and contributing to its wellbeing.

Yusuf (2004) points to an interesting anthropological distinction that is used to divide cultures between those that are shame cultures and those that are guilt cultures. He suggests that Islam elevates shame so that a person is aware of everything they do (he defines shame as a 'quality' that needs to be nurtured in order that it deters people from acts that may seem vulgar or displeasing in the sight of God), but an individual can internalise both shame and guilt when exposed to a variety of cultural influences. It is difficult to think of shame as a quality to be nurtured, but it may play a part in racialising notions of *izzat* or honour as something peculiar to historically 'Asian' families, and today increasingly applied to communities from South Asia and the Muslim world as motivations for acts of denial of life, opportunity and lifestyles, for example, honour killings. But it would be difficult to convince an unemployed Durham miner that honour and shame mean less to him or, for that matter, a soldier, who will also deny life. The racialisation of honour is unhelpful in seeing how beliefs about honour are located and played out in different communities and groups.

Honour can raise a sense of self-worth and enable a consciousness of one's actions, elevating characteristics of dignity and integrity. Tragically it can also generate extreme censorship that names honour and dishonour. Here, honour is elevated beyond every other value, generating a consuming pride in which any price is worth paying, including the lives of children, for its maintenance. This elevation of family or tribal honour is fundamentally challenged by the Prophet (pbuh) in both Mecca and Medina as his message challenged both tribal loyalties and a patriarchy that marginalised and devalued women through rights of inheritance and practices such as female infanticide.

The relationship to community is often expressed through the invocation of the *ummah* as an aspirational reality. *Ummah* as a term appears 65 times in the Qur'an and its meaning develops and changes according to different contexts. It is used in the singular and the plural *umam*. It is used to denote the original, one humankind created by God, but more often than not refers to the transnational Muslim community. For many Muslims today *ummah* is an ideal type worldwide religious community of Muslims that they aspire to being part of and contributing to. It is a 'pure space' that can take them out of cultural politics, ethnic loyalties, caste snobbery and oppression, community, kinship and gender, and realign attachments that proportionalise the importance attached to the former. Pnina Werbner refers to the way that at certain critical political moments, Muslims 'invoke the Ummah' (Werbner 2002).

It appears that just as the terms *fatwa* and *jihad* have been de-legitimised, the same Islamophobic discourse is now constructing *ummah* as something sinister, a primordial loyalty before all others, as a distinguishing marker between 'us and them' that forever compromises meaningful integration and common ground. These sentiments politicise expressions of empathy and understanding in relation to Kashmir, Palestine, Iraq, Afghanistan, Chechnya and so on by young Muslims, and can label them as apologists to terrorist causes according to the CONTEST strategy (July 2011). This politicisation disempowers by creating resistance to how *ummah* can be conceptualised as a political and learning tool for understandings of community and belonging. In the same manner, *jihad*, as the concept of individual struggle and renewal, is virtually impossible to employ in this context due to the meanings and feelings that have become attributed to it.

Another term used in the Qur'an meaning 'people' is *qaum*. It is a word that appears much more frequently in the Qur'an than *ummah*. A person's *qaum* is their party and their kinsfolk or tribe. This term refers to kin and ethnicity and could also mean nation. At a local level this can exist in the dynamics of representation in the political sphere. It can be argued that, for example, the Labour Party, in seeking the votes of the Asian or Muslim community in Britain or, as they probably saw it the Pakistani community, appealed to notions of loyalty based on ties of kinship and community to vote for them in Britain, so what they were appealing to was *qawm*. In the process, they were aware or unaware that this contributed significantly to the replication in Britain of historical tribal loyalties and forms of patriarchal representation that made little recourse to any previous national identity. It is now necessary to revisit this strategy, as those historically involved in the *ummah* project and prepared to challenge the current political relational landscape are challenging familial and tribal loyalties. Before the advent of Islam, tribal identity had always claimed the primary loyalty of the individual. The *ummah* was meant to be an ideal type that made visible tribal injustices, a model that provides a level to aspire to as an individual in a community, and not how it has often been presented, as a system to overtake and to become the supreme loyalty of all Muslims overcoming inter-tribal feuds and territorial loyalties (Castells, 1996). The ideal still exists as a painful contrast to human excesses, nepotism and advantage, as found in the relational or tribal nature of power and governance in Saudi Arabia.

The *ummah* ideal can be a problem when it is treated as an ideal that refuses to acknowledge the messy reality of some young people's lives. Youth movements in particular aim to realise this ideal in the way the *ummah* is used to transcend differences of 'race' and ethnicity. The *ummah's* relationship to class is, I believe, much more problematic as an aspirational ideal, and although Janine Clark's study is on Middle Eastern middle-class networks in relation to Islam and charity (2004), the lens she applies to look at how class is activated in power relations could easily be applied in the UK and other parts of the world as it appears to be a generalisable phenomenon.

Relationship with creation or environment

> That which is impenetrable to us really exists. Behind the
> secrets of nature remains something subtle, intangible, and
> inexplicable. Veneration for this force beyond anything that
> we can comprehend is my religion. (Albert Einstein)

The relationship with the environment or creation is a powerful
relationship that overlaps with the relationship with the self, with God
and with the community. Sardar (1985) states that as human beings our
future is intrinsically linked to our attitudes to the environment and that
there needs to be a cognitive shift from the way that our connection
with nature has been constructed as a battle for control and as an act
of consumption rather than as a relationship.

Creation or environment, depending on your beliefs, has a key role
in the transmission of prophetic duties and relational signs, but it is a
relationship that is often ignored. For example, the power of the story
of Hagar and Ishmael, when Hagar is looking for water in Mecca, takes
on different meaning and awe when one actually visits Mecca and
imagines, from what is left of the barren, cold or hot, inhospitable and
unwelcoming nature of the landscape, in which the miracle of *zam-
zam* took place and on which some of the rites of the *hajj* (pilgrimage)
are based. Today it takes a significant imaginary leap to visualise this
as it now hosts shopping centres and residences. This relationship is
constantly referred to in the Qur'an as necessary for self-actualisation
and for an understanding and relationship with God:

> Behold in the creation of the heavens and the earth and
> the alternation of night and day – these are indeed signs
> for men of understanding. Men who celebrate the praises
> of Allah standing, sitting and lying down on their sides, and
> contemplate the (wonders of creation) in the heavens and
> the earthy…. (*Surah*, 3:190-191)

And again:

> Not for (idle) sport did We create the heavens and the earth
> and all that is between. (*Surah al-Anbiya*, 21:16)

This particular aspect of alienation has taken on real urgency as regular
natural 'disasters' seem to symbolise this alienation based on the ideas
of consumption, economic development and profit. The relationship

between the activities of global capitalism and global warming may be disputed, but the regularity of natural disasters says that if the earth were a person, than it would definitely be an unhappy one. As creation is a trust on humanity, abuse of this trust is a sign of alienation from its creator. There is a real gentleness advocated in the Qur'an towards creation: 'the servants of the Most Gracious are those who treat the earth gently, and when the ignorant speak to them, they only utter peace' (25:66). According to the Qur'anic account of creation, humankind is entrusted with the responsibility of looking after the earth and its resources of minerals, water, plant life, animal life and so forth. Creation is a gift from God and God consciousness includes appreciation of that gift, leading to responsible care of it. We have been given abundance, materially and spiritually:

> To thee have We granted the fount (of abundance). Therefore to thy Lord turn in prayer and sacrifice. (*Surah al-Kawthar*)

Alienation from nature and creation is seen as the cause of squandering of resources, neglect and mistreatment of living things, pollution and environmental disasters that could have been avoided if humans took better care. When the *khalifa* (vice-regent) is in a state of *jahiliyya*, creation suffers neglect:

> it is He who gives life and death; and He has power over all things. (*Surah al-Hadid*, 57:2)

On the whole the earth belongs to the Creator. Yet in the Qur'an there is a concept of humanity as God's trustee or vice-regent on earth (Khalifa, 2:30): 'Behold, thy Lord said to the angels: "I will create a vice regent on earth" with special abilities and liberties and corresponding responsibility.' Relationship with creation involves responsible use of the earth's resources and relationships with other living things, such as plants and animals. It can be understood as a relationship with our environment and with the other life forms in the eco-system that we are part of. Waste of resources is strongly criticised in the Qur'an (for example, *Surah*, 17:26-27). Our responsibility for the treatment of animals is illustrated with the image of mistreated animals accusing their tormentors on the Day of Judgement.

Sardar (1985) connects the notion of the *khilafa* or the vice-regent to that of *amana* (trust), and explains this as a moral responsibility that is placed on the shoulders of humankind, a trust that can be used for benefit but over which can be no dominion or ownership, a trust that individuals are held accountable for in life after death.

The reciprocity between humanity and the environment in this relationship pales into insignificance compared to what is received. The relationship with creation is called for in the Qur'an for a variety of purposes, and the following themes emerge from Leaman's (2006) understanding of the relationship between the natural world and the Qur'an:

- Education: 'say: "travel through the earth and see how God initiated creation; in the same way will God produce a later creation: for God has power over all things"' (29:19-20).
- Balance and proportion – in nature and in one's conduct, the Qur'an makes mention of the perfect balance of everything (15:19).
- *Dhawq* (meaning taste) or quality of life – affected by the earth through the resources that have been made available for humanity.

In terms of activity that can inform a person's consciousness, the need to see creation through travel is necessary to evoke feelings of awe, wonder, challenge, enjoyment, struggle, distance, isolation and so on, which are all able to generate a cognitive shift in the self and in an individual's ability to see the *ayat* (signs). While the notion of *khilafat* appears to be applied and discussed in relation to modes of governance of people and societies, it is rarely applied in relation to the environment. This is surprising given the emphasis placed on creation as a sign of the Creator. The importance of the relationship with nature is being made possible by the experience of its absence, especially in urbanised centres, where nature is either extricated out or managed in. Nasr (1997) refers to this absence as an external void that is also internally present in individuals, that can emerge from inside individuals, despairingly and violently. Societies based on a co-existence or a relational approach to the world around them have suffered greatly at the hands of societies that are based on models of domination over nature and have goals of economic progress. Nasr uses the metaphor of the relationship between 'mountains and men':

> Men no longer climb spiritual mountains – or at least rarely do so. They now want to conquer all mountain peaks. (Nasr, 1997, p 19)

The danger of the mantra of a 'complete way of life'

The seamlessness in the interconnectedness of these relationships can in itself be a barrier to understanding their depth and purpose.

The theoretical framework and its relational nature is presented as a means of framing educational with youth work purpose and outcome, but doubts can be raised by organisations about the division of the theoretical framework into a series of relationships, that there is actually just one relationship and a reluctance to explore specific relationships, for example, 'Islam is a complete way of life, you cannot divide life'.

They are all relationships that find their basis in the Qur'an. The reason that they have been presented in a circle format is that when they are all invested with balance and proportion, the possibility of movement is enabled for the individual and for society. The relationships are personal, asking a critical consciousness, and due to the types of engagement asked with the community, they are also political. This paradigm suggests that the relationship should be the end goal, not used as a means to an end, as is so often the case in services to young people, and which activates and gives legitimacy to a variety of existing curricula and questions what happens in the pedagogic space, wherever that space is.

The fear of indoctrination strongly associated generally with religion and Islam in particular has led us to ignore the affirming qualities that spiritual traditions bring to bruised and battered identities. In a societal context that is powerfully reconfiguring primary relationships, especially between the state, the market and the individual, religion can and has become an important locale of resistance, as is the case for Muslim young people.

It asks questions of theology, policy and practice that often informs a discourse that pathologises individual agency, family or community, which then works to disconnect subconsciously in the name of emancipation and reconfigure this connection rather than make it stronger or healthier – 'individual arrival' being about independence rather than an awareness of our interdependence – happiness found in the freedom achieved when free from the restraint of others (Cray, 1996).

A tentative application of this theoretical frame suggests to me that there appears to be a powerful connection between religion and society; how effective it was in processes of individuation or connecting to a relationship with God leaves challenging questions:

- How are relationships to the self invested in by faith-based organisations?
- Is the direct relationship to God invested in or actively mediated or even denied?
- How does a Muslim rhetoric, so often heard from *ulama*, that asks resistance to the world and talks about it in a similar way to the Christian concept of the fallen world in which salvation is found in Jesus, reconcile itself with a God expressing perfection in creation?
- Do the activities and services invested reflect the relationships being prioritised? The next question is, why?

For this and other reasons, theoretical frames such as these may be resisted (as I found), but are key in youth work practice and thinking with Muslim young people. This resistance will, however, come from all quarters as the development of Muslim youth work may not necessarily need to sit among Muslim organisations with strong confessional agendas but among 'Muslim-literate informal educators' for whom the development of a theoretical and practical resource is necessary to articulate practice and to explain activity.

FOUR

Anti-oppressive practice and Muslim young people

He asked: 'Where is it most pleasant?'
I replied: 'In the Emperor's palace.'
He asked: 'What did you see there?'
I replied: 'A hundred miracles.'
He asked: 'Then why is it so desolate?'
I replied: 'For fear of the robber.'
He asked: 'Who is the robber?'
I replied: 'This feeling of blame?'

Mevlana Jelaluddin Rumi (1207–73);
translated by James Cowan (1997)

Antonio Gramsci developed the notion of hegemony to describe how dominant ideas and interests were being adopted by working-class people which maintained the vested interests of the establishment/ elite (Apple, 1990). The picture of society being saturated by a particular idea or message which then determines political outlook, personal relationships and professional networks seems to be an appropriate analogy to describe the incessant and powerful nature of the portrayal of Islam as a moral marker that forms an 'us and them' and the Muslim caricature as the folk devil. Cohen's definition of a moral panic seems particularly precise, naming key protagonists in this exercise:

> Societies appear to be subject, every now and then, to periods of moral panic. A condition, episode, person or group of persons emerges to become defined as a threat to societal values and interests; its nature is presented in a stylized and stereotypical fashion by the mass media; the moral barricades are manned by editors, bishops, politicians and other right thinking people. (Cohen, 2005, p 1)

The outcome is the cultivation of a discourse that leaves little room for manoeuvre, with Muslim expression frequently expressed from the 'back foot' – a constant act of explaining shaped by the agendas and fears of others. Those working in professions shaped by a strong value or ethical base can be particularly prone to internalising this discourse which is often manifested as an act of preservation and defence of values through, for example, notions of liberal equality or as rescuers of young Muslims in general and young Muslim women in particular, through problematising family, community and belief.

The cumulative impact of a historical presence on the occidental 'front page', whose headlines have had Islam in the foreground or the background, has generated a powerful discourse that informs the practices of organisations and the lives of people. The impact of the everyday nature of this discourse is captured by the feminist notion of micro-inequities which describes the small everyday way people are made to feel through a gesture, tone of voice, body language and use of language, inflection in voice and the withdrawal of courtesy that is felt but that is impossible to challenge or name. Individually and cumulatively they can lead to issues of self-esteem and self-worth, and within organisations, self-isolation. It is the drip, drip, drip rather than a visible overt event that is felt so intensely; it exists mainly in the realm of perception and is experienced alone and often unsupported.

Neil Thompson's PCS model theory is probably the most well-known model used in the training of youth workers and social workers to make sense of how these three overarching sites, personal, cultural and structural, manifest practice and experience that is oppressive or discriminatory. It is a useful model that can be applied to understand Muslim experiences, but here I use a model developed by a colleague, Steph Green, a tutor at Ruskin College. The 'I's' model developed by Green charts a relational trajectory of how injustice, discrimination and oppression are experienced and reinforced by different realms, and it is useful in terms of the theoretical frame for Muslim youth work proposed elsewhere in this book. It follows a trajectory that names and follows oppression, moving from the international to the institutional to the interpersonal and ultimately to the internal (see Table 4.1).

The naming and challenging of oppressive practice, given the strength and prevalence of a powerful Islamophobic discourse across these realms, is a fraught exercise. Elizabeth Kubler-Ross' (1970) work on death and dying is particularly interesting to frame responses to 'news'

Table 4.1: Green's 'I's' model

Internal : developing a strong resilient 'internal' level is crucial to being anti-oppressive. Developing confidence in our own identity and worth is central. Questioning our own beliefs and attitudes, building our understanding of the oppression we experience and the way that we oppress others, is essential.
Interpersonal: we can build our own understanding of the oppression we experience by examining it with other people who also experience it. We can develop ways to challenge oppressive behaviour, be open to challenges ourselves and actively seek to find out about other people's experiences. How we behave and work with others is important. There is no point in having the right rhetoric if we treat other people in an oppressive way.
Institutional: we are all part of many organisations and communities of practice, family, social peer groups, schools, work, religious groups and so on; we also contribute to wider institutions of business and government through what we buy and the taxes we pay. Identifying and challenging oppressive organisational cultures and practices can mean questioning ingrained, unspoken shared beliefs and ways of doing things as well as addressing policies and written rules. Collective action, building alliances and working together, across our differences, are essential if we want to challenge oppression.
International: global politics, economics, media and religion are present in our everyday lives. Our clothes, food, household belongings and other everyday products are made and sold within an international market. Our lifestyles have an impact on the global environment. Our taxes are used to fight in international conflicts and to maintain the power of the UK and the Western world. War, asylum and terrorism are facets of international power relations in which we are implicated.

that challenges a person's mortality or, in this case, morality, as this is how it is often received. We spend most of our lives not questioning our mortality in our unconscious minds and rarely in our conscious minds. The consciousness of our mortality with our focus or occupation with the affairs of the world is challenged by practices associated with death and burial in Islam. The funeral is meant to take place soon after a person's death, preferably the same day. There is no week's notice to give people time to make arrangements. There is a cognitive kick generated to focus on the deceased – it is customary to see the face of the deceased as a reminder of the fragility of our mortality and a reminder that there is an accounting for our actions.

In much the same way, in our unconscious minds we are not racist, sexist, homophobic, Islamophobic or ageist; our sense of self is more than likely to be made of being fair at best and tolerant at worst – an ethical spine that provides a moral compass, that 'I am a fair and just person'. Kubler-Ross (1970) identifies five stages in the responses from individuals when they are told that they have a fatal illness. These stages may also be useful to understand people's responses when their moral compass is questioned on grounds of, for example, racism or Islamophobia. While Kubler-Ross's stages seem appropriate for racism, as Table 4.2 below seems to suggest, it does not seem to apply fully for Islamophobia.

There is another stage, that of hope which follows acceptance. It takes us to a place where our actions are born out of hope rather than hopelessness, denial, guilt or blame.

As mentioned earlier, this trajectory cannot be accurately followed in the case of Islamophobia, which is much more confident in its expression than racism, politically and ideologically, because it adds to it. The death of Stephen Lawrence and its aftermath left middle England needing to appropriate the message that racism was not part of its moralising vision, and therefore today it is much more difficult to challenge yet no less prevalent, while Islam has continued to act as the public marker of what can and what cannot be tolerated. Former Prime Minister Tony Blair's comments on the veil as a 'mark of separation', a symbol of the 'difficulties faced by British Muslims trying to balance their loyalty to their state and to their religion'[1] gave political legitimacy, provided policy direction and magnified the public and political gaze on Muslims. Charles Husband (2005) captures the contradiction between New Labour's progressive but low-key approach to challenging discrimination and inequality through legislation and the

---

[1] www.aljazeera.com/archive/2006/10/200849161625566914.html

Table 4.2: Kubler-Ross stages of grief

Stage	Death	Racism
I	Denial and shock	Shock and denial
2	Anger, rage, discomfort to towards those around	Anger, moral rage – where the person challenging has to defend her/himself. This place becomes uncomfortable
3	Bargaining for an extension of life if you are good or a time that is pain-free	This bargaining takes place through defences, for example, saying that that you have Black friends; a commitment to diversity and inclusion that leave institutions' racist practices unchallenged are also examples of bargaining (Barndt, 2011)
4	Depression that comes from no longer being able to deny your illness, feelings of guilt and shame	Feelings of guilt or shame as you can no longer deny – but it is important not to linger here too long and try to move on to the next stage
5	Acceptance	This is the stage of acceptance and liberation – a greater comfort with uncertainty about what to do. There is the acceptance of the inevitability of internalising such powerful discourses and the need for vigilance and self-critique through anti-racism

Source: Kubler-Ross (1970)

front-page rhetoric on asylum or immigration and Islam to reassure a 'concerned middle England' and the scared White working class. This rhetoric exacerbated the vulnerability and the marginality of these communities and seemed to pathologise the White working class as 'instinctively racist' in order to feed a discourse that generated a public opinion that was supportive of the 'War on Terror'.

The experience of anti-racism approaches seems to be generally contingent on whether you consider yourself Black or White. For Black workers it was a context in which micro-inequities could be named, the perceptual put forward, and the contradictions of a meritocratic society challenged. For White workers it could feel like victimisation, as an inducement of guilt, of legitimising the chip on the shoulder, the enforcement of pc (politically correct) practice and a feeling that you were being blamed. This may have been partly as a result of 'over-simplification or reductionism – reducing a complex, multi-level phenomenon to simple single level responses' (Thompson, 2006, p 10). Discourses, whether racism, Islamophobia or homophobia, have an impact on every one irrespective of religious, racial or ethnic identity.

They are metaphorically clouds we all stand under, and are covered by – for some they provide shade; for others darkness; some are made to feel normal; others abnormal; some are reassured and strengthened; others made fragile and unsure; some self-hate and deny others, blind to the privileges afforded. The analogy of a cloud also visualises the fact that we are all drenched by messages that are homophobic, racist, sexist, ageist, misogynistic and Islamophobic; we all internalise them and all enact them, and so all need to see the damage they do to ourselves and how we then damage others.

Thompson (2006) makes reference to the way this simplification often became reduced to appropriate and inappropriate language, but so much of what differentiates life experience on the basis of colour or gender operates in the realm of the taken for granted, what is considered as common sense or the normal, and the invisibility engendered by the factual connotations that underpin these notions and phrases. Yet when so much of institutional power and oppressive practice remain invisible, it is language that *is* visible, revealing something of the values and beliefs that may underpin them.

Fred Halliday explores the post-9/11 impact of the of the military operation in Afghanistan and Iraq and the 'War on Terror' on the English language, making reference to new coinage such as 'embedded reporters', 'global *jihad*', and euphemisms such as 'rendition', 'detainee', 'collateral damage', 'precision bombing', 'detention facility' and so on. He points to the importance that 'those that seek to control events, people and their minds also seek to control language' (Halliday, 2011, p v).

This struggle for control of the meaning of language has had a profound and debilitating impact on a concept that is central to a Muslim understanding of challenging oppression – *jihad*. Its connotations are so powerfully fixed as something associated with terrorism, injustice, a sign of radicalisation, Muslim fundamentalism, as something '*they*' want to do to '*us*', that it is difficult to make a case that this is central to Muslim anti-oppressive practice. The war against terror, while euphemising its activities, has corrupted the meaning in the public imagination of key empowerment notions – most importantly, *jihad*. It is virtually impossible to convey this as a concept infused by notions of struggle against self-oppression and oppression in society. Any youth and community course developing notions of anti-oppressive practice from a Muslim perspective cannot do so without exploring this as a central idea; however, the discourse cultivated on notions such as *jihad* also act in censoring its use legitimately – it is an act of disempowerment by disabling the use of language and ideas that challenge and empower. At the least it may be understood as an activity of apologists of terrorism, as may be understood under new government strategies (for example, the Prevent strategy, 2011).

Muslim young people are caught between two ideological discourses: a discourse that sees no good on the one hand (Islamophobia), and on the other, a protestation of the 'beauty of Islam' that sees no bad, and young people end up living with the ugly side of both. Between these two claims of fact it may be in the realm of fiction that dilemmas, experiences and realities of the 'Muslim condition' are explored under the protection of suspended reality by writers such as M.Y.Alam (2002), Elif Safak, Alifa Rifaat (1987) and Michael Muhammad Knight (2007), to name but a few.

Those working in social care, schools and colleges and as a youth workers are well aware of the complex nature of the situations faced by young Muslims to which terms such as 'alienation', 'self-esteem' or 'socio-economic disadvantage' provide little detail. In her paper, 'I's model: understanding oppression', Steph Green names four interrelated realms that are sites of oppression and anti-oppressive practice (see Table 4.1); her model is specifically developed for those working with young people. Green names this as the 'I's' model because the 'model starts from one's own identity and experiences' and their impact on the 'internal', while identifying that 'oppression in all these realms works simultaneously' (Green, 2010, pp 2-3).

In this model, the use of the 'I' is deliberate and central – here, oppression works from the out to the 'in', but challenging oppression as informal educators is about working with the individual, it is a journey from the in to the out. For those working with young Muslims this model is very pertinent as it captures all the domains that are captured in mind maps that try and make sense of the Muslim relational experience, from the individual to family, neighbourhood to the institutional and the global political.

The feelings and beliefs of those of influence around you can have a profound impact on the way that you feel about yourself, good and bad, therefore confidence in yourself and your identity is very important (Khan, 2006; Green, 2010). Kerry Young (1999) writes about youth work being about 'identity work', but the challenge of an identity already made either fragile or uncompromising by the 'bad news Islam' brigade is a difficult exercise. In the case of the former there is a need to comfort, support and affirm identities, not challenge identities that are already unsure and defensive. Secure identities are more open to reflexive approaches to constructions of self.

Muslim Youth Helpline, a counselling and support agency based in London, finds relationships a key area of worry and concern for young people. The need for a secure and confident self is important, as Green states, to be able to talk, share and work with others in building support and networks that can challenge oppressive practice and discrimination. Enormous courage is involved in taking the risk to be open to the challenge of another and to challenge others in a way that builds shared understandings. The interpersonal relational space is one of enormous risk and potential; the internalisation of expectations of friends and family, and the experience of your identity in the street, with colleagues and peers. For young women and young men this interpersonal relational landscape can be a fraught place. A common refrain often heard from people is 'What should I do?' or 'How should I behave here?', and this can be interpreted as sign of identities that are externally learned rather than internally cultivated. The vulnerability of young women to messages that sexualise and practices that commodify the female body are responded to or mirrored by an equal desire driven by motives that can be about either resistance, piety, spirituality, protection or control. The following verse of the Qur'an touched on earlier is useful to explore in the way it challenges oppressive practices in central interpersonal relations, and what can be described as the cult of obedience to, for example, parents:

> Kill not your children for fear of want: we shall provide sustenance for them as well as for you. Verily the killing of them is a great sin. (*Surah*, 17:31)

I imagine that all of us understand or feel this verse in our own particular way. When I previously looked at it I thought, does this mean that we can do pretty much anything except kill our children? The word 'kill' in Arabic is derived from the root *qa ta la*, and this includes notions of denying or disabling; therefore this verse could also be understood as denying or disabling someone so that they cannot reach their full potential, and it also poses the question as to why parents are given assurances about sustenance, but again, it is important to consider that sustenance takes many forms – food is the obvious one, but how many of us are sustained by dreams, hopes and aspirations? And so it can also mean not to constrain children and young people by our dreams and aspirations but to empower them to pursue their own; nor should we, as adults, deny our own aspirations and dreams and frame them in the plans of a third person.

The challenging of deeply help beliefs requires networks of support often emerging from, or as extensions of, interpersonal relationships. The role of institutions in conducting our lives has been a significant characteristic of the last century; health, death, education, work and safety are mediated by institutions such as healthcare providers, schools, arms of the criminal justice system, such as the police, courts and probation – these are some institutions that immediately come to mind. The exploration of the Muslim experience of these organisations needs careful unpicking. The Muslim youth experience, revealed and visualised by Maurice Cole (2008) below, uses a variety of identity markers:

- the under-achievement of Pakistani and Bangladeshi pupils;
- that 31 per cent of British Muslims leave school with no qualifications;
- that a community that represents 3 per cent of the UK makes up 10 per cent of its prison population;
- Muslims are at the highest risk of being victims of racially motivated crimes;
- 35 per cent of Muslim households have no adult in employment;
- just under 75 per cent of Pakistani and Bangladeshi children are living in households below the poverty line;
- Muslims have the highest rate of reported ill health and high rates of incidence of special educational needs.

Cole provides the above examples from government and non-government sources, but which experience is due to an individual's religious identity and which is due to another socio-economic identity indicator is a useful exercise when considering interventions. Jeffs and Smith (1989) make a valuable point when they state that 'less is said about the subordination of young people as a consequence of their class' (1989, p 179); instead, Jeffs and Smith state that class is referred through 'coded references' such as 'inner-city youth', 'alienated' and 'disadvantaged', essentially terms that became associated with the experience of minority ethnic communities. The invisibility of class as an identity and experiential signifier is reflected by the perceived experiences and claims of being ignored (invisible) by White working-class communities. This same invisibility of class as an interrogator of these experiences also compromises the complexities in understanding Muslim experience. Class is a dynamic alongside those of other socio-economic characteristic (such as race and faith) that plays an often unacknowledged role in life expectancy – your learning needs being recognised by the school you go to and the support you receive. It is associated with where you live and the risks that it exposes you to, such as the likelihood of being stopped and searched by the police.[2] Young people's career options are pretty much decided by the school they go to as schools trying to climb the results ladder reduce options to study English literature or to study the three sciences to achieve the five A–C grades, including maths and English language (just English language will suffice for a school to achieve 5 A–Cs), thereby limiting possible study options and career options as well denying the cultural capital that is gleaned from the study of literature.

bell hooks (1994) observes a reluctance of 'privileged black folks' to problematise class but an equal eagerness to commodify blackness; something similar can be observed in the Muslim context with the added dimension of the 'equalising and beautifying qualities' of the *ummah* notion in which we are all 'brothers and sisters'.

There are two other institutions within the institutional realm that need to be acknowledged as important for young people and which indicate a need for Muslims to consider oppressive practices that they themselves may be vulnerable or party to. The first is the family and the second religion, as represented institutionally by *masjids* (mosques). Camila Batmangelidjh (2006) makes reference to the importance of parental perception to a child's self-esteem and identity. She makes particular note of the need for secure attachments, making reference to the work of John Bowlby (1969). Her observation that state institutions that work with people do so under the assumption that there is somebody 'back home' who will support them, and under this assumption fundamentally fail them, is insightful, as this is something that youth workers do not often take for granted. In the case of Muslim young people there is a reverse 'danger' where the 'place back home' is something institutions and workers consciously and unconsciously work against rather than work with.

There are a number of locales that Muslim organisations can consider as vulnerable to oppressive practice or in creating mental and physical conditions that can compromise safety and potential. The following categories informed by key informal education principles try to identify these arenas, but with some nervousness of the danger that they may add to the problematisation of Muslim organisations and families that continue to put communities and individuals on the permanent back foot.

---

[2] www.guardian.co.uk/uk/2012/aug/24/black-teenager-met-police

Pedagogy: the practice of *taqlid* or emulation is practised by Jewish and Christian organisations through ideas of Jewish literate *teachers* or youth *leaders*, street *pastors*, and by Muslim youth organisations developing similar youth leader roles, for example, *emirs*. For *masjids* and *madrasahs* claiming to deliver youth work it runs into problems. In *madrasahs* *taqlid* is a pedagogical approach that cultivates obeyance as part of the acculturation of young people into the etiquettes of the space and the etiquettes associated with the position of the *imam*. The facilitation of two opposing and distinctive pedagogical approaches and their implications on space is an important challenge for *masjids* seeking to develop youth work. *Taqlid*, as a concept, facilitates reproduction rather than creation. It resonates very strongly with Freire's (1970) notions of the banking model of education, a pedagogical approach that leaves no power or voice and which can make the student vulnerable to abuse. Cases of young boys and girls being abused are not commonplace, but neither is it the case that they do not take place, and when they do, the strength of this power silences powerfully. Freire's reading of power in the student–teacher relationship is characterised by this statement:

> The teacher teaches and the students are taught; the teacher knows everything and the students know nothing; the teacher thinks and the students are thought about; the teacher talks and the students listen meekly; the teacher disciplines and the students are disciplined; the teacher chooses and enforces his choice. And the students comply; the teacher acts and the students have the illusion of acting through the teacher; the teacher chooses the program content, and the students adapt to it; the teacher confuses the authority of knowledge with his own professional authority, which he sets in opposition to the freedom of students; the teacher is the subject of the learning process, whilst the students are mere objects. (Freire, 1970, p 53)

The latter part of this quote is particularly pertinent as the validation of the position of the teacher is an important part of the outcome sought. It is an extension of a pedagogical approach that characterises God and the Qur'an as the objects of worship rather than a relationship that is open to questions, doubt and direct inspiration, with vestiges of this pedagogy used to cloak the teacher in the same aura.

Participation: Janine Clark's (2004) point about Muslim organisations operating class-based vertical power relations rather than horizontal power relations is one that can be used to critique all organisations; this dynamic is not exclusive to Muslim organisations but Muslim organisations do demonstrate it. The lack of access to decision-making structures, to inform organisational culture and practice, is profound for young men and even more so for young Muslim women, especially in relation to *masjids*. Those *masjids* that use a separate entrance for women invariably locate it at the side of the building or at the back, and in doing so are increasingly finding this act interpreted as an act of either tribal patriarchy, institutional religious marginalisation or spiritual inequality. The importance of a place reflecting the diversity of its people is necessary for it to be able to reflect the concerns, experiences and positions people take as well as to benefit from the wide range of expertise within its community. Muslim women are visible in society at large in many professional fields as people who have something to offer, but due to the positioning and organisation of *masjids* and representative organisations as extensions of a patriarchy, they are denied the political and theological 'position of Aisha', the wife of the Prophet Muhammad (pbuh); they are therefore increasingly adopting the strategy of the Prophet's first wife, Khadija, a business woman, operating outside religious patriarchal structures to make needs visible and to respond to them.

Person-centred: this means working from where young people are at, where their feelings, thoughts and experiences inform the direction of the conversation, revealing the dilemmas and issues young people may encounter, whether of identity, ethnicity, family, sexuality, unemployment, relationships and the potentialities that sit in them. It requires a pedagogical approach that is about asking the critical question rather than providing the 'ruling', the answer or the Islamic position. It requires a Muslim pedagogical approach where being Muslim is an act of self-definition, and attaches a value to a condition of dialogue based on what Freire names, that is, love, hope, faith, critical consciousness and humility, as characteristic of this relationship and learning experience for both parties.

The idea of 'equalness' through the mutuality of seeking, knowing and learning in this relationship is captured by the Sufi saying that 'The teacher seeks the student as a student seeks the teacher' that draws from the following *hadith* found in the collections of both Bukhari and Muslim:

He who comes closer to Me one span, I come closer to him a cubit; and he who comes closer to Me a cubit, I come closer to him a fathom; and if he comes to Me walking, I come to him running.

The person–centred approach is spiritual and political where politics is understood as an act of participation and not as an act of power through the privileging and imposition of, for example, status, gender, age or sexuality. Hamza Yusuf (2010) makes reference to the danger of the exploitative possibilities of hierarchical systems, and how 'religion has been used by the powerful to maintain certain hierarchies and social practices at the expense of the oppressed' (2010, p 16).

Islamic perspectives on oppression

The Arabic word *zulm* is familiar to all Muslims irrespective of which part of the world they come from. In most cases it has been accommodated into existing languages and used to describe an act that violates another and names the oppressor as the *zalim*. It is not a term that is used lightly. The Arabic saying 'Those who possess, oppress' (Yusuf, 2010) indicates this as an act in which power is often sourced from economics and politics.

The Arabic root of *zulm* is *za la ma*, meaning oppress, suppress or tyrannise (Berjak, 2006), and occurs in its various forms nearly 300 times, signifying the importance of this to the Qur'an. According to Rafik Berjak, there are three types of *zulm*:

- The oppression or suppression that a person does to themselves – that oppression damages the person themselves as the Qur'an states, 'It is not the eyes that go blind, but the hearts within the breast that go blind' (22:46).
- The oppression of one human being over another, which can also be experienced as mental oppression through, for example, pedagogical relationships that cultivate blind obedience, referred to as *zulmat al-taqlid*.
- From a person to God.

Struggle against oppression is reflected in the life of the Prophet (pbuh) and the context in which the Qur'an is revealed and its purpose, as exemplified by the following verse:

> And We revealed the Qur'an to be a healing (for hearts).
> (17:82)

A prophet who is an orphan, poor, illiterate and without much material prestige and has no son as a successor challenges the purpose of literacy or status of education, the significance of the accumulation of wealth, the importance of status and importance attached to sons as legacy. In his opening chapter to *The prayer of the oppressed*, Yusuf captures the challenge made by the Prophet's life and beliefs:

> It was a hierarchical and unjust place where some people were considered superior to others because of their lineage and complexion. Initially the Prophet was persecuted for teaching that women were not chattel but had rights, that slavery was immoral, and that indentured bondage should be liberated. He taught that feeding the hungry and homeless was one of the greatest acts of charity ... he prohibited domestic violence, child abuse and economic exploitation of the poor. (Yusuf, 2010, p 25)

Yusuf goes on to state that gender, 'race' or even beliefs did not raise one above the other as all are created equal before God, but what elevated one individual above another was conscientiousness.

The most powerful institution of pre-revelation Arab society was the tribe, and the above challenges were to its economics, to the privileges of patriarchy and its systems of survival and dominance; therefore Yusuf's example shows the Prophet (pbuh) naming and challenging oppression and also acting on transforming systems of thought and belief through challenging and transforming values seen as a weakness or a vice to something that was and is virtuous, as was the case with forgiveness. Yasien Mohamed (2006) points to the move of morality as something tied to tribal loyalty, to one of a personal ethic. The following verse questions a society for whom vengeance was seen as an act of healing:

> The servants of the merciful are those who walk humbly upon the earth, and when the ignorant address them, say 'peace'. (25:63)

Honour killings particularly come to mind when writing the above; the tribe as an institution is very powerful and continues today. Whether called extended family networks or gangs, it continues to be a place of significance and status, of security, protection, solidarity and support;

it can be a place of ostentatious acts of courage and generosity that elevate a person's name and reputation, or the creation of myths that are carried from one generation to the next, but it is a place where moral boundaries are enforced by the preservation of the 'name' and therefore ultimately shaped by the tribe or the gang. In this context women often become both chattels and symbols of honour. For women, the unaware 'revel' in the latter and the aware struggle in the former.

Yusuf's book *The prayer of the oppressed* (2010) and Esack's book *Qur'an liberation and pluralism* (1997) have been very helpful in providing and informing the following frame by which oppression takes form and can be interrogated (see Table 4.3). Oppression, the oppressor and the oppressed have a considerable presence in the Qur'an, as the following verses suggests (translated by Abdullah Yusuf Ali):

For tumult and oppression are worse than slaughter. (2:191)

... and fight them until there is no more tumult or oppression. (2:193)

Table 4.3: Muslim sites of oppressive practice

1. Oppression as a state of being: oppression requires disconnection from the context and those who are oppressed for the oppression to take place. It is an act of alienation from the self. This makes tyranny possible and the tyrannised vulnerable. The role of interpersonal relationships in critically challenging the oppressor is important to challenge the development of this disconnect and this personality.
2. An act of selective hermeneutics: Esack's book (1997) is located in the struggle against apartheid in South Africa, and this location becomes the lens through which the Qur'an in this instance is understood. This locational lens is employed by Fatima Mernissi, Asma Barlas, Nimat Hafez Bazarangi and Saba Mahmood in relation to gender in unreading the patriarchal interpretations of the Qur'an, and Scott Siraj al-Haqq Kugle in relation to sexuality, but it is also employed by every translator, as Sardar points out in his text *Reading the Qur'an* (2011), where interpretation is an act of meaning making and meaning control.
3. As an act of possession: this is in terms of resources affecting others' material welfare, but also of human possession that, for example, creates indentured labour, a practice so often employed in Gulf States today, and the treatment of any dependent or disempowered group.
4. As an act of suppression: this particular category is inspired by the Qur'anic verse 17:31 referenced earlier, and the meaning that can be derived from the root *qa ta la*, that is, to deny, to kill, to essentially disempower.

> Tumult and oppression are worse than slaughter. (2:217)

> To those who leave their homes in the cause of Allah, after suffering oppression.... (16:41)

> A book revealed unto you ... your heart be oppressed no more.... (7:2)

A study of the Qur'an will reveal many examples of what it understands to be oppression and justice; both are powerful themes and both are understood as acts of being and acts of politics. The selections above and many like these are unequivocal about the duty to challenge oppression, but to challenge it there is a need to be able to see it, to know it and be moved to do something about it. This is an act of knowing and conscientisation that individuals are required to reach by employing a will incapacitated by statements that are acts merely of sentiment. Seyyed Hossein Nasr's (1999) observation of a separation in the relationship between knowledge and the sacred and knowledge and the self as a postmodern condition that externalises and desacralises knowledge seems to find resonance with this incapacity.

Yusuf (2010) names three responses to challenging oppression: patience, a focus on the struggle and not the outcome, and the need to recognise the tyrant within. The latter condition finds resonance with the following verse:

> Verily, never will God change the condition of a people until they change what is in themselves. (13:11)

This verse has significant implications in terms of pedagogical approaches and seems to sit well with Green's model discussed earlier, in which she views the anti-oppressive journey as something that is from the individual outwards. The verse is suggestive of an inner *jihad* (struggle) before any external struggle. At its heart for informal educators is the agency of the individual as somebody who entertains transformation or change out of choice. It is the Muslim version of the feminist perspective of 'The personal is political'. In this verse the personal is political and it is the personal that is the starting point of changing the 'condition of people'; therefore its impact is at the individual level and also at the interpersonal level, as the verse seems to suggest. It indicates change as a process and as something voluntarily entered that has an impact across Green's 'I's' model rather than being imposed or done to people. It informs the principles set out in Chapter Two.

The history of Islam is replete with examples that aim to cultivate values that challenge oppressive practice, discrimination or impoverishment, as the following excerpt from the Prophet Muhammad's (pbuh) last sermon, delivered shortly before he died, suggests:

> ... an Arab has no superiority over a non–Arab nor a non–Arab has any superiority over an Arab; also a white has no superiority over black nor does a black have any superiority over white except by piety and good action.

Notions of anti-oppressive practice are central to the philosophical underpinning of informal education, whether that is in forms of pedagogy or relationships in all their spheres, as discussed in the Muslim youth work theoretical frame. This chapter has been an exploration of the concepts, ideas and histories that can be employed to give a Muslim meaning or perspective, and these are essentially political due to the importance attached to the experience of oppression and justice, the need to understand it and the wisdom and courage to respond. The possibility of all this is found in the way the Qur'an describes the act of creation and willing something to be (2:117;16:40): 'Kun faya kun,' meaning 'Be! And it is.' Therefore what we 'be' 'is'.

FIVE

On anthros and pimps: researching Muslim young people

I changed my style to silver
I changed my clothes to black
And where I would surrender
Now I would attack.

Leonard Cohen (1934–)
from the song 'I came so far for beauty'

'Theyification'

Academic knowledge generated out of research on any marginalised community rarely finds itself in verse, careful as it is about the validity of its methods to secure the expertise of the researcher and the factualness or correctness of its data for potential generalisability.

The following examples aim to express the feeling and impact of being researched. The first example is an extract of the lyrics from a song by Floyd Red Crow Westerman (1936-2007), a Sioux actor, political activist and musician, titled 'Here come the anthros':

> And the anthros still keep coming
> Like death and taxes to our land;
> To study their feathered freaks
> With funded money in their hand.
>
> Like a Sunday at the zoo
> Their cameras click away –
> Taking notes and tape recordings
> Of all the animals at play.
> Here come the anthros, better hide the past away.
> Here come the anthros on another holiday.
>
> Then back they go to write their book
> And tell the world there's more.
> But there's nothing left to write
> It's all been done before.
> And not a cent of funded money
> That the anthros get to spend
> Is ever given to their
> Disappearing feathered friends.
>
> And the anthros keep on diggin'
> Our sacred ceremonial cite
> As if there was nothing wrong
> 'Cause education gives them the right
> But the more they keep on diggin'
> the less they really see
> 'Cause they got no respect for you or me.

The second example is titled 'Ethical pimping' that I wrote and which was published in the *Muslim News* in 2007 in their ' From another shore' column:

> I grew up in the 1980s in Balsall Heath, Birmingham; it was a well-known and busy red-light district where kerb crawlers often left little room on the pavement. The exchanges taking place were obvious to even the youngest amongst us and made us witnesses to the exploitation of lives that was visible in all the ways ours was not. Even to a child it was hard not to notice young women grow very old, very quickly, and all that was vulnerable and fragile giving way to survival and bare life. The traffic has slowed down somewhat since the prostitutes and the pimps were driven out but the lust for and trading on 'experience' has re-surfaced in different guises on the kerbs of our neighbourhoods, and with it, a new kind of pimp. A new type of go-between, extortionist and entrepreneur has emerged living off the exploitation of 'experience' and trading on its current hyper-inflated political and academic currency: the researcher.
>
> Some will find this analogy between dissonant experiences and exploitations unpalatable or downright objectionable. Some may see it as merely metaphorical. But exploitation is exploitation, whether of another's body or experience. My assertion that research can become a form of pimping is not one that I make without experience or observation and by doing so I put myself under the same charge. As a former Youth Worker there were often and in recent years an increasing number of phone calls from consultation companies, research houses, 'think tanks', Government departments and researchers hoping I'll procure them 'ten Somalis', 'five Kashmiri vegetarians', or just generally 'your yoooth'. As an academic the demand to 'capture and analyse the Muslim experience' has never been greater. Articles, surveys, questionnaires, focus groups, charting and polling all aspects of Muslim life proliferate in a manner suggestive of the colonial survey groups of old charged with mapping terrain, territory and tradition. For the 'Aden survey group' of old read 'British Muslims' today.
>
> It would, by the way, be a mistake to assume that these research 'visitors' are 'outsiders' (though I am never really sure who the insiders and outsiders in the Muslim community

are); and though some within, as Muslims, struggle with this dilemma, others 'extract' and 'map' unperturbed. For what purposes? To whose benefit?

The question facing individuals in the research community, it seems to me, is simple: Pimp – is that who I am; am afraid of becoming; am asked to be; or need to be for a living. Rather than face it in this stark and unsparing form, the reflexive response of the researcher is a reiteration of the mantra of 'professional ethics', a cleansing formula that turns on the purge of the bad apples of methodological fault, failures in data collection or ethical transgression, rounded off with the benefits of empirical research of proper standards to avoid facing the deeper, more disturbing question. But this evasion can sometimes itself be a sign that pimping is exactly what is happening. Medicine and law, after all, are the professions with the most codified ethical standards, but doctors and lawyers are often also those from whom we are the most distant; it is with butchers and mechanics that we know exactly where we stand! Focus and fixation on ethics can help to professionalise endeavours through process, ritual or ideology, which is also a distancing and separation; a justification for walking away because we have norms, guidelines, duties and obligations. Ethics not only legitimises research activity, it often underpins and justifies the process itself.

In community research ethics can afford us a neat protective capsule; a vehicle that takes us in and safely and untouched brings us out again. It is an effective way of setting boundaries creating an 'us' and 'them'; helping us decide how close we should or 'can allow' ourselves to become, or how distant we must remain; whom we are allowed to speak to, and whom not. Others' experiences become data, and when they do, the focus shifts to the researcher and the data, rather than the researched who can no longer be trusted with it. This is one reason why Yunis Alam's recent book, *Made in Bradford* (Pontefract: Route Books), is such a breath of fresh air: people were trusted with their experiences and he gives neither reason nor right to get in their way.

The rawness and directness of the experience finds expression through poetry in the case of Westerman; the terms used to name this experience, 'anthro' or 'pimp', generate reactions of denial, anger, rejection, hurt and in some cases, recognition. The examples recast the educational and ethical intentions and safeguards that legitimate the intention and the outcome. The terms are Freirean acts of naming an experience and, as Westerman writes 'hide your past away', his lyrics call for a preservation of knowledge and experience that should only be possible to know through belonging. The hiding of the 'valuable' from educational intentions is a poignant statement of the feelings of the objectified as people and culture. I have sat in on research meetings where nothing unethical could be felt about attaching recording microphones to children in *madrasahs*, so that what they talk about could be researched. There has been a 'theyification' of me in other research exercises in which much of what was me in terms of community, religion and ethnicity was extracted as indicative of the generic characteristics of an externally defined 'they'. There is therefore a process of 'theyification' – a researcher's creative act of power in rendering me into something that existed outside the room, something they brought in as an a priori knowledge of me. The Turkish language uses three words to differentiate the distance of an object to the person – *bu*, *su* and *o*. The *bu* is the near, the *su* the nearby and *o* the distance. In these exercises it was the *o* that was being used as the something distant, beyond reach. It was an example of the impact of language in the subliminal transformations involved in the 'othering' processes. The process of disconnecting experience and knowledge from its 'belonging space' is possible to trace simply by looking at the language being used in research – experience becomes data, places and relationships become research sites and people become focus groups, respondents. For MacIntyre (cited in Lee, 1993) this is not just the expression of a discipline, but evidence that the discipline is the expression of a wider culture, and therefore the researched should be wary of its intentions and practices:

> Our culture has one idiosyncratic feature that distinguishes it from most and perhaps all other cultures. It is a culture in which there is a general desire to make social life translucent, to remove opacity, to reveal the hidden, to unmask.... A secret in our culture has become something to be told. And social science research cannot hope to avoid being in part an expression of this same tendency. (MacIntyre, cited in Lee, 1993, p 18)

To name this experience is not easy; it is not meant to be offensive. It is a reflexive necessity for those who research Muslim young people, however they define themselves, as Muslim or otherwise. The dilemmas are not any less if you are a Muslim researching Muslims; in many cases they are more, although it is often received as offensive and as questioning professional practice and personal relationships and thus the experiences, feelings and expressions of those being researched often get crushed under the weight of the indignation of the researcher.

The wariness of those being researched to research as the handmaiden of imperialism and colonisation is often dismissed as something of the past and not of the present (Asad, 1973). Yet initiatives by the US military, such as Project Camelot in 1965, clearly saw the importance of research in understanding indigenous structures, sensitivities and sensibilities in which interventions can be made to achieve military objectives – they demonstrate the importance of social science research to the imperial intentions of subjugation and control. Talal Asad (1973) captures this in the following:

> Bourgeois disciplines which study non-European societies reflect the deep contradictions articulating this unequal historical encounter, for ever since the Renaissance the West has sought both to subordinate and devalue other societies, and at the same time find clues to its own humanity. Although modern colonialism is merely one moment in that long encounter, the way in which the objectifiers understanding of these modern disciplines has been made possible by and acceptable to that moment needs to be considered far more seriously than it has. (Asad, 1973, p 104)

The creation of the 'other' as the 'object' is aided and abetted by first having some knowledge of the people or the place. Edward Said (1993) refers to the rise of ethnography, a research approach that normally entails the direct observation through participant observation of a group (Marshall, 1998) to codifications of difference, naming a causal relationship between research and domination. In Orientalism, Said (1978) refers to the deliberate creation of interest, whether commercial, religious, cultural or military, that merges into the notion of, for example, 'British self-interest', that then needs to be defended culturally and militarily. For many, Islam is still symbolic of the 'Far East', the different, the alien, but there is also now a 'Near East' captured by notions of 'Londonistan' or 'Bradistan', that the establishment sends out a message that it no longer knows.

The search for beauty, the different and idealist intentions to know compromises and endangers the researched more than the researcher, the powerless more than the powerful, at the same time that it leaves us with the questions as to whether there can be a 'virtuous concern', an innocent curiosity or an ethical position. Is the idea of virtuousness already overly laden with notions of morality? And who are these determined by? Can I, in the pursuit of beauty, the different, pursue an idealist wish *to know* – to comprehend 'the other'? Can I have not only an innocent gaze on someone else's life, but in fact, a virtuous concern with understanding? These are claims that could be said to be at the core of some of the current claims being made for the cosmopolitanism of a shared universality plus difference (Appiah, 2006).

The Qur'an itself names difference and the need to know as a divine decree, as the following verse seems to suggest:

> O mankind! We created you from a single (pair) of a male and a female and made you into nations and tribes that ye may know each other. Verily the most honoured of you in the sight of Allah is the most righteous of you. And Allah has full knowledge and is well acquainted. (*Surah Al-Hurriyat*, 49:13)

This verse is a reminder of the need for wariness of absolute assumption of bad faith, or at least, of hegemonically compromised intent, on the part of all researchers, yet fears and, for that matter, anger in relation to the latter, are difficult to marginalise. It suggests a dialogue, a two-way process of knowing, an equal relationship in which something of the self can be revealed by the other. This desire of a giving and receiving relationship is poignantly stated by Chief Dan George in his most famous work, 'My heart soars' (1974):

> Everyone likes to give as well as to receive.
> No one wishes to receive all the time.
> We have taken much from your culture....
> I wish you had taken something from our culture ...
> for there were some good and beautiful things.

At the heart of the thought of the Jewish philosopher Emmanuel Levinas are descriptions of the encounter with another person, an encounter given a primordial importance by tracing his philosophy to the encounter between two human beings rather than between God and a human being. What is possible between this encounter between one human being and another is often taken for granted, overlooked even, and yet the impact that we have on one, both uplifting and destructive, can be profound indeed.

Experience suggests that research on Muslims has often focused on the proximal, 'them', their families, peers, neighbourhoods; this research often reifies public policy discourse and maintains the focus on Muslim young people which informs a public policy that targets change in 'them' rather than in meta narratives and meta structures that bear down on them through policy and strategy. The case of Åsne Seierstad, the journalist and author of *The bookseller of Kabul* (2003), reported in *The Guardian* on 14 December 2011, powerfully reveals the feelings invoked by the invasion of privacy of the 'bookseller' that she described and wrote about. Seierstad got to know Shah Mohammed Rais and his family and painted a picture of a local hero and a ruthless tyrant. Shah Mohammed Rais accused her of invasion of privacy, treachery and of humiliating him, his family and Afghanistan as a nation, and took her to court in Norway. An inconsequential bookseller in Kabul, he seemed to have had the clash of civilisations being played in the public gaze through his and his family's life. The ruling by the Norwegian Court found the author 'not to have acted negligently, and the content of the book was essentially deemed true' (*The Guardian*, 14 December 2011, p 21). The truth of the meanings of the life of Shah Rais and his family became contested. The feeling of humiliation and the felt violation of space and trust may be experiences others can also relate to.

The reification of government policy occurs when the discourse generated within government departments in the unequal, and less than rational, dialogue between ministers, their departmental staff and their advisers is taken unquestioningly as an objective language of concerned policy: where the concepts that come to be the anvils on which policy is beaten out are taken as unproblematic. For example, Field (2003) and Arneil (2007) provide a revealing account of the enthusiastic importation of the conceptual language of social capital from the US, when in fact that concept was both problematic in its foundational definition and in its application in the UK (Husband and Alam, 2011). The hegemonic power of government to set the terms in which we come to locate other people's lives as objects of 'benign' state policy is one of the most potent and potentially oppressive forces shaping research and its interpretation. Funding tends to follow policy, rather than the other way round. The Economic and Social Research Council (ESRC), for example, has become an increasingly obvious vehicle of government policy, with research agendas set a priori and funding increasingly being given to those who have had previously large grants.

Something of this process can be seen in the emergence of a new category of problematic Islamophobic behaviour, namely, the insidious offence of being an 'apologist'. The Muslim Youthwork Foundation designed a series of posters that sought to capture the experience of being young and Muslim in the 'Preventing Violent Extremism (PVE) world'. One of the posters titled 'How much can you carry?' captures the labels being generated by the wholesale labelling of the Muslim community as a terrorist threat (see Figure 5.1).

Figure 5.1: How much can you carry?

© Muslim Youthwork Foundation 2013

This poster was designed and produced in 2008; there is not much that can be taken off it as most of these labels continue to exist, but the new CONTEST strategy (published in July 2011) names a new kind of offender, the 'apologist', and this has been added to the front cover of this book . While this policy seems to ignore the supremacist narrative that informs the racism of the English Defence League (EDL), it defines Muslim extremism as grounded in a supremacist narrative. The EDL is therefore a reactionary manifestation of the Muslim presence. This discourse has evolved rather than shown any sign of listening to Muslim grievances, and with this new label then disabling the ability of young Muslims to name underlying, structural inequalities that inform the experience of young British Muslims in Britain and

Muslims internationally. It can also be interpreted that those who have engaged with government have done nothing more than help reify this discourse, acted as much needed representatives and experts with whom dialogue can be shown – in the case of New Labour, an ethical preoccupation with evidence-based collaborative policy.

The interest in access to young Muslims is an ethical concern for youth workers who not only act as gatekeepers but often as mediators and negotiators with and between structures for young people (Imam, 1999). Imam, writing in 1999, touches on the questions of primary loyalty with which Black youth workers were or are often faced. This role as mediator and gatekeeper, and the ethical issues of exposing young people to unequal power relations in the context of a highly politicised and visible discourse informing government policy towards Muslims in Britain and 'Muslim lands' abroad, is ethically loaded for the worker and the young person. It questions the role of consultation as a maker and shaper of policy, and it all too easily positions the researcher or consultant as a reifier of policy. As somebody involved in the initial dialogue with the Department for Communities and Local Government in the establishment of the Young Muslims Advisory Group (YMAG), these ethical tensions were very clear to me as a Muslim outsider (of government) youth worker, but not so clear, it seemed, to insider Muslim government civil servants. The YMAG started life conceptually as the Young Muslims Consultative Group, a group that government consulted with on issues affecting young Muslims but whose name was later changed to the Young Muslims *Advisory* Group – for a government seeking approval, to have an advisory group was much more preferable than a consultative group. This change of title may have made the young people feel more significant *if* they were involved in this change, but it is definitely more in the government's interest to claim to have people who advise rather than people who they simply consult about their ideas. This is but one example of the ethical dilemmas faced by young Muslims in consultation processes in terms of exposure to unequal power relationships where there is comparatively little control of the image and the word – that is, how they are presented and what they say.

The strength of the discourse between Muslim young people and terrorism compromises the presence of young Muslims in wider policy debates areas; it generates a suspicion to consultation processes that exacerbate the absence of this voice in wider policy issues. Khalida Khan's assessment of the impact of PVE (2009) captures this wariness and the language being used to describe it – infiltration, mapping, monitoring, spying. Khan captures this in two quotes from her report, the first from Kris Hopkins (2008) in a BBC Newsnight interview and the second from Mary Bousted, General Secretary of the Association of Teachers and Lecturers: 'What they [the government] said is if we were willing to go out and monitor the Muslim community and use the resources of the local councils to do that'; and '… teachers are not trained to deal with radicalisation. We're not spy-catchers.' Khan herself uses the phrase 'intelligence through the backdoor'.

It is no surprise that the cumulative effect of these kinds of experiences can generate a research resistance, with individuals and groups feeling both over-researched and under-resourced, without any real tangible benefit in return. This experience generates an attitude that is ambivalent at its best to the idea of research. The research in itself may not be an anthropological exercise, but it can feel like one.

This feeling can be the strongest from communities that already feel the impact of social, economic and political marginalisation; therefore there can be a class and political dimension to the accommodation of research support and research resistance. The experience of being researched, however, generates discernment to the 'critical question', that is, 'Who is it critical to?' and 'What purpose does it serve?' and latterly, 'What's in it for me?', challenging the objectification of people, places and relationships. It brings to the surface questions that you want to ask of yourself and your communities. The post-9/11 research interest on Muslim young people has come from a variety of sources including universities, think-tanks, local authorities and central government, some named as research, other as consultation or mapping, and for many of these, youth workers have played an important role, especially as *border pedagogues* as they often are, that is, operating at the edge of communities, on the interstices of community life. This is the location of the encounter because this is where people live and develop a sense of belonging. It is the place where credentials for access are most critical and where researchers' claims to insider expertise are most significant. It is not a place of being one or the other, but it is the place of difference and the acting out of indifference, and this is the place that youth workers often inhabit. Knowledge that comes second nature and relationships that are a normative part of their personal and professional worlds have considerable value to researchers who have an interest in both. Young people will meet researchers on the strength of their relationships with youth workers, and this places significant responsibility on youth and community workers. The credentialisation of researchers through their own, or borrowed by association with others, claims to being trustworthy and simpatico to the researched, is itself is a major area for exploration. The credentials of 'credentialisers' are themselves only as good as their last case of support for an incoming researcher. The trust question that is invoked is rarely tested in terms of the researcher's 'performance' as a researcher within the community, since often their findings are not published until 18 months or two years later, and may never become known to the researched.

Lave and Wenger's notion of peripheral participation (1991) is extremely useful to understand the relationship between knowledge, relationships and peripherality for youth workers. 'Youth work knowledge' emerges from the interrelationship between all three. This is the locale of visibility and an invisibility for youth workers. Youth work more often than not exists on the periphery, involved with those on the periphery, marginalised and alienated in terms of identity, socio-economics and/or geography or with those who just don't seem to fit in with the ideas and expectation of the centre. The connection between relationships, locale and knowledge are eloquently described by Lave and Wenger, describing knowledge as something that is both inseparable from practice but that is integrated in the life of communities, their value systems and ways of doing things. For youth workers and community workers this locale is a position of privilege and responsibility, and many who are conscious of this can come across as obstructive and objectionable to voyeurs.

Researchers view research as something that broadens knowledge, improves understanding and as something that can make a positive difference in people's lives. It is something that is a 'social good', carried out more often than not by well-meaning people, but how it is used can be unexpected. The unexpected uses of research are anecdotally illuminated by George Smith who was the Co-Director of the Social Disadvantage Research Centre at the University of Oxford from the 1990s to 2005. The Centre's pioneering work on the development of 'multiple deprivation indices' was meant to inform how government could target resources to need geographically – therefore the enquiry from the Council of Mortgage Lenders (CML) to use the indices to grade risk geographically was not the first enquiry expected. A system that was meant to develop profiles that could inform government grants to the most needy could also be used by the CML to weight lending and risk through geographical profiling.

It is revealing that while government, through consultation exercises, mapping exercises, special advisers, pet organisations and research exercises, seeks knowledge of young Muslims, young Muslims do not return the compliment of seeking this knowledge of themselves from government consultation reports and qualitative research papers.

Muslim societies have been the subject of research interest long before its most current manifestation of 'researching Muslim young people'. The following typology gives a broad brush idea for the possible motivations for researching Muslims and Muslim young people in Britain or Europe today:

- A governmental approach in developing evidence-based policy.
- A historic exercise rooted in suspicion, fear and interest in Islam.
- A necessary activity in the act of colonising people or places.
- Revealing knowledge that can 'make a difference' in how Muslims can be known, accommodated and related to.
- Knowledge for the sake of knowledge.
- An attraction or interest in the exotic, the mysterious, the unknown.
- To know something of the self through the other.
- An interest in what has been lost in the self (community) but existing in the other.

Much of the above is indicative of the potentially highly political nature of this activity in terms of intention and in how it can be received; experience suggests that being Muslim does not equate to an automatic understanding or sensitivity to this, nor can one assume that not being a Muslim equates to an inability to understand this dynamic. Philosophical standpoints, political consciousness and ethical reflexivity are all means by which one can be sensitised or not to this research experience.

Muslim as an identity label is expressed through a variety of cultural practices that are informed by, for example, ethnicity, gender, 'race', geography, language, kinship, sexuality, and class. As somebody born in a Muslim family, my journey and experience as a Muslim or Muslim researcher (an insider) and being researched may not be the same as that of an English White Muslim convert. For example he/she will have grown up with a different experience of racism to me; he/she may well have been exposed to an internalised, stereotypical and racist messages of the 'other', but not the experience of being at the butt end of them. We may share aspects of the experience of Islamophobia as Muslims, but at the same time, I will not share the experience of the non-Muslim reaction to 'one of their own' turning to Islam. It is important to acknowledge that the *ummah* is not a level playing field; it is a place where privileges attached to 'race', gender, age, class and sexuality can and do get played out despite a rhetoric that seeks to resist. Such, however, is the power of the label Muslim that I, for example, am immediately viewed as an insider, ignoring the myriad of differences that exist within this identity label that will influence the 'in group' location. The experiences and depths of feelings evoked are dependent on context and one's class location alone can bring to the surface any of the below, as Sayer explains:

> We are evaluative beings, continually monitoring and assessing our behaviour and that of others, needing their approval and respect, but in contemporary society this takes place in the context of inequalities such as class, gender and 'race' which affect both what we are able to do and how we are judged. Condescension, deference, shame, guilt, envy, resentment, arrogance, contempt, fear and mistrust, or simply mutual incomprehension and avoidance, typify relations between people of different classes. (Sayer, 2005, p 1)

The insider–outsider paradigm in any research activity implies something static, a viewpoint on what is being observed, but within this lies the assumption that you can see more the further away you are, and you see less the closer you are. The insider's perspective in this model can be referred to as subjective, not generalisable, emotional, courageous even, all of which can be 'nicely' dismissed as methodologically compromised, but the insider–outsider location is not always able to convey the movement that happens in the course of any question looking for an answer. Those on the outside can move inwards and those on the inside can move outwards, and the feelings that this movement generates can be revealing of the realpolitik of the landscape being researched. Feelings, whether gratefulness, acceptance, respect, anger, frustration, revelation, disappointment or confidence, themselves become useful insights. Vickers (2002) quotes Ranjan and Clegg (1997) about the dangers of conducting insider researcher in a society (and, I would add, a community), politicised and pathologised like I believe Muslim communities are. As an insider, the dilemma is in saying how 'you are feeling it and understanding it', personally and professionally, even when this challenges the informal and formal negotiated settlements or understanding being built between respected researchers and the researched and between government and community institutions. There is a danger to the powerful and the powerless in revealing symbiotic relationships that are about securing and pacifying the powerful, of reifying the discourse being cultivated that eventually, as Said (1978, p 94) observes, 'texts can create not only knowledge but also the very reality they appear to describe' in much the same way as funding reifies the policy discourse by an application process that asks to demonstrate a connection to, and an awareness of, the reality that it wishes to intervene in. Community Cohesion and PVE are excellent examples of this, where Muslims may reject the wholesale labelling of the Muslim community as potential terrorist, but then have to affirm its presence or dangers in funding applications – this viewed both as a survival tactic and as an act of betrayal. Although Vickers is writing here about insiders in organisations, the dynamic she describes is not exclusive to them, and she refers to the danger to the insider in challenging consensus:

> Frankly it can be dangerous to write about what goes on in organisations. Those of us who survive organisational life recognise that the speech of survivors can be highly politicised. Telling it like it was (or is) can threaten the status quo, and powerful political, economic, and social forces continue to pressure survivors either to keep their silence or to revise their stories. (Vickers, 2002, p 614)

An advantage of the personal voice in the research exercise is to provide a connection, a hook that draws in the reader and makes the research more accessible to the general public and the research; it is unclear if Shah Mohammed Rais would have known what Åsne Seierstad had written if it was written as an academic paper and published in an online journal.

In youth and community work many enter the profession with a story that is rarely far from their side, a story that often has elements of resistance, challenge, inadequacy, injustice in the context of family, education, work, the criminal justice system and so on, and part of the process of finding an identity as an informal educator is the working out of these stories. This often means that these stories have to be put out, to be heard. For Muslims, many of these stories have been externally politicised by the events of recent years, and the opportunity to be 'heard' has become an increasingly difficult exercise due to the strength of the 'Muslim imaginary'. So, chances to be shaped by the other's narrative and to shape ours are less possible, and yet it is unavoidable that the narrative of the other will have some effect on one's sense of self, but it makes the task of finding the common humanness that Cottle (2002) describes here all the more difficult. For Cottle it should:

> Evoke the matter of our humanness along with those vexing questions involving our definitions of self at the very deepest levels of our capacity to reason and feel. The narrative

possesses the potential to push us inward to those places that feel to us to be the farthest limits of our self knowledge.... And painful and difficult as it may seem, this inward turning to ourselves may denote the best that we can do as sensate beings, for it may represent our attempts, however feeble, to make sense of the traces of meanings and sensations of our humanness, our own internal miraculous being. It may also be the best that we can do in our encounters with the traces of others, friends or strangers, as we seek to construct a sense of self. (Cottle, 2002, p 543)

There is a danger in the presentation of the personal narrative that the actual research becomes secondary, but this complexity seems to be highlighted as more of an issue for some researchers than others, and 'race' and faith seem to play a part in this. In this book my reflections are not confessions about my fallibility that seek to gain some form of authenticity through this fallibility. They are my thoughts, feelings and reflections. These may be affirmed or rejected (Cottle, 2002), but for me, in order to express what I understand and observe, they need to be said. I did not enter research to make friends.

Academics may be among the best equipped to speak out, to share, to de-victimise the victim, to de-silence the wrongdoing, to lift the veil on the unspeakable and the undiscussed. What remains for researchers who choose to tell their stories is to know that they are truly writing on the edge – and there is no safety net. However, the reward and the excitement come from sharing with others and sharing with those who want to know. (Vickers, 2002, p 619)

SIX

The voluntary sector:
values and worlds

I see you standing on the other side
I don't know how the river got so wide
I loved you, I loved you way back when –
And all the bridges are burning that we might have crossed,
But I feel so close to everything that we lost.

Leonard Cohen (1934–)
from 'The tower of song' (1993)

Introducing organisations

In his text, *Modern organisations*, Amitai Etzioni (1964) observed that we are born in organisations, educated by organisations and most of us spend much of our lives working for organisations. We spend our leisure time paying, playing and praying in organisations. Ultimately most of us will die in an organisation, and consent for our burial place will be given by an organisation. Scott (2003) observes that the rise in organisational types and numbers has been a defining feature of the last hundred years, principally because organisations have become the main mechanism by which, in a highly differentiated society, it is possible to get things done. This level of differentiation is reflected in organisation types, activities and in organisational size.

The voluntary sector comprises organisations that have budgets of millions of pounds and those that have struggled to have a budget at all. It encompasses organisations that are part of the cultural landscape of Britain, such as the Scout Movement and YMCA, and organisations that are embryonic, local and with no history to demonstrate capacity or expertise and everything to prove; organisations that do not have to explain themselves and their credentials; and organisations that have to spend most of their time explaining themselves to funders, government and politicians, before they can or are allowed to do anything. More often than not Muslim organisations happen to fall into the latter group, and those that claim to do work informally through youth work have to explain not only their youth work, but the meaning of 'Muslimness' and its relationship to social policy and government agendas with regard to the management of difference, diversity and, of course, community cohesion. They have to demonstrate their 'niceness' before their 'nous'.

Belton and Hamid (2011) provide a helpful map of the type of organisations claiming work with young people, their affiliations and their emergence such as the Young Muslims, Muslim Association of Britain and Islamic Society of Britain. The New Labour government and its localisation and regeneration agendas and the post-Cantle and 9/11 landscape culminated in a proliferation of organisational activity that identified itself on a variety of bases including need, gender, ethnicity and locale. Every city and town will have examples of such organisations, such as the Nida Trust and Muslim Youth Helpline in London and Local Leagues and Ulfah Arts in Birmingham. These organisations are new to an established Muslim organisational field comprising organisations who can trace their roots of their relationship to the British state from British colonialism, such as Jamaat-e-Islami and the Muslim Brotherhood, and their later expressions, such as the UK Islamic Mission, the Islamic Foundation, Muslim Association Britain and Young Muslims, are all related to this history.

Organisations make complex claims about their values, their relationship to their objectives and their 'community', which is further complicated by the culturally amorphous nature of the term 'youth work', used to describe practice in all kinds of contexts. This is its strength and its weakness as it does not easily reveal youth work as the practice of a set of values or principles or just simply as work with youth.

This chapter aims to explore these claims, but this is not an easy task in a climate in which the voluntary sector itself is subject to a struggle for its identity and survival. It is no coincidence that both Bernard Davies, a leading thinker and historian on youth work, finds himself alongside Colin Rochester, a leading thinker and writer on the community and voluntary sector (CVS), as directors of the National Coalition for Independent Action (NCIA). In a series of papers for the NCIA (2010-11), Rochester described the relationship between the CVS and the state as one of colonisation. The postwar relationship between the CVS and the state has been reconfigured by successive governments, including New Labour, to the point that notions of mutual aid, the Big Society and David Cameron's invocation of muscular liberalism (2010)[1] and the Christian 'we' (2011)[2] hearken to a world left behind by two world wars.

The development of any theory on the voluntary sector has been made more difficult due to its changing nature in the last 40 years in particular, but David Billis provides a theoretical frame that can be used to understand organisational identity today. His model stems from Weber's notions of 'ideal types' and of the 'bureaucratisation of society' (Parkin, 1982; Andreski, 1983). Religion, bureaucracy and capitalism were key themes in Weber's work, his observations synthesised within a sociological perspective (Slattery 1991, Andreski 1983). Weber constructed 'ideal types' or model examples, yardsticks against which to compare, evaluate and to analyse society, including institutions or bureaucracies. Billis, in his turn, created an ideal type theory in which he described the sector as operating in three 'worlds' (see Figure 6.1): the personal, associational and bureaucratic. Although conceptualised for some years and revisited by Billis in 2010, as discussed later it seems that his theory is still useful in revealing the realpolitik of organisations.

---

[1] www.number10.gov.uk/news/pms-speech-at-munich-security-conference/

[2] www.guardian.co.uk/politics/2012/apr/04/david-cameron-god-easter

Figure 6.1: The personal, associational and bureaucratic worlds

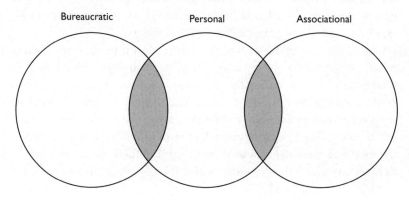

The personal world is the arena in which social problems are resolved by friends, peers, family and neighbours on a private basis. This category may be helpful for acknowledging the level of support available for young people informally in neighbourhoods, and through localised informal networks of peers and congregational contacts. Although not 'constitutionally' evident, this world is significant in its presence operating on a daily basis, offering associational activity, place and meaning to young people.

   The personal world can also be interpreted as the world identified by Singerman (2004) when describing informal networks operating in the urban Muslim world that have become the focus of study since 9/11 (Ramadan, 2004; Werbner, 2005; Abbas, 2006). In the global post-9/11 landscape, organisations operating at this level have also been given a clandestine label that can damage the normative nature of their actual practice. In this way Muslim personal space and informal activism has become politicised. The feminist perspective of the personal being political appears appropriate. Groups that work with young people or that seek to develop some work or make a response are vulnerable to this politicisation label, especially if their work focuses on issues of identity, faith and belief, with Islam understood as something that one can only be indoctrinated into. Therefore the idea of Muslim approaches to youth work receives significant resistance. The phrase is almost seen as an oxymoron, and approaches and organisations are labelled as subversive or, at best, inconsistent. 'The personal is political' therefore comes to have particularly powerful resonance for Muslim young people. Consequently organisations with an explicit ethos or politics of operating in this 'personal world' of Billis may choose to 'face away' from the political agendas carried by the 'bureaucratic world' and the conditions they impose for support. Wiktorowicz (2004) refers to this world as the space of 'social movement communities' in which informal institutions and social networks operate as a recruiting locale for social movement organisations.

The personal world in Billis's model aims to retain a high level of relational activity; it is about the sense of significance and solidarity generated from the company of others that at times requires a pretext of social good. It is reminiscent of the 'conviviality – the enjoyment of festive company' – that Rochester touches on in exploring the roots of voluntary action in his papers for the NCIA. This relational or convivial dimension is used by aid agencies in the Muslim world in particular, such as Islamic Relief, through fundraising dinners and charity events.

This relational and convivial world is the arena in which access is being sought to embed what are termed 'community-based counter-terrorism approaches'. It is access sought by Prevent, but it is also of interest to the PURSUE elements of the CONTEST strategies. State interest in this arena has been described as the 'ungoverned space', and Rochester's claim is that government policy has been to eradicate such spaces through surveillance and restrictions to rights of assembly, financial support and so on. Community activity that presents problems of definition sits outside the realm of 'state knowing', its communal and political dimensions described here by Cnaan and Mislofsky:

> Their boundaries are permeable. They often are more about the process than the products of their work or the tasks people seek to accomplish. They disappear when their signature problem is not present as a community concern only to reappear when a new crisis arises. They may change character when new members join. Their expressive value is often equal to or even greater than their instrumental value. They may not own resources but rather depend on what is needed when time comes for work to be done. Their leaders may not be self-conscious entrepreneurs but rather maybe citizens who are raised up by acclamation or be it the needs of the moment. They are settings or venues where community happens and as such are inseparable from the larger system that is this amorphous thing we call community. (Cnaan and Milofsky, 2007, p 2)

This personal world is also a world of committees, although this is not the committee that may come to mind as a group of people with some organisational oversight function. The term 'committee' in

My first death committee

It happened when I was eight. I found myself in a gathering of men, some of whom I knew, others that seemed more familiar with one another. It wasn't unusual for me as a child to be there, age demarcations hadn't quite set in and I was drawn to the way the smoky atmosphere had added intrigue to their serious intent. They had gathered to establish a death committee, and gave me, in what I am sure was considered as a sign of respect, the job of writing down the names of all those that were meant to be part of this group. I am fairly sure that I wrote the names of all those that I was particularly close to last, even when they were given to me first. It seemed to me that I was writing the order of their death and not just a list. Children can have a strange understanding of their influence on death.

This happened 32 years ago and every year since collections for the death committee take place – and for your information death hasn't followed the course that I sequenced on that list. For those who still can't see past the smoke, these are not death squads or *jihadi* prep groups. These types of groups where individuals make a contribution to cover the costs of their funeral expenses are fairly common.

The contributions are normally gathered at the beginning of February for the death committee I belong to, but if truth be told, it can take anywhere from two to three months, no reminder letters are issued or debt collectors informed, then again neither are there ever any receipts given nor are you asked to provide three quotes when services are required to ensure that you have gone for the most economical option. A couple of weeks ago I came across a membership list at a wedding function as there was some issue with one or two members and a group informally gathered to discuss the matter (the nearest that it comes to a meeting). Since its inception despite there being over four hundred 'active' members no list had been typed up and the repeat photocopying had made some of the names difficult to read.

The story of this death committee takes on many different meanings depending on the reader, their imagination and their prejudices and job. At one level it can be taken to be typical of the organisational capacity of given communities, no minutes, written record of decisions, clear trail of income generated, end of year accounts or annual report is issued, nor the potential of the reserve funds optimised. A perfect example of a lack of organisation that I often have to respond to.

Seen from another shore it is evidence of a service that has required the minimum of bureaucratic investment and where the organisation as a mediating agent between the members is kept to a minimum. There are no salaried staff and if you happen to keep the bank book, and you say all is well, then all is well – report concluded. Those who have not paid know they have not paid and they will;

frustrating, but such are people. Organisations, though often understood as a sign of a modern society can also be the requirement of a fractured community where relationships and services are mediated by them rather than by people themselves.

Events of late in Birmingham have brought into sharp focus how this type of informal activity can become self-indicting. There is an organisational language that is increasingly applied to activities by Muslims whereby talk of networks, groups, and informal gatherings takes on a sinister connotation that envelops every Aunty Shamma or Uncle Aftab's fundraising group in the same cast of suspicion as tentacular terror cells and transnational money laundering operations. Informal discussions at weddings, or sudden visits to Pakistan can take on meanings for the criminal justice system that can introduce you to a parallel reality that you wish was just kept for the silver screen.

The problem is that we are not people who easily trust in organisations as the events around the Kashmir earthquake again proved. It is more often than not individuals that are entrusted to be of service to those that need it. For this act no receipts, written reports, agendas, business plans or strategies are required nor are you likely to keep them. It is therefore difficult to follow the trail of our good intentions. And this is where, as in so many other ways, the new 'terror legislation', and the distorting lens through which it frames and interprets ethnic and Muslim communities and lives is again causing untold damage. It is and will have lasting disruptive effects on the nature of community and the ties and relations of recognition, solidarity and exchange that bind it, criminalising a way of being.

To be of service is a privilege or activity that has more dimensions than you can safely imagine if you happen to be a Muslim. Under the presumption of guilt Muslims in the mutual self-help informal sector are at risk of not being able to explicate the innocence of their activities. *Khidmat*, serving Allah by serving others, was a form of socialisation and character building upon which communities are built. Today, as the raids in our streets make news and fill our screens with a larger than life reality here to stay, the modern Luqman's advice to his sons is to think of themselves before anybody else.

some Muslim communities has little connotation of oversight; rather it is more reflective of mutual aid societies where groups of people contribute for some personal benefit such as funeral expenses, or to meet the expense of something, and as somewhere one can turn to in times of hardship. It is a world in which you are forced to save but there is no interest to be earned, and notions of trust and respect or shame make it a self-regulating activity. The emergence of committees is symptomatic of distrust, especially in banks, to support people at time of need. I wrote the above article for *Muslim News* as the implications of the Terrorism Acts were beginning to be felt and understood by this 'world', and the article explores the implication of the provisions within the anti-terror legislation to entities such as committees in the Muslim community.

The irony for Muslims dependent on or servicing this personal world is that it is David Cameron's Big Society in action, yet those who are the most vulnerable are the most likely to experience its limitations. The claim and experience of political marginalisation is not altogether the same as social marginalisation, although there is an important connecting relationship. Muslims marginalised through factors that challenge social norms are aware that this realm is not enough to meet needs that fundamentally challenge the message of the consensus, or see it as representative of them, or whether it will wish to challenge the oppressiveness of local consensus.

Government distrust of differing cultural formations and expressions and the desire to have all activity within the 'knowledge of the state' makes this realm both subject to 'state gaze' and the state sponsorship of dominant agendas such as PVE or Community Cohesion that then seem to have an impact on and overlay all other issues. The message of the 'Big Society' sits in sharp contrast for many Muslim communities and networks because contingent features of cohesive communities, such as trust and altruism, are fundamentally questioned by a preventing extremism message that suggests that you cannot trust anyone.

The personal world inside Muslim communities is the locale for the formulation of contention and grievance that sometimes finds expression in increasingly diverse organisational forms, objectives and activities. This diversity is along a number of lines that reflect society at large, including denomination (historical schism), generation, sexuality, ethnicity, age, gender and class. Gender and class are particularly significant dynamics in organisational activity. Yasmin Ali (1992) has highlighted this in *Refusing holy orders* in terms of the patriarchal nature in which state multiculturalism historically, and community cohesion today, operates. More recently it has been explored by Yavuz (2004a), Singerman (2004) and Clark (2004) in terms of the vertical nature of power dynamics between a middle class that engages in organisational activity and those who use their services. The class and gender dynamic involved in the relationship between the state and communities and organisations is, to a degree, reflective of the society that it finds itself in, whether in Britain or Jordan, as in the case of Clark's study.

The voluntary world

Voluntary associations are where individuals or loose informal networks within the private world begin to form themselves into groups, to be visible to the state and to the community. In so doing, a need or objective is identified and often boundaries are drawn between 'us and them', and notions of membership emerge and become important. The 'them' can include the local or national state and/or other Muslim organisations. This level may be useful for exploring how Muslims and Muslim young people begin to get organised and to develop a distinctive group character. This is an opportunistic landscape, the organisational shape appearing to be determined by the types of organisational worlds that this emerging entity is in contact with. The step into this world can be part of a movement toward mobilising resources to meet a need, of people giving time, sharing expertise, willing to cover organisational costs. It is a place where assumed, shared, collective identities are routinely made salient through the process of developing voluntary association.

It seems that Muslim social activism and Muslim radicalism have come to mean very similar things in the way they are understood. Individual processes in both require a cognitive shift emerging out of something, whether an event or an experience that informs a personal and political consciousness. Wiktorowicz (2004) lists the following reasons for Muslim activism:

- institutional incapacity
- structural strain, which is connected to the above
- erosion of intermediary groups that integrate individuals into society but that also represent the voice and needs of people
- the linking together of modernisation and Westernisation
- the gaps between those who have and those who do not within the Muslim world and outside it
- socio-economic reasons
- the move from rural to urban environments and the discrimination or anomie that this can cause
- as a response to cultural imperialism.

And, I would add, a powerful sense of injustice and hypocrisy from Western governments which fundamentally distrust the compatibility of Islam in any democratic process, even when the other option is oppression, suppression and murder, as the examples of Egypt and Syria have suggested.

Billis (1989) suggests that the direction of the voluntary association is determined by which particular world it overlaps with or is moving towards – voluntary associations linked to the government become government-orientated associations; those linked with business bureaucracies become profit-orientated associations; and those linked with the personal world become informal groups. In a later work Billis (1996) differentiates between these organisational types through income types: fees associated with the business sector; donations and legacies associated with the associational or voluntary sector; and tax and revenue connected to the governmental sector; and, I would suggest, 'profit' associated with social enterprises. Billis's model demonstrates real vision as Rochester's (2010-11) analysis of the CVS in the second decade of this century suggests. Just as the post-Beveridge state institutions modelled themselves on the hierarchical structure of industrial firms, larger voluntary sector organisations have followed suit as the best resourced are able to reflect state organisational models to engender trust and demonstrate capacity. New Labour's frustration with the inability of smaller CVS organisations to deliver *its* targets despite the heavy investment in capacity building has meant that these organisations became increasingly marginalised in favour of large non-governmental organisations (NGOs) and private sector companies looking to deliver state contracts, for example, KPMG or the Office for Public Management (OPM). The latter claimed to play a leading role in the development of social enterprise and mutual aid initiatives with the National Council for Voluntary Organisations (NVCO), and were also awarded the contract to support the YMAG when the Muslim Youthwork Foundation carried out much of the foundational work. This is an example that reinforces the 'access model' in government relationships with Muslim organisations, that is, that they are there to either access the Muslim community or to deliver something to it – an example of an organisation being used as a 'condom'.

The development of commissioning models, outcome cultures and the language of social enterprise has meant that this sector has been increasingly drawn away from the personal world. They are models that commodify a particular expertise and experience, set a price and find the buyers.

It therefore seems that the voluntary sector is, in effect, a business partner of the state, and this 'facing' to the bureaucratic state world questions 'value claims' made by the voluntary sector that it is closer to the community and is more innovative. The 're-direction' of this sector has been an exercise assisted by a sector seeking to show itself as delivering best value and resentful of a stereotype of a woolly and ill-defined but well-intentioned people, as parodied by the Parish Council in the television series, 'The Vicar of Dibley'.

The voluntary sector is the realm within which organisations place themselves in their role as mediators and creators of a relationship between the individual and the state (Sunier, 1998). Berger and Neuhaus (1996) suggest there is a need for mediating influences between the individual and the state, because as the apparatus of the government becomes more complicated and distant the lack of a meaningful relationship between the state and the individual becomes a cause of alienation and disconnection. The implication of adopting this is that it suggests that better information or advocates who can translate policy would improve relationships, but its critique does not go beyond this. Tariq Ramadan (2004) also discusses the role of mediating organisations to the experiences of Muslims in Europe. He notes a danger that mediating organisations could operate in a manner that kept individuals as members of a, for example, Muslim, Black, Turkish community, rather than as citizens of a nation. As citizens of a nation we are likely to invoke the language of 'rights', whereas as members of a community we invoke belonging and shared values to the community. As citizens our key relationship is with the state, but it is the member and community relationship that seem to be a subject of constant attention for Muslims perceived as being loyal to the latter at the cost of the former. This relationship to community can also be one in which a dependency is cultivated that challenges key principles in the practice of informal education. Nevertheless, Berger and Neuhaus (1996), both key figures in the neo-conservative intelligentsia, argue that mediating institutions should actually be strengthened as, among other roles, they provide the marginalised with opportunities for leadership and help in the creation of civil society. A failure to engage with or support and strengthen religious institutions is therefore a hindrance to the agendas of renewal and cohesion, a dynamic possibly evident in the British government investment in the Church Urban Fund and its Near Neighbours programme in 2010.

Muslim organisations themselves can reify the perspective mentioned earlier, in which Muslims are perceived simply as community members alone by problematising community and the relationships to family trans-nationally. These relationships treated as examples of 'not letting go' as something that sits outside of, or compromises, emotional and financial investment in a British Islamic identity, the irony being that

Muslim organisations can themselves consist of a core of family-related or class-related members for reasons of limited resources but also possibly of preservation, protection or, ultimately, control.

The third world that Billis identifies is that of the bureaucratic world. There are different types that exist in this category and their distinction, according to Billis, comes from their 'legitimising philosophy', for example, profit motive for the commercial bureaucracies and democratic process for the government sector. In essence, in this world he describes a bureaucracy as something that employs people in some form of hierarchical structure. Voluntary associations are normally more collective, impromptu and self-appointed than organisations that have moved into the bureaucratic world. Weber's notion of bureaucracies was initially based on government institutions, but it has become increasingly relevant to the voluntary sector.

It would appear to suggest that local authorities and central government would be interested in commissioning services to organisations that have models that they can recognise as reflective of their systems and structures. They would also lean towards organisations with an established history and the capacity to demonstrate spend and outcomes. As cautious entities it is unlikely that comparatively new organisations (as Muslim organisations often are) will be in position to respond unless they are able to replicate these models – by demand, the state is asking the voluntary sector to face Billis's bureaucratic world.

An increasing number of organisations have come to define themselves as social enterprises. Unlimited, supported by the Millennium Awards Trust, has played a significant role championing this model in supporting individuals who wish to develop an idea to meet a social need. It has had significant political support, particularly under New Labour in creating the Social Enterprise Unit and launching the Social Enterprise Coalition (Billis, 2010). It is a model that seems to commodify the skill or service being developed as something distinct, that others would be interested in purchasing, or learning from.

Values, the voluntary sector and the Big Society

The historic picture of the voluntary sector is unhelpful in understanding it in all its manifestations in the 21st century. It came to be defined originally by the goodwill of the people involved and the blurred relationship between the management and those whose role it may be to action the mission. It was shaped by two types of giving: money (philanthropy) and time (volunteerism) (Rochester, 2010-11). The manner in which this relationship was played out has often been perceived as amateurish, and this caricature has remained with the CVS for a while, but it seems to be one that has been increasingly applied to the state sector in cultivating a discourse that can allow the 'minimal state' through withdrawal from services directly delivered by the state, while the voluntary sector, especially the large established organisations, has positioned itself as the 'third sector' – as efficient, innovative and in touch with communities and needs. The language of 'citizen and rights' so powerfully associated with the state has been replaced by the language of 'consumer and choice' associated with the private sector, and in some cases adopted by third sector organisations because of the privilege given by the political discourse operating, but there is a warning due to what else is associated with identities that are informed by consumption, as Salecl states:

> Unfettered consumption tends to lead people to consume themselves; with self-harm, anorexia and addictions being only the most obvious forms. (Salecl, 2011, p 4)

The use of the language of the consumer is deliberate due to its associated connections with choice; however, securing choice is predicated on the securing of legal rights and emotional belonging, both struggles for marginalised communities. The variety of terms used to describe what was traditionally known as the voluntary sector is reflective of Billis's later recognition of an organisational hybridity that makes reference to his three worlds which he has also described as the personal, public and the private, as already mentioned (Billis, 2010). This choice of self-definition is used opportunistically it seems, and when necessary it can place a multi-million pound international organisation with an organisation that is very local and has no budget, as if they are somehow the same entity. But for national and international organisations, such a connection in people's imagination can be very helpful to demonstrate local connection and need for continued support.

Religious or faith-based organisations are especially characterised by the idea of mission, acting out of goodwill and of being associated with a higher purpose, principles and values.

Harris (1998) terms those individuals who conceptualise, start and lead social organisations as 'guardians'. Who these guardians are may vary depending on the type of organisation. Harris (1998) places organisations into types by analysing the relationships between 'guardians', beneficiaries and paid staff. Examples of 'guardians' are: founders, parents or members in a self-help group, highly motivated and driven staff and volunteers. They are the defenders of the original aims of the organisation and protectors of the cause. Yet their conservatism or entrenchment can stifle new development and the involvement of beneficiaries in the organisation. Their passion can also ensure its survival, but this does not mean that they are essential to an organisation's continuance. New funding regimes can shift the aims and purposes to a point that they become far removed from their original mission, commonly referred to as 'mission drift'. The relationship between guardians and the development of bureaucracy would also be interesting in an environment where leadership is idealised and politicised. Guardians are sought-after commodities, especially in relation to strategies such as Prevent, from the Muslim community for the following purposes:

- As 'condoms', to provide safe entry into Muslim communities, to deliver a message or policy, or to secure an outcome. The metaphor of the condom is deliberately being used to convey the crudeness and disrespect with which this strategy is often applied.
- To transform into advocates and social engineers in relation to social policy. Leaders, as Harris observes, can be problematic as they don't easily compromise, and the service or activity dimension creates room in which small compromises send big messages.
- Leaders are cheaper than funding an organisational infrastructure.
- Leaders can buy both silence and consent for the state.

Values are often portrayed as a defining attribute for those in the voluntary sector – their values a key factor that may critically differentiate them from the private or the public sector. The claim is that theirs is a different agenda to that of the profit margin or the 'one size fits all' services of the state; they claim to play a significant role in religious and humanitarian-orientated voluntary sector organisations and are integral to the cultural value system of the organisation, by default suggesting that neither is as strongly present in other organisational worlds.

Muslim organisations face another challenge as faith organisations: they span the spectrum of personal lifestyle and faith to organised religion, as demonstrated by the oft-cited belief that Islam is not just a religion, it is a way of life. This notion is similar to Quaker thought between personal and professional ethics and actions. The use of social enterprise in many ways legitimises activity through the monetary value placed by the demand of a given expertise. This 'monetary or expertise value' rather than 'religious value' may be particularly useful for women for whom the latter is often denied due to the comparative lack of position and influence in institutions perceived to be as representative or as 'leading' the community which generally remain a male domain. Islam as a religion is a 'claim problematic', while Islam as a business is a world of opportunity and opportunism. The development of regulatory bodies to capitalise on 'brand Islam', especially brand *halal* (for example, ritually slaughtered meat and poultry) is a multi- million pound business. The *halal* brand provides a psychological consent to consume. While there has been enormous activity to 'regulate' what is *halal* or not, in terms of slaughter there has been a marked absence of thought on the high levels of meat and poultry consumption and its impact on the health and wellbeing of both the individual and the animal. This is a contradiction that reveals something of the opportunities and meanings being privileged by the commodification and commercialisation of religious practice and the comparative absence of concern of the impact on the 'chicken and chips' generation.

For Paton (1996), a number of reasons need to be considered to understand the volatility that can exist in the voluntary sector and the passions that seek to define its existence as separate to and in opposition to the statutory and the private sector. Paton (1996, pp 32, 33) asserts that the values the voluntary sector seeks to appeal to are higher values and they therefore take on an ethical dimension in the practice and management of the organisation and the work:

• Values become a 'this is what we stand for' for the 'guardians' of the organisations (Harris, 1998).
• The problem with this values emphasis is that there is a limited scope for compromise, because disputes are on matters of principle.

The danger with this is that conflicts over principles and values are likely to escalate because beliefs are at stake. This moral high ground is, however, questioned by Marshall (1996), especially when this is claimed at the expense of the statutory sector:

> The fact that the statutory sector is framed in terms of legal rights does not mean that those legal rights are not ultimately based on moral decisions, rather than ones of calculation. (Marshall, 1996, p 51)

Marshall's (1996) analyses and challenge to the voluntary sector continues to be relevant and poignant given the funding cuts visited on statutory services during the 2010-elected Conservative-Liberal Democrat coalition government. Marshall questioned core voluntary sector beliefs such as that the voluntary sector is more personalised and closer to the community than the statutory sector, and that the voluntary sector is more hospitable and reflective of minority issues and representations. For Marshall, closeness to the community is a matter of resources, and the accusation of excess bureaucracy of the governmental statutory sector actually goes some way in trying to ensure some forms of accountability in terms of practice – youth services have often humanised an organisational edifice perceived and experienced as unsympathetic, overly bureaucratic and distant. This challenges Weber's ideal type of the bureaucracy as unsympathetic, uncaring, inflexible, and an arrangement in which personal volition and feeling are extracted out (Parkin, 1982).

Marshall questions the voluntary sector claim that it is more trusted and embedded within community life than statutory organisations, and seeks to represent views and concerns of those communities to services and political representatives. The movement evident using Billis's model of the facing to the bureaucratic world in the contract or commissioning culture seems to support Marshall's challenge (although this challenge was made in 1996, it has proved to be accurate), and poses a further problem. The post–Second World War Beveridge world extracted the service delivery functions of the voluntary sector and placed them in the hands of the state as universal services such as education and health as part of the social contract between the individual and the state. This social contract emerged as the blood money of two world wars and is now being fundamentally dismantled by the Conservative-Liberal Democrat coalition.

This postwar reconfiguration meant that the voluntary sector developed identity claims to secure relevance and resonance to need and community. The extension of services to minority communities was resisted by some voluntary sector organisations and claimed by others, often on the basis of racism or 'race'. The CVS, as an experience for disenfranchised minority communities, can be summarised by three broad categories of organisations that lay claim to communities and services.

The national established voluntary sector: some have been mentioned earlier, and include organisations such as the Scout Movement, YMCA and Barnardo's. These are national and international, and often have the infrastructure, networks and relationships to respond to, for example, the NCS, either as standalone or through regional networks.

This sector has risen to 'prominence as a central player in the policy arena' (Billis, 2010, p 9), locating itself in the space between the public and the private sector generated by Giddens' third way (1994), blurring both boundaries and accountability for a public used to clear-cut organisational sector boundaries.

The local established voluntary sector: by this I mean pre- and postwar organisations that only had a regional or city presence, such as Settlements, and postwar organisations that became active in the late 1960s and 1970s, often based in ethnically diverse areas and that responded to the integrationist agenda being centrally determined, and to socioeconomic issues that were locally visible.

Emerging voluntary sector: these are organisations or self-expressions including from BME communities, often locally formed and based, and seeking to make local responses to visible needs with a high degree of local knowledge. The advocates come from the communities and position themselves critically against the statutory sector and the established voluntary sector. Marshall points out that the established voluntary sector organisations have often actively resisted the emergence of 'indigenous voice' as the survival of some established voluntary sector organisations is based on a BME organisational absence.

The emergence of new organisations was or is often a direct challenge to the legitimacy or relevance of the services of established organisations, their expertise and their representational role, often associated with territory, neighbourhood or a particular service, while there has been a willingness to appropriate new leaders into these organisations or to develop organisational offshoots to accommodate 'entrepreneurial' Muslims. Those that have sought to organise independently have received a great deal of resistance. The investment of New Labour in programmes such as the New Deal for Communities and the Single Regeneration Budget revealed communities with a more confident relationship to their neighbourhood and to their believed right to determine investment than during the Urban Aid programmes within which this established sector was much more active.

Marshall's challenge to the raison d'être of the voluntary sector is to its claims that it is:

- more concerned with disadvantage
- that it is the community that controls the voluntary sector, and
- that it is more innovative and creative than the statutory sector.

The voluntary sector has continuously presented itself as being concerned with the disadvantaged, and this is the discourse in which it is mainly seen and understood. It has been historically shaped by two distinct forces, namely philanthropists who have hugely influenced the shape of young people's services today, and social movements such as trades unions, feminism and the civil rights movement. Class and religious beliefs have played a significant role in this due to the class and religious profiles of these philanthropists. The issue of whether an organisation is a *'for'* or *'of'*, for example, *for* Muslim youth or *of* Muslim youth, is a significant difference and dynamic. The challenge posed by the emergence of *'of'* organisations is often first received by the *'for'* organisations, and this can become the first institutional, cultural and relational barricade that needs to be navigated. The pathologising of these new organisations as angry, radical and inexperienced was, as often happens, in a way an institutionalised response as the world of capacity building and business plans was thrust on emerging organisations that were responding to a landscape being changed by the month by political imperatives and world events. The comparative absence of infrastructure engendered grand claims of significance and objectives beyond their resource capability, but nevertheless was politically valuable. A case of big houses and empty fridges.

Marshall (1996) discusses class and privilege in this sector and suggests 'there may be a reverse tendency in some respects, as the more advantaged have the greater skills and resources to organise themselves'. In youth work history there was real resistance to the move from charity to welfare, that is, from the 'services to youth sector' (Davies, 1999a). In practice this means that there is a pecking order based on cultural capital that may include some and exclude others in the search for resources. Historically and to this day, it appears that the voluntary sector has been a middle-class exercise that has always included the following dynamics: self-preservation, a mission and the need to 'be of service'. Marshall's contention is that in the space between the disadvantaged and the state the most effective, active participants have been the culturally most articulate, and Muslim communities are no exception to this. The rise of Muslim social and organisational activism is influenced by a British Muslim middle class that places itself between the state and Muslim communities as representatives, reifiers of dominating discourses, leaders and/or as an expression of a collective contention locally, nationally or internationally inspired.

In the 'heyday' of multiculturalism, under the label of 'Asian', it was the most articulate or affluent who benefited, and the experience of the disenfranchised may be the same whether under the label of 'Muslim' or 'Asian'. Each label provides opportunity that its most articulate constituents benefit from. For organisations dealing with disadvantage, the nature of the claim of the voluntary sector, whether rooted in location, values, leadership or governance, implies a rootedness in disadvantage that then enters into a relationship with the state and bureaucracy in which class is a significant factor. Differentiation on the basis of faith is not a guarantee that marginalised Muslim communities disenfranchised under the label of 'Asian' will be made visible under the label of 'Muslim', but there is at least an acknowledgement of the significance of the Muslim identity by this naming.

The role values play in the voluntary sector is extremely important as they provide a moral platform to legitimise opinion that is meant to be the voice of the community, an expression of an issue or the acting out of sentiment. This interrelationship between community, values, opinion and representation is also employed by the Muslim community in Britain and by Muslim organisations. Under British charity law religious activity can be an objective of a charitable organisation; this makes what you believe in important and your ability to 'translate' these beliefs critical. Where beliefs are guided through to action or organisational practice then the relationships (between belief, values, attitudes, behaviour and action) become important. For example, if the belief is that all non-Christians or non-Muslims go to hell, how does this sit with the value that all religions have equal respect, the requirements of funders for equal opportunities policies? How does this inform the approach to the other? The interpretation of beliefs to facilitate access to platforms and resources is therefore a key 'ability'.

The existence of 'values-based' identity in a 'rights-based' society is touched on by Abdolkarim Soroush (2000). The same formula can also be applied to organisations operating on a values-based platform in a rights-based society. Youth work is both person-centred and rights-focused, so how organisations work with individuals who challenge these morals or values, sexuality being an oft-cited example (drugs, relationships, dress being some others), is important. In this exercise it becomes evident that the way Islam is understood becomes critical to the access, participation and experience of the young person.

Leadership in organisations

Weber's idea of the 'charismatic leader' who relies on no hierarchy or office, who gains and maintains authority solely by proving 'his' strength in life and who, if 'he' wants to be a prophet, performs miracles and, if he wants to be a hero, performs heroic deeds (Gerth and Wright Mills, 1964, p 249), is useful in this subject. Charisma is seen here as something that needs to be constantly proved, and authority is maintained on this basis of proof; when the proof diminishes, so does the authority (Parkin, 1982). The history of the voluntary sector has many charismatic leaders and philanthropists such as Robert Baden-Powell and Joseph Rowntree, as well as people such as Neville Chamberlain, and the early Cadbury's family. In the examples of the organisations established by these individuals and others, particularly in the history of youth work, charisma has given way to other types of authority, according to Weber's typology. Traditional authority within his typology means authority rests on established beliefs, in the sanctity of tradition and the legitimacy of those exercising authority, while rational legal authority rests on a 'belief in the legality of rules and the rights' of those elevated to positions of authority. For Scott (2003), this move from charismatic leadership to forms of rational-legal authority are necessary for the 'project' to survive and be maintained, as charismatic leaders are exceptions rather than a rule, often arising in special circumstances. This also means that the relationships that exist within the organisation change – for example, personal ties being replaced by formal arrangements. Authority and leadership are important concepts in any field of organisational studies. Leaders, unlike managers, define the mission of the enterprise. They can construct a structure that embodies the values that they subscribe to and the criteria for those whom they wish to serve and the ability to defend, interpret and renew the mission of their organisation (Selznick, 1957).

Notions of authority take on distinct features in faith-based organisations (Harris, 1998). In mapping the early history of the church, Harris describes how distinctions between the laity and the clergy appeared that were based on the acceptance of religious doctrine rather than religious inspiration. This distinction is also possible within the Muslim world between the struggle for legitimacy, often simply polarised by those with knowledge of doctrine or law, and those inspired by God, the literal and the spiritual. Charisma seen as the gift of grace from God can be still relevant in the relationships of power and authority in faith-based organisations. There is a symbiotic relationship between charisma and inspiration; the latter as a continued connection between God and human beings is important given that in the Muslim context, the revelatory relationship, according to Muslims, was completed by the Prophet Muhammad (pbuh). Inspiration can therefore be understood as the presence of this relationship between individuals and God.

Inspiration and congregation are valuable political commodities. According to Rochester (2010-11), religious organisations that bring together, synthesise inspiration and congregation are key social policy tools or partners, especially in relation to BME communities providing access and engagement to people; they have resources such as a building, donation of time and money, and committed and respected individuals who are 'repositories and transmitters of social values' (Rochester, 2010-11, p 120). Congregation-based organisations are particularly useful to government as access points due to the relatively little power that congregations may exercise as a result of the blurring of the boundaries of the role, purpose and expertise or inspirational status of the *imam* or the leadership. However, what emerges in the convergence of space, people, time and values can vary widely across faith and denominational lines in every religious tradition. Yet Rochester's (2010-11) faith-based organisational typology is very helpful in distinguishing types of organisations that all claim to be 'inspired' by religion and the activity they engage in, and this is explored next.

Which world are you facing?

Billis's model is extremely useful in revealing the 'movement towards ...' of organisations of the direction in which they are heading; it is able to locate Muslim organisational presence and the issues that it may face in each of these worlds. It asks in whose hands is the destiny and control of an organisation, as does Rochester. Rochester sums up the relationship between people and organisations with the following categories: shareholders, stockholders and stakeholders. The worry is that in each case the group of people involved are narrowly defined and with vested interests. The poem or lyrics in the opening of this chapter, for me at least, capture the familiar and the distant that the third sector can represent; it seems to reflect the frustration and resignation that I have sometimes encountered from individuals seeking to be clear again about why they set up an organisation or why they work for a particular body, whose agenda they are serving and what happened to what they wanted to do – not sure whether they want to let the bridge burn so that they can build it again or try and fight the fire.

SEVEN

The Muslim organisational landscape

The relation between what we see and
what we know is never settled.

Berger (1972)

We have attached each human being's fate to
their neck, and on the Day of Judgement we will
present him a record that he will find unsealed:
'Read your record! Today your own self is
sufficient to take account against you.'

Surah, 17:13–14

Searching authenticity and making change

In 'The politics of recognition', Taylor (1992) linked identity with the notion of authenticity, of being true to oneself rather than constantly trying to be accepted by others, your difference only exacerbated by your efforts to fit in. In youth work, authenticity appears to be a major issue for Muslim organisations seeking to develop an active and viable presence in the youth work organisational landscape, yet there appears to be stubborn persistence with Muslim organisations, only taken seriously when followed by a constituency or membership, and this limits the vision of what is possible. This mono view of the emerging Muslim organisational landscape is symptomatic of closed views of different societies and communities, as defined by the Runnymede Report (1998) on Islamophobia. Political necessities may require appropriate representational organisations for dialogue, but these representational structures have a considerable struggle themselves within the Muslim communities in valuing informal education or youth work and in supporting anything other than *masjids*, Muslim girls' schools or international relief charities. This struggle is compounded by the absence of the political will to support the development of models of practice, either through the use of space or in the training of Muslim-literate informal educators. The development of a Muslim youth work degree at the University of Chester was a significant development, and its closure both disappointing and sad in the opportunities it could have afforded for the development of narratives to inform Muslim pedagogy.

David Billis's original organisational worlds theory (1989) is helpful in locating organisational practice, as discussed in the previous chapter. In a more recent edited book, *Hybrid organisations and the third sector* (2010), he has revised this visual model to understand the movements and relationships that have developed between these worlds in response to notions and demands of collaboration, the state interest in third sector partnerships, the development of commissioned services, the bypassing of the local state through localisation agendas and the rise and public culling of quangos (quasi-autonomous non-governmental organisations) as well as the investment in capacity building of the small CVS organisations and the state investment and championing of social enterprises. There are implications of all this for organisational identity, that is, which world/s they face and by implication, work in and serve, as well as the impact of this on their 'base world', as pictured in the previous chapter in terms of accountability, the ownership of decisions, their governance and who sets the priorities about what they should be doing, and the impact of all this on the public perception of an organisation's identity and location.

Billis's ideal-types model, whether unrealistic or flawed due to the ideal nature of the models it puts forward, is useful in providing a frame, a map to understand organisations and the people organising them. It is often by the presence of ideal types that identities, contradictions, achievements and the exercise of influence and power become visible. The proliferation of organisational types in the last century is also reflected in Muslim worlds through the development and presence of associations, 'professional societies', charities, sports clubs, study circles, 'Muslim product businesses' such as those selling heritage holidays, perfumes, clothes and so on, youth movements, interest groups, disaster relief charities, 'death committees', savings committees, media (online chatrooms, television and radio stations) – these are all examples of the multitude of ways people are organising their time, interests and creating spaces for the facilitation and expression of Muslim identities, and Muslim needs.

Each decade brings rapid changes and new organisations, such as the emergence and presence of the Muslim Council of Britain (MCB), Hizb ut-Tahrir (Party of Liberation), Khilafah, the Gulen movement, Islamic Society of Britain (ISB) and Muslim Association of Britain (MSB), as well as numerous city-based organisations such as the Mu'ath Welfare Trust in Birmingham, An-Nisa Society and Nida Trust in London and humanitarian relief charities such as Islamic Relief, Muslim Hands, the development of 'visual and the virtual' organisations such as the Salaam portal or Noor TV, Peace TV and the Madani Channel. The organisational landscape has new types of participants whose names allude to the constituency that they seek to serve and advocate for, such as ethnicity, nationality, school of thought, age, activity and profession and preference of medium of connection. This cursory glance clearly demonstrates that seeing Muslim organisational forms through *masjids* and *madrasahs* was a limiting lens, whether applied in the 1980s or the 1990s, but it is limited more so today in an increasingly diversified organisational context; *and yet* there has never been a greater state engagement with *masjids* individually or through their representative bodies than in the last 10 years, primarily because they have been the most responsive organisational types to the PVE agendas of at least New Labour.

This interest from the state could not have been better timed as it seems that there has never been a greater threat to the position and role of the 'Muslim clergy' than today due to the access to Islamic literature through the availability of texts and the internet independently to people. It has meant the development of powerful discourse in this act of self-preservation in which individual agency and capacity are being questioned, resulting in the need for an 'SAS' of Islam, that is, scholars, alims and shaikhs, to interpret beliefs and positions.

Roles, positions, constituencies and dilemmas

The acting out of a Muslim piety has broad equivalents in a variety of political and religious traditions; for example, organisations such as Oasis founded by Steve Chalke aim to enact both a Christian piety and mission, and also an action to locate a 'Christian-ness' in the community. The motivation for this 'locating' may vary depending on theology, need and attendance for worship, but it cannot be assumed that the same motivations and opportunities apply across religious and political beliefs and ideologies.

For *masjids*, attendance is often not a motivational factor, but the 'War on Terror' and the symbiotic relationship between PVE and Community Cohesion has enabled a move in purpose, politics and political relevance from a role that negotiated an identity between a community or an individual with God and themselves to intermediaries in the relationships between the state and/or the community (Nielson, 1997). It places them in a position in which they have to embody aspects that have at times been described as in opposition to one another (Yavuz and Esposito, 2003), that is, contemporary social and political concerns and the preservation of an authentic Muslim identity (the first positioned in the language of modernity, and the second positioned in the language of tradition). The move from bodies constituted by spiritual capital defined by the facilitation of religious observance to those that hold relevant political capital especially in relation to agendas of de-radicalisation and the war against terror has been unexpected, it seems, and in the main welcomed by *masjids*, but what impact it has had on their spiritual capital remains to be seen.

The above repositioning primed by state interest appears to be an act of necessity rather than choice by the state, as generally Muslims and Muslim organisations find themselves caught between two different forms of secular tradition, described by Yavuz (2003), through the notions of French Laicism which is anti-religious and seeks to eliminate or control religion, and the Anglo-American experience which seeks to protect religion from state-based interventions but sees a role for it in supporting civil society. The problem with 'dealing with Muslims' is that you have to then acknowledge Islam, and even in systems that use the Anglo–American model, there is a strong undercurrent that is about an 'unhappiness with Muslim consciousness' (Modood, 2005, p 167).

The terms 'Islam' and 'Muslim' and how they are employed by organisations can give some but essentially limited understanding of their vocation. The issue of faith as a primary identifier has been problematic in a state and local government context that has historically focused on facilitating ethnicity rather than religion in organisational forms in relation to Muslim communities. In response, organisations that would identify their motivations and identity in relation to their experiences as Muslims or their values or motivations from Islam have used 'code' to make reference to this through, for example, gender, religious concepts, ethnicity or historic figures for references, as in the case of the Mu'ath Welfare Trust based in Birmingham, which began life as a supplementary language school for Yemeni children. It was established by a number of postgraduate university students from the UK and abroad who, by chance or fate, found themselves studying and living in Birmingham and the surrounding cities. The Trust emerged from this group, also known as Amana (meaning 'a trust'); Mu'ath was the name of the emissary of the Prophet Muhammad (pbuh) who first invited people to Islam in the Yemen. The school developed a city and regional profile attracting Yemeni children and young people from across Birmingham and its surrounding areas. Its influence and reputation spread nationally, with families moving to Birmingham in order that the children could attend the school and be near the centre.

The collection of individuals that conceptualised and developed this project were also networked with the individuals that established Islamic Relief, the largest Muslim charity in Britain. The centre was first established for Yemeni or Arabic-speaking students and is identified with the Arabic-speaking community in Birmingham, both actual (from Arabic-speaking countries) and aspirational (for whom Arabic is the language of the Qur'an and the *ummah*). The Mu'ath Welfare Trust is a possible example of how organisations may privilege certain aspects of their identity over others in order to develop services to meet educational and social welfare needs.

Yet ethnicity as a community signifier is still powerful, as in the example of the Khoja Ithna Asheri Jamaat. The Khoja community that emigrated from India to East Africa and now to Britain is the key driver of the *jamaat* (congregation). The *jamaat*, it seems, refers more to its 'Khoja' ethnicity than it does to its 'Shi'a' belief/theology. It sees itself as part of a worldwide *jamaat* through its connection with the World Federation of Khoja Ithna Asheri Jamaats.

Ultimately I have found, as Wiktorowicz (2004, p 2), when looking at types of Islamic activism, which he saw as 'the mobilization of contention to support Muslim causes', that it is very difficult to define what is Islamic due to the plethora of differences in the Islamic world – any definition would include some and exclude others. One difference that does exist in common discourse is that when the 'Islamic' label is used, it is often to describe a 'truth', while Muslim is often used to describe something personal or communal. Therefore 'Muslim' as a term becomes safer to use as it is applied to the individual or the individual as part of the collective. It is understood that their experience and belief is subjective rather than an essential, objective truth. Again this would not apply to all organisational scenarios. Simply speaking, under the label of Islam, nothing defamatory can be attributed, while under the label Muslim, things can be more 'flexible'.

Muslim organisational forms

Religion in the organisational sphere is depicted as a source of mobilising ideology and a means to combat injustice (Wiktorowicz, 2004). But religion has also become a matter of identity, and the Muslim turning to religion is often an instinctive response to challenges faced, as acts of belonging and identity. Wiktorowicz lists these collectivisations in the name of Islam as prayer groups, propagation movements, terrorists, study circles, political parties, NGOs and cultural societies, and states that Muslim activism is the most common form of activism in the world today (2004, p 5).

Sunier (2002) lists the emergence of Muslim organisational activism in three stages:

- creation of prayer space, as discussed earlier;
- migrantisation – greater involvement in the political process with a mediation role with governmental organisations;
- creating 'influencers'.

In the third phase Sunier argues that each emerging generation becomes more active through a cognitive shift of orientation that tries to disconnect Islam from the homeland, and, I would add, from the cultural. Sunier proposes that these are neither cultural organisations nor migrant organisations because these young people no longer see themselves as migrants; rather they are participants in social movements engaged in rational attempts to mobilise outside, impenetrable, formal institutions. Muslims involved in the Stop the War movement in Britain was an example of young Muslims willing to make alliances (for example, with the Socialist Workers Party) on common interests and from Respect, which then provided the political platform necessary to be legitimately politically visible; for example, Salma Yaqoob, formerly a member of Young Muslims, then chair of the national Stop the War movement, became a parliamentary candidate for the Respect Party.

The Muslim organisational models discussed are examples of the acquiring and using of cultural capital to meet social, educational or welfare needs and to address marginalisation and disadvantage, but it must not be forgotten that there is a distinctive history of organisational models and forms from the Muslim world that include:

Waqf meaning religious endowment. Such is the extent of this activity in the Muslim world that in some countries there are government departments that assist in the management and regulation of these endowments. (Newby, 2002)

Tariqas and *taifas* as manifestations of Sufi Islam have also now begun to receive academic attention as examples of transnational communities (Trimingham, 1998; Nielsen and Draper, 2006). *Tariqa* is the mystical path; *taifa* is the organisation. In Birmingham an expression of this Muslim organisational type is Ghamkol Shareef (Werbner, 2003) in Small Heath, Birmingham. As a *tariqa* it operates on as the relationship between the sheikh or spiritual teacher and the student. As the *taifa* or the external organisation, it has entered into relationships with local government, colleges and other external agencies, adopting the appropriate organisational form for it to engage in work with these organisations, such as registering as a charity, or a company limited by guarantee. The *tariqa* provides the basis of an almost unquestioning legitimacy for a *taifa* at communal level. The *tariqa* and the *taifa* can become conflated in the eyes of the wider community, with the questioning of one being seen as a challenge to the other.

Just as the history of the 'British' established voluntary sector is marked by charismatic figures whose work and mission have been institutionalised, the Muslim organisational landscape in Britain is appearing through similar processes. Werbner's *Pilgrims of love* (2003) uses the example of Sufi Abdullah who established the Ghamkol Shareef Mosque in Small Heath, Birmingham. It is unfortunate and disrespectful that she uses the language of the cult to describe this organisation, and cites his charisma as a key element of his success, but there is also an ability to acquire the skills and knowledge to put an organisational infrastructure in place that is flexible and contingent on context and opportunity. The *tariqa* and *taifa* model is not exclusive within Sufi traditions; more literalist schools of thought also use the same model, with the place of the sheikh as guide replaced by the sheikh as the law-giver as well as fulfilling the function of teachers.

Longstanding organisations such as the Muslim Brotherhood and the Jamaat-e-Islami, initiated by charismatic leaders, for example, Hassan al-Banna and Abul Ala Maududi, have become structured bodies that have have sought to build on the legacy of the founder. Individuals who appeared in exceptional circumstances (colonialism and a waning international Islam) started these movements; since the death of their founders they have developed an organisational infrastructure that has ensured the survival of the organisation. Who is affiliated to each of these groups provides some insight into dynamics of class, as well as city-village dynamics. Ansari (2004) and Lewis (2002) comment on the affiliate profiles of groups and the class and professional determinants or influences of their membership. These individuals and organisations above arose from middle-class urban constituencies and leadership. Today ties between and within different groups may accommodate a variety of differences, whether ethnic or national, but cross-class ties within an intra-ethnic context would be an interesting exploration.

The other types that will be discussed in more detail using Rochester's typology are:

Mosques/*masjids* – traditionally have not been purely a place of worship but also of debate, discussion and meeting. This public space role can be seen constructed into mosques whether in Istanbul or Moorish Spain through courtyards and so on.

Madrasahs has become the catch-all term suggesting the schooling or the training of young Muslims. Post-9/11, *madrasahs* have been associated with the schooling of terrorist sentiments. They are involved in teaching children to young adults, and have a variety of manifestations and degrees of presence within the educational infrastructure in different parts of the world. In Britain what we find are historically knows as *kuttabs* (Qur'an classes) which mainly focus on the teaching of the Qur'an, which is largely what is found in local neighbourhood *masjids*. *Madrasahs* are traditionally associated with the teaching of subjects such as the life of Prophet Muhammad (pbuh) (*seera*), jurisprudence (*fiqh*), Qur'anic interpretation (*tafsir*) and the saying of the prophet (pbuh) (*hadith*).

I have attempted to provide, below, a typology, building on the faith-based organisational typology that Rochester (2010-11) identifies. Rochester's typology seems to be based on Christian faith-based activity, but it is useful in providing a frame that can be used to try and construct a Muslim organisational typology:

1. *Places of worship:* the early *masjids* that emerged in Britain were motivated by the idea of creating a space that could allow the duties of the faith to be performed (Lewis, 2002; Sunier, 2002). They were often, but not specifically or intentionally, intracommunity organisations that had little design on mediating a relationship between themselves and the state. However, as the demand more than the need to represent became stronger, and the external requirements for this legitimacy were internalised, loose organisational structures or roles appeared, such as *masjid* committees, boards of trustees, treasurers, secretary or the chairman, that meant, according to Billis's ideal-type theory, a move from the purely 'personal world' to that of a voluntary association. Abdolkarim Soroush (2000) uses the notions of rights and duties to distinguish between the modern world and the classical worlds. This distinction could be used to differentiate between the early *masjids* and *madrasahs* established by the different communities and the new organisations appearing on the Muslim organisational landscape. The first organisations were committed to providing space in which duties (*fard*) could be performed, and were very inward-focused, operating in much the same way as Weber describes collectivities, 'as particular acts of individual persons' (Parkin, 1982), rather than a collective organisation. This is unsurprising for Soroush (2000) for whom the language of religion is also the language of duties. They were interested in the *masjid* space, while the new organisations being established and determined by the emerging second and third generation Muslims could be both much more outward and interested in the context and equally, in some cases, reluctant to outside engagement, particularly policy-related.

2. *Congregational services:* this is connected to the above. They are services that emerge to meet congregational need, for example, children's and adult classes, funeral services and in some cases, youth activities and study support. They are not, however, separately constituted bodies. Organisations such as the Khoja Shia Ithna-Asheri Jamaats have a sophisticated committee structure providing activities and services, while many others, due to restriction of space, 'activity orthodoxies' about what a *masjid* should and should not provide, focus on traditional activities such as children's Qur'an classes.

3. *Faith-inspired organisations,* Rochester's third category. These are non-congregation organisations, outward-facing, inspired and animated by belief to acts of service – aid charities such as

Islamic Relief or Muslim Hands are examples of these. Welfare organisations would sit under this type. Although inspired by faith, they do not necessarily claim to be confessional in their approach. There are, however, organisational manifestations that are confessional, that remain closely linked to a congregational base and an inspirational figure, and will develop separate formal organisational manifestations, such as Noor TV.

4. *Youth movements:* they are not based on a congregation but normally have memberships. They aim to connect young people to a narrative that can inform their lifestyles and identity – much as Jewish or Zionist youth organisations in Britain can be described as movements that aim to make young people Jewish or Muslim-literate. They aim to teach and support young people through a variety of activities to an awareness of their religio/political identity. Young Muslims and Hizb ut-Tahrir can be seen as examples of this type of activity.

5. *Federations:* the above organisations may also participate as members of regional or national bodies such as the MCB to generate political support, to inform social policy and to make audible a Muslim voice and position. There are also professional and interest-based federations such as the Muslim Doctors and Dentists Association.

6. *Needs-inspired organisations:* these are non-congregation organisations that emerge out of an identified need. They do not work to take forward a faith-inspired agenda, but have insight or expertise on realities confronting young Muslims. There is an importance in acknowledging young people's religious, cultural and ethnic identities, and they will symbolically demonstrate this understanding through programmes of activity, dress, language and so on. Muslim Youth Helpline, Muslim Women's Helpline and in Birmingham, Learning Curve, Pioneers and maybe the Bangladesh Youth Forum, are examples of these, although the latter can also be understood as an ethnicity-inspired organisation. Mu'ath Welfare Trust in Birmingham defines itself as serving the Arabic-speaking communities in the Midlands, therefore the needs of Arabic-speaking communities have a particular focus for the organisation.

7. *Muslim interest or specialisms:* these are also non-congregation, either developing or informed by a Muslim or Islamic aesthetic, insight or expression. Organisations such as the Khayaal Theatre Company, the Association of Muslim Social Scientists (AMSS) and Ulfah Arts are examples of these; organisations such as An-Nisa (London), can also be seen as needs-inspired organisations.

This 'map' is by no means comprehensive; it is a first attempt inspired by Rochester's typology that will hopefully be refined by reflection and feedback. The emergent point is not necessarily the *masjid* for many of the above organisation types, yet their activity and its cause may reflect a contention towards *masjids*. It is clear that there are organisations that may sit in a number of these types, and some in their journey may change their defining characteristic. A significant difference between these organisations, especially the first three, and Christian organisations, particularly those from long-established traditions such as the Anglican and the Catholic Churches, is the infrastructure and hierarches that sit above them, providing emotional and intellectual support, information, training, funding, political support or connection, as well as the power to compel and instruct, all these finding themselves in the development and critique of practice. There is no similar infrastructure for Muslim organisations; this comparative absence of infrastructure does provide a high degree of local autonomy and reliance on local initiative as well as financial and political vulnerability. Organisational platforms have appeared that have sought to respond to these and other challenges, such as the Council for Mosques, Bradford, MAB, MCB, UK Islamic Mission, British Muslim Forum and the Sufi Muslim Council (SMC) (Joly, 1995; Lewis, 1997; Nielsen, 1997; Ansari, 2004). National organisations such as the MCB and Islamic Foundation both endeavour to position themselves in this 'infrastructure' role, but 'their offer' is developing, and the experience in the meantime can be one of 'herding cats'; as they enact this role through political presentation and developing resources or initiatives that can be of use to their members.

Being an umbrella oranisation suggests an affiliation structure. Both the Imams and Mosques Council and the MCB state that they have over 400 affiliate organisations nationally, while the British Muslim Forum claims 300-500 affiliate organisations whilst the shi'a Khoja Ithn'a Asheri Jammat as a federation exists nationally and internationally. There are also other networks that exist that emanate out of charismatic leadership figures, for example, Pir Maroof in Bradford and Sufi Abdullah in Birmingham, as mentioned earlier.

In organisation literature, the role and relationship between the 'headquarters' and the affiliate has attracted academic attention (Billis, 1993; Harris, 2001a) in efforts to understand roles, function and relationships. Lave and Wenger (1991), in their notion of communities of practice, have placed this relationship in a number of developmental stages, ranging from being just an affiliate member and therefore part of a loose network to that of being part of a transformative exercise. These stages provide a framework of what is possible in this affiliate relationship and the role that the umbrella body can play. In the case of the major Muslim umbrella organisations, the relationship does not appear to be hierarchical or instructive. In the Muslim context, umbrella bodies have come into existence:

- through political opportunity (Sunier, 2002);
- through policy imperatives – government demand;
- emerging out of the work of charismatic leaders such as the late Maulana Nisar Ahmed who first established the Sparkbrook Islamic Centre, Sufi Abdullah in Birmingham and Pir Maroof in Bradford (Werbner, 2003);
- organisations inspired through a particular community such as Sufi *taifas*;
- as a form of opposition;
- through denominational presence.

The affiliated organisations can and do exist independently of the umbrella body, other than through representation on the governing structure, as is the case with the MCB and the Imams and Mosques Council. It is also possible that there are umbrella organisations affiliated to a larger umbrella organisation, as is the case of the UK Islamic Mission's affiliation to the MCB. It appears that the relationship is neither top-down nor bottom-up to any large degree. Rather, it is about having a required platform that can demonstrate the strength of voice necessary to attract serious political attention. This helps to understand the role that is expected of the umbrella organisation and the dangers associated with it becoming local and therefore in competition with its affiliates.

The London-centric nature of umbrella organisations introduces a further dynamic in their representational credentials and the intra-organisational competition for representational hegemony. The relationship between the affiliate organisations and the umbrella organisation appears to be horizontal, but the relationship between the umbrella organisations and the people is difficult to assess as a matter of both capacity and influence.

Umbrella bodies such as UK Islamic Mission have initiated organisations such as the Islamic Youth Movement that was re-launched in the 1980s as Young Muslims, members of these moving on to form the Islamic Society of Britain. The Federation of Student Islamic Societies (FOSIS), based in universities, provides a forum for young Muslims in higher education. These and similar revivalist organisations share a doctrinal base and are characterised by recruiting the aspirational with an impetus to connect young people back to their version of the faith. The presence of organisational entities, such as Hizb ut-Tahrir and Al-Muhajiroon, is particularly interesting. It appears that they have targeted the street as well as academia. The fact that they appear to be outside the historical and relational ties of existing revivalist organisations allows a great 'meritocracy' in their structures and hierarchies, and opens access for young people to have a more participative role.

The use of the *masjids* as a means of claiming public space and dialogue with the state does not necessarily always mean that this dialogue is necessarily informed by or is representative of the congregation, or that it can demonstrate consultation and participation, or that the dialogue has been used to empower in some way – all of which are important youth work principles. The use of the *masjid* five times a day, seven days a week by a congregation does not therefore equal consultation or participation, and if it does, this participation would be in many cases comparatively absent of the voices of young women, in the cases of many *masjids*. This lack of genuine consultation is felt particularly by the young people whose expectations of consultation and participation may be much more robust. The absence of their perspectives in the messages that do or do not emerge from their *masjids* is something that fuels the work of organisations such as MPACUK (Muslim Public Affirms Committee UK). bell hooks (2003a) makes reference to Martin Luther King, Jr, of the temptations of conformity experienced by 'clergy' and the temptations of symbols associated with status and power, but essentially symbols of this world. Equally, this absence of perspective in the consensuses generated can attract young people to the 'pure politics' of social movements.

A number of the previously mentioned established national and international organisations emerged out of the colonial encounter with Britain in the South Asian context at least, that have now established themselves in Britain. These organisations sought to shape Islam in the context of British and European imperialism but also saw themselves as renewers and purifiers of the faith and the faithful in this imperial context. The organisational forms that they took were familiar to the British. Lewis (2002) lists and describes these in the South Asian context as: the Deobandis who in Britain established a seminary in Bury; Tablighi Jamaat, which has a seminary in Dewsbury; and the Jamaat-e-Islami, established in Pakistan by Maulana Maududi that is closely connected with the UK Islamic Mission and the Islamic Foundation, initially through students such as Professor Khurshid Ahmad. Each has been commented on by Lewis (1997) and Joly (1995). For the sake of this chapter, what is relevant is that these organisations did not appear out of a British Muslim context but have moved and adapted to this context. A movement that exists outside of this type is the Barelvi *masjids* that have influential organisations that have trans-city and transnational links, such as Ghamkol Shareef in Birmingham or Pir Maroof's Jamiyat Tabligh ul-Islam in Bradford. The Barelvi *masjids* have played a role in the establishment of the Muslim Forum in 2005 as a challenge to the MCB, which it saw as Jamaat-e-Islami-inspired and unreflective of its constituency.

Janine Clark's (2004) study of Islamic social movements in the Muslim world provides some insight into the dynamics that may be considered when analysing Muslim institutions and organisations in Britain. She argues that these organisations are an arena of cross-class recruitment in which the middle classes mobilise the poor or the working class in a relationship that treats the masses as objects of social reform and control; and where institutions are established, she argues, they are run for the middle classes by the middle classes. It is by strengthening the middle-class membership base that the survival of the organisation is secured. Therefore, according to Clark, these organisations operate relationally on class and kinship lines rather than vertically through the class and need spectrum; in the context of Britain, using Malcolm X's well known phrase, 'the house nigger is representing the field nigger'. The role, function and use of class has many shared dynamics to the way class, organisational activity and political representation is played out in non-Muslim White working-class and middle-class communities.

Shaikh (1992) carried out a similar exercise within a context of Islamic revivalism and the spread of Islamic militancy. Shaikh noticed a changing perspective from a move to accommodate Muslims and Islam with modernity at the turn of the 20th century to a demand for pure Islam (Shaikh, 1992; Sardar, 2004). The manner in which individual Muslims mobilise themselves has some distinctive features in the organisational landscape that are a result of the socio-political context. Shaikh (1992) notes the difficulty in finding information about the structure and organisation of Muslim movements or organisations. This, in Billis's model, would not be an issue, as the structures of voluntary associations connected at a personal level are often very loose and difficult to grasp as a matter of character. It may be that this is the stage that they operate at until an event or opportunity brings these informal networks to the surface. It is in this context that one can understand Werbner's comment that the *Satanic verses* affair brought out the hidden politics of the Pakistani community (2002a). I would say it forced loose associations and networks to formalise and become visible to non-Muslims. Informal networks operate in all layers of all societies; just because they happen to be Muslim does not necessarily mean clandestine activity.

The process of mobilising communities by 'social movements' has been given the following phases by Snow and Benford (1988) that could also be used to place voluntary sector agencies or NGOs in terms of their development and maturity:

• diagnose the problem and cause
• offer solutions and tactics
• offer a rationale to motivate collective action and bring new players on board to make observers into participants.

Although organisations do appear out of social movements, equally organisations develop outside of any social movement or without a structural connection to a social movement. For many youth projects that appear at a local level it would be too grand to place them as part of a social movement. They are often a response to an identified need by individuals affected and willing to take some responsibility for action. They may share sentiments with those that inspire social movements and may become inspired by social movements, but they will remain localised voluntary associations, according to Billis's ideal-type model, dealing with local issues and needs. The acknowledgment of the impact of globalisation on young people in youth work practice has been evident for some time (William, 2001), but it has often worked from the development of understanding globalisation as a north–south dynamic; but the East–West intersection that exists in Muslim young people themselves appears to sit outside the global youth work narrative of the young as global consumers. Yet so many of the front lines of resistance to and accommodation of global capitalism have Islamic or Muslim involvement. The global dimension is crucial to addressing the alienation of Muslim young people as the causes of their alienation or disenfranchisement can be connected to their witnessing of the oppression of Muslims as well as Muslim oppression. The attraction of Islam as a symbol of global resistance to Western cultural imperialism is making Islam by default perceived as a social movement, and finds expression in a more localised and personal resistance to practices that deny young people agency and choice.

The notion of a loose social movement, connected by a discourse of Islam in the West and the development of Islam challenging neo-orientalist presentations that demonise Islam and do not acknowledge local Muslim transformations (Cesari, 1998), is also useful in placing

Muslim organisational activity. This activity includes localised organisations appearing to make localised responses, with a proliferation of activity encouraged by a system that requires organisational forms for dialogue and conduits for enacting policy. There is equally a danger, however, that Muslim activism in Britain is wholly framed as part of a global social movement rather than social activism, that has at its heart local issues of socio-economic deprivation, marginalisation or discrimination and identity.

The tension between discourses of ethnicity as the primary form of identity within which religion, language and custom are constituents, and Islam being the primary form of identity which then seeks to extract ethnic specific culture out, is discussed by Samad (1996) as a struggle that is subordinating cultural linguistic and religious affiliations to Islam (Samad, 1996). He observes and fears that ethnically and culturally diverse groups may be reduced to Islamic essentials; this extraction can take place in the name of religious purity and in fashioning an authentic British Muslim identity (Khan, 2011).

Muslim communities are often perceived as distinct social and cultural worlds of urban villages or ghettos, or as self-contained communities (Lewis, 2002). According to Lewis, the size and the self-contained location of these communities have made them create and sustain an independent institutional and economic infrastructure that has been interpreted as essentialist, impenetrable and exclusive (Cantle, 2001). In this picture the regional variation of how space, ethnicity, class and faith have been played out needs to be considered in the context of individual cities; and the local organisational landscape that has appeared reveals something of the presence, interrelationship and dynamics of these factors in the locale. The 'Bradford-centrism' that seems to be applied to Muslim communities nationally doesn't even acknowledge the movement of people within Bradford of similar origin or the challenges of the dynamic nature of these neighbourhoods and the communities that live in them, let alone acknowledge the contrasts across Britain, as Finney and Simpson's (2009) study of Bradford's demographics demonstrates.

The idea of Muslims organising seems to draw people to the idea of this action always being a part of some form of collective social movement. David Snow and Susan Marshall (1984) connect 'Western' cultural imperialism and Islamic movements in that one has an impact on the mobilisation of the other. In this case, religion is used as a mobilising tool that activates resources against cultural imperialism, in much the same way as the Black church was used by the civil rights movement (Sunier, 1998). Lost in the 'clash of civilisation' discourse of Islam (Huntington, 1998) is a history that Islam, for many young people growing up in Britain and Europe, was and is a legitimising factor that enabled a cognitive shift that made Britain home. In the 1970s and early 1980s at least, the beard and *hijab* were more symbols of rebellion against the family and ethnic community than of compliance with it, and part of a new reflective identity taking shape out of the minority experience (Nielsen, 1997). These have been appropriated and mainstreamed by the Muslim community and have moved from cultural and identity symbols of resistance to those of belonging, piety and politics, as well as being used as a provocation to the wider community or perceived as being so. For Yavuz (2004a), these symbols have also been commodified through a process that views this identity both as a marketplace in which context, product and client have been identified, and as a site of *jihad* in which the meaning of symbols is reinvented. Today it is viewed as a means of access into the public space, whereas before the *hijab* may have been viewed as a symbol of seclusion by Muslim young women. Just as symbols of dress became important for young Black men and women, at the same time they contributed to the 'racialisation of the street'; a symbolism is taking shape that is being determined by a challenge to global capitalism and in response, Muslim spaces and symbols are being problematised.

There is an imposed conversation about leadership and representation that legitimates and allows the minimum of investment. This may be a historic subconscious exercise with BME communities that is financially inexpensive, but by default, it legitimates particular expressions of Islam that creates resentment, isolating in particular the idealist young who come to see politics as an exercise in compromise. This is particularly so today where dialogue with government is connected with the badge of 'moderation' that sits uncomfortably with the 'righteous anger of youth' at what they see is being inflicted on the Muslim world by the 'War on Terror'. Their understanding of the *ummah* experienced by this 'witnessing' their understanding of *masjids* as places either appropriated, infiltrated or deemed inconsequential by the Prevent agenda.

But there are also demonstrations of leadership in other areas appearing that challenge, for example, the exclusion of women. Recent organisational developments such as Noor TV – 'led' by Pir Alau'udin Siddiqui, although steeped within a Pakistani Sufism and an emulative pedagogy, with the young people on the programmes behaving as the faithful but not so complete copies of the key Pakistani clergy presenters – have used the 'mood music' of Turkish Sufism and presented a powerful defence of the participation of women in marches that celebrate the birthday of the Prophet Muhammad (pbuh), known in the vernacular as *Milad mawlid, mevlid, mevlit, mulud*, despite criticisms received.

Taniya Hussain (2006), a social worker in London, in an issue of the journal *Youth & Policy* dedicated to Muslim youth work, reflected on an approach that many Muslims working with young people had to consider at some point, about what it meant to work in a Muslim way in both Muslim organisations and in secular bodies. She provides a useful insight that shed some light on organisations that make a distinction between identifying themselves as Muslim or Islamic and working in a 'Muslim way'. The ability to demonstrate a value base is important in conveying what is being done and informing collaborations; equally, the absence of resources that can help with this articulation can leave individuals and organisations frustrated in their inability to contribute to the policies that they eventually have to 'interpret' for local resonance, disabled by their professional focus in an arena where events search for and bring out representatives and little else.

Hussain describes this working in a Muslim way as something that:

> ... involves firstly respect for young people, having a child centred approach, and balance in assessments in terms of justice to the young person, victim and society whilst taking in to account the welfare of the young person. (2006, p 108)

Hussain's position and coinage of working in a 'Muslim way' is contained, it seems, in a set of values that she draws from her Muslim identity, which then inform her practice and relationships and which she feels give the personal meaning in the intervention as a social worker working in a youth offending team.

However, working Islamically, understood as a set of values, cannot always be assumed to be present in, for example, the sale of a 'Muslim product'; here the nature and label of the product, whether Islamic, Muslim or *halal*, helps a perceived assumption of a set of values in the practice of the organisation and in the content and process of the making of a product by the recipient, due to the 'piety value' attached by the label to the product.

Much of the above activity finds itself either in the creation and commodification of Muslim products and/or in the acting out of a Muslim piety through the establishment of 'needs organisations'.

What is clear is that mainstream youth work as we know it is facilitated today by a myriad of agencies that are all, by and large, able to have a dialogue with power without the 'representative label'. This infrastructure is far from representative of Muslim youth concerns and this unrepresentativeness will be exacerbated further still due to the indications given as to the 'preferred partners' of David Cameron's coalition administration, that is, established and known and therefore 'trusted', in which Christian NGOs will stand in good stead.

The question for the Muslim community is not one of whether the infrastructure is diverse enough – the speed of change in organisational interests and specialisms and so on – but what supports it, informs it, trains people in it and provides critique over the dimensions of quality of practice, equality and participation. The emergence of a Muslim youth work degree at the University of Chester was one such opportunity, and its closure is a real loss of opportunity in having the space to bring forth articulations of issues for those working with young people, of what it means to work in a Muslim way, an opportunity for developing Muslim-literate informal educators, testing out theoretical frames, and so on.

Courses such as the Chester course needed to have a support infrastructure around them such as the support of organisations for placements, qualified individuals to act as fieldwork supervisors, participants in practice assessment panels, and this needed time to generate trust in a field that is suspicious of 'separatist' approaches.

The Muslim youth work degree could have played a powerful role in the training and support of those seeking to work with young Muslims, and knowing that just being a Muslim is not enough because of the issues, challenges and complex needs of young people.

International relief agencies such as Islamic Relief, Muslim Hands and so on hold enormous potential for the development of a Muslim informal pedagogy, the development of activity that provides meaningful engagement for young people interested, informed and affected by the global dimensions of their Muslim identity. These organisations may have the infrastructure in terms of national presence, funding and the attraction to give value to informal education processes within Muslim communities allied to the experience of Muslim young people seeking to making a difference to others and in the process, transforming and enriching their own lives. Given the population profile of Muslim communities in Europe, the need to engage and support the needs of 'funding communities' for these aid agencies can also generate enormous emotional capital that such organisations can turn to, which they do, as monies raised in fundraising in cities across Britain demonstrate. It is a step hesitantly being taken, it seems, despite attention paid to this area by the Red Cross and Oxfam through its Oxfam Youth Action Groups who make a point of investing through staffing, activities and resources.

The Muslim organisational sphere is not a mystery; its politics are reflective of those that are found across all communities organising around class, gender, faith, sexuality, age and so on. To view it purely through the lens of *masjids* and *madrasahs* is a narrow lens through which to view this world and the diversity of its activity, and it is extremely unfair on *masjids* themselves that then have to account for aspects for which they do not have the expertise. The comparative absence of a support infrastructure generates significant autonomy but also a sense of isolation as an infrastructure also includes systems of communication, the ability to establish networks across areas of practice and with it, the development of communities of practice that provide grounded insights and solutions. There is an organisational base with significant energy for working with young people – but it needs an infrastructure that can support it, not grand claims, as there is always someone out there who has thought of or done what has just come to one's mind.

Experience suggests that grand claims are essentially acts of self-assertion or self-preservation. They serve political necessities far more effectively than they serve community need, but we all succumb to their enticements, some more regularly than others.

EIGHT

Youth work, community cohesion, preventing violent extremism and Islamophobia: a symbiotic relationship

The master's tools will never dismantle the master's house.

Audre Lorde (1934-92)

This chapter explores the symbiotic relationship that exists between community cohesion, preventing violent extremism and Islamophobia, and how this relationship has been experienced and has found expression for those working with young people. I suggest that one cannot exist without the other, and attempt to reveal the relationship between them and the impact that this relationship has had or is having with those working with young people.

In considering what preventing violent extremism brings to understanding Islamophobia and what Islamophobia brings to understanding community cohesion, and what each brings to the understanding of the other, there is much to be gained in identifying their interrelatedness. Husband and Alam (2011) look at the operational implications of the two and their experiential and perceptual impact on those working with these remits in local government, suggesting that Islamophobic assumptions that underpin community cohesion have laid the foundations for the acceptance of strategies employed by preventing violent extremism and the allegations and perceptions that underpin it.

There has recently been increasing respect and attention afforded to the 'journey' of the researcher, finding ultimate expression in heuristic research where the researcher becomes the object of the search (Moutakas, 1990;Vickers, 2002). For example, Claire Alexander's book, *The Asian gang*, while maintaining a focus on the youth group she was working with, makes it clear that she was close up rather than a distant observer, involved in a 'rubbing together' that revealed as much about herself as it did about the young people she was working with. Accounts of personal journeys have become viewed as authentic writing, and writing as an obligation with knowledge of the risk involved (Vickers, 2002). An element of this risk is that, as people train and practise in the gathering of information of others' experiences and of the subsequent interpretation and analysis, we need to expose our thinking and experiences for analysis (Vickers, 2002).

This chapter does not chart a personal journey, but the topic is personal to me and will be personal to many youth workers working with young people who have chewed over how to respond to the CONTEST Strategy conceptualised and rolled out by New Labour and the Conservative-Liberal Democrat coalition governments respectively. Youth workers and youth work has been a meeting point, an intersection where Community Cohesion and PVE agendas seem to find their way, in much the same way as the millionaire in the 'Secret Millionaire' television programme always gravitates to a community or youth centre to know more and meet those in need and local heroes, relying on the local expertise, relationships and relational skills of the youth or community worker.

Youth workers have always relied on generating funding to meet the cost of what they do; where there has been funding for posts this has often been without funds for projects and activities, projects that can expose young people to new experiences that can generate cognitive shifts, strengthen relationships or just simply provide time out from difficult situations. Where this funding has come from has rarely been an issue, until PVE.

A symbiotic relationship

The PVE programme emerged out of the Preventing Extremism Together (PET) taskforce, set up after the July 7th bombings in 2005 to develop practical recommendations for tackling violent extremism. Due to the relatively short time frame, this process seemed to be a continuation of the discourse on the merits and responses to the notion of community cohesion put forward by Ted Cantle following the northern city disturbances of 2001, based on a fear of religiously segregated towns and cities. PET not only added extremism to the perception, it also charged Muslim communities with self-segregation, of over-cohesion.

This presentation of Muslims as some form of congealed mass unable to integrate or penetrate connected discourses of Community Cohesion and PVE that emerged out of the CONTEST Strategy, managed by the Office for Security and Counter-Terrorism (OSCT) in the Home Office to measures in a variety of provisions in 'terrorism legislation' since 2000. Legislation and policy sought to challenge this over-cohesion and the informal nature in which such communities organised and the mutuality of trust that underpinned them.

The seamless interrelatedness has been helped by a cross-party political consensus that has consistently sought to outflank each other in collapsing together issues such as terrorism, immigration, Britishness or British values under New Labour and later muscular liberalism (2010)[1] and the Christian 'we' (2011)[2] by David Cameron – fixing content and meaning to the slippery notion of community cohesion. The relatively short time frame of the events and responses mentioned earlier made these connections possible in people's minds, and indistinguishable in their policy implementation and practice (Husband and Alam,

---

[1] www.number10.gov.uk/news/pms-speech-at-munich-security-conference/

[2] www.guardian.co.uk/politics/2012/apr/04/david-cameron-god-easter

2011). Community cohesion is not an ethical or moral premise – it is a political premise as it is politicians that have sought to define its meaning or purpose.

The political rhetoric generated by the need to demonstrate toughness and to reassure White Britain, according to Kundnani (2009), narrowed the gaps between government messages and the British National Party (BNP), and with it, legitimising the anti-Islam and anti-immigrant sentiment and far right activity through the programmes of the BNP and the EDL. Muslim communities are witnesses to city after city, town after town being shut down to accommodate EDL marches – shops shuts on weekend shopping days, traffic re-routed, diversionary activities laid on for Muslim young people and young people generally who may be attracted to counter-protest, the trouble to accommodate suggesting that activity of the EDL is understood as an act of politics rather than radicalisation or extremism. The accommodation of viewpoints that terrorise Muslim communities, reifying their 'otherness', while remaining unsympathetic to the fragility, vulnerability, frustration and anger that it cultivates, that the statements of 'Of course we appreciate your position,' 'We understand the distress this may cause,' 'We have every sympathy for the fear this may cause,' do little to mitigate. Such sentences are the standard anaesthetising prefixes to any engagement with the wronged, that disable and silence because knowledge is already assumed of your experience and position, so there is nothing more that you can really say.

It is understood that the term 'Islamophobia' emerged into common discourse from the Runnymede Trust report in 1997, and has come to mean an irrational fear of Islam made up of open and closed views. Allen's (2010) analysis of the dangers in the dualistic definition of Islamophobia, that is, Islamophobia or Islamophilia, highlights its lack of nuance and its susceptibility to creating polarised positions of those taking a view on Islam and Muslims. He argues that this position does not allow a nuanced understanding of Islamophobia or Islam, and helps challenge it. This positioning of people into those who fear (phobia) and those who love (philia) can stem from a number of positions:

• it may be a legacy of White responses to racism where White love or immersion in Black culture was meant to be a signifier of non-racism or anti-racism;
• a genuine interest and fascination in 'the other' as an extension of the self, as articulated by the philosophy of Emmanuel Levinas;
• 'the other' as fascination, difference, embodying the hidden or lost.

The Runnymede Trust report and the critique and criticism that it has received (Allen, 2010; Sayyid and Vakil, 2010; Husband and Alam, 2011) is testament to the impact it made in naming a reality that was experienced but not named. Yet critiques like Allen's point to unanticipated consequences, such as the increased sophistication employed by the BNP in developing anti-Islam rhetoric, employing the binary understandings used by this report and leaving little room for those who neither love nor hate Islam or Muslims. Sayyid's (2010) analysis is particularly helpful in identifying the implications of this absence of 'Muslim nuance' when compared to an earlier report by the Runnymede Trust on anti-Semitism – *A very light sleeper* (1994) – in which no such good or bad split is presented 'in the case of Jewish communities: there are neither moderate Zionists nor extreme Zionists, let alone good Jews and bad Jews'; nor, as Sayyid goes on to suggest, is there a 'clear endorsement of Muslim autonomy or its political expression' (2010, p 11).

Halliday (1999), in his analysis, prefers the term 'anti-Muslim' as being more able to differentiate between the historical, cultural and political specificity of Islamophobia. Husband and Alam (2011) use it as an overarching term, as a moment in history 'which placed anti-Muslimism on the political and policy agenda' (2011, p 99). The anti-Muslim notion seems to reflect the very personal experience of this hostility by the Muslim community and with it, as Kundnani (2009) suggests, ethnifies and radicalises this phenomenon:

> To be a 'Muslim' in the 'war on terror' is to belong to a group with common origins, a shared culture and a monolithic identity that can be held collectively responsible for terrorism, segregation and the failure of 'multi-cultural' Britain. The 'Muslim community' becomes, effectively an ethnicity rather than a group sharing a religion. (Kundnani, 2009, p 29)

Pnina Werbner (2005) explains Islamophobia by describing it as the fear of Muslims and Islam constructed on the basis of three types or tropes: slave, witch or grand inquisitor. They are helpful in visualising the relationship between Community Cohesion, PVE and Islamophobia. Husband and Alam (2011) also use them in their helpful text critiquing the relationship between counter-terrorism and social cohesion.

The first trope is the *slave*, or the subordinate, the dangerous street mugger who threatens the law and order of society, a figure reflecting fear of rebellion and insurrection. This is the fear of the ghetto and of the street. It is a fear of a Muslim physicality expressed through a language that has found itself in public policy (the language of self-segregation or segregated communities; see Cantle, 2001; Ouseley, 2001), of a congealed unmovable mass unable to integrate or penetrate. It is a space whose counter-values have been fostered by multicultural egalitarianism that has compromised the cohesiveness and safety of Britain. Fekete (2009) and Kundnani (2009) draw on speeches by leading politicians who have sought to express this 'fear' and a need to reclaim space and values:

> 'We will give you back your country.' (William Hague, 2001, quoted in Fekete, 2009, p 7)

> 'We have downplayed our culture and we need to reinforce pride in what we have.' (David Blunkett, quoted in Kundnani, 2009, p 34)

> 'We need to reassert faith in our British values which help stability, tolerance and civility.' (David Cameron, quoted in Kundnani, 2009, p 29)

These, alongside more recent statements by Prime Minister David Cameron on muscular liberalism in 2010[3] and the Christian 'we' (2011)[4], express a reclaim of territory and values that have somehow been surrendered by British accommodation to 'space' and identity. This is the well-rehearsed trope of the 'enemy within', given a new religious script in which alien religious values underpin the fanatical dangerousness of 'the other'. It is a fear that invokes the language of tolerance and expressions of intolerance in everyday interactions in supermarkets, bus stops, schools, hospitals and so on. For many Muslims there is a marked experience of intolerance that leaves little room for 'mistakes' in everyday etiquette. The need to reveal the hidden and to assuage fear is also played out on the Muslim female body. In 2006, Jack Straw sparked controversy when he revealed that he asked Muslim women to lift their veils at his surgeries in his Blackburn constituency – for Straw, the veil was a mark of separation and manifestation of

---

[3] www.number10.gov.uk/news/pms-speech-at-munich-security-conference/

[4] www.guardian.co.uk/politics/2012/apr/04/david-cameron-god-easter

the development of 'parallel communities'. It seems that New Labour cultivated sentiments that gave confidence for the expression of greater intolerance to the expressions of Muslim identities, and sought to legalise it through legislation, such as the proposed Private Members' Bill by the Conservative MP Philip Hollobone to ban women in the UK wearing the *burqa* or *niqab* in public places, following the example of France in 2010. Zizek (2011) suggests that the 'intimidation and alienation' of the *burqa* is based on the 'feared other', of being subject to the gaze of 'the other'; without being able to see the 'feared other', it is the ultimate expression of the 'feared subordinate'.

The second trope is the *witch*. Not all victimised groups have been poor – some may have been the well off, such as the persecution of the Jewish community in Nazi Germany. The fear of this group is a different kind of fear: a fear of the disguised, the hidden; the stranger seeking vengeance or retribution. This fear exists in the breakdown of trust within a community or nation, leading to it becoming divided against itself, neighbour suspecting neighbour, colleague suspecting colleague. Government initiatives can be placed here that ask ('placed a duty', according to the Terrorism Act 2006) teachers, lecturers, sales assistants, neighbours and families whether they have seen signs of radicalisation in their colleagues, students or children (the Channel programme). It conveys the fear of a hidden agenda, of an intelligence planning and designing. Whereas the slave and the subordinate is fixed by an impenetrable locale, isolated by their economic, social and cultural peripherality, the witch is much more difficult to position but no more difficult to generate. The witch is the middle class, whose allegiances, alliances and associations remain with another; whereas the slave and subordinate are distrusted for their anger, the witch is distrusted for the opposite reason, for having the cultural and social capital that can locate it as a 'subversive insider'.

The fear of the witch is based on its perceived dangerousness and so, too, within Islamophobia there is a rhetorical empowerment of communities that de facto include some of the most socially deprived and excluded elements of the British population. The focus of the Prevent Agenda is on the behaviour of young Muslims, not on the social forces that reproduce the poverty and the marginalisation of these communities. The intrusive powers developed by the state in its anti-terrorism strategies and embedded by its counter-terrorism approaches require the widespread acceptance of imminent threat in order to legitimise the erosion of human rights and the specific targeting of whole communities that are perceived as overly cohesive due to an emphasis on locale and ties of kinship and territory. The witch trope captures the 'invisible intelligent' that has helped profile Muslim communities. The demographic profile of individuals arrested for terrorism offences only reinforces this trope.

The third trope is the *grand inquisitor*. Here the fear is of the 'dominator', a force that seeks control of a person's body and soul, how they live, work and believe. This is also the fear of an ideology capable of dominating and taking over. Language is often used to convey the 'otherness' of this dominator. The way *shari'ah* is reported and responded to in the popular press is an example of this, as are notions such as *jihad, ummah* or *kuffar*. The construction of these terms in the popular imagination by the media are so powerful that it borders on the impossible to get individuals to understand or 'feel' them any differently. For Muslims the latter is particularly damaging as notions such as *jihad* are conceptually important as they are intertwined with individual self-development and societal conscientiousness.

The 'grand inquisitor' trope is a classic instance of constructing a perceived symbolic threat. It is the values, beliefs and ways of being of the majority that are presented here as being challenged by an alien, non-European (Muslim) force within the context of the international reach of Islam and the transnational reality of British Muslim lives that feed the belief that Islam constitutes a formidable force that has powers beyond the territorial boundaries of Britain. So Islam in this way is perceived not just as a symbolic alien threat; it is simultaneously a territorially alien power. Again, difference and power are intermingled in constructing a profoundly threatening 'other'. Within counter-terrorist policies the linkages between young Muslim citizens and religious communities overseas are, in this light, infused with ambiguous risk and potential danger; all networks become suspect, oaths of allegiance necessary and duties and obligations as citizens taught through citizenship in schools, and learned and tested by making it an exam subject, as many schools have done by introducing the GCSE in Citizenship.

Werbner's model (2005) is particularly useful in understanding the relationship between Islamophobia, PVE and measures within the different terrorism legislation. It provides a frame in which the multiple manifestations of the three can be located and understood. Within this conceptual frame it becomes possible to scrutinise the different forms through which Islamophobia becomes realised, through preventing extremism, community cohesion and anti-terror or counter-terrorism discourses. This includes manifestations as:

- a *belief* in a challenge to British values or culture in which there has been movement from 'Britishness and Englishness as something non cultural and non-ethnic' (Clarke, 1993) to claims of a 'nativism' embodying at-risk values and culture;
- an *approach* by institutions, organisations and professions in their work with the Muslim community or in their employment or deployment of Muslim staff;
- an *attitude* – experienced in the micro detail of the transactions of everyday life, whether on the street, driving a car, in the workplace, in a child's schooling, at the shop counter, at a restaurant, or passing through customs at an airport, expressed by the feminist notion of micro inequities;
- a *threat* to Britain as a cultural space, its skyline, neighbourhoods, in which facets that exist to serve non-Muslim communities, restaurants, post offices, taxi firms, are tolerated or celebrated, but those that are meant to serve the community itself, such as *madrasahs* and *masjids*, can be perceived as markers of difference or places that cultivate difference.

Looking for the Heineken effect

The 2009 HM Government strategy to counter international terrorism (HM Government, 2009) known as CONTEST through its strategy document and managed by the OSCT, has four strands of operation:

- Pursue: take action to stop terrorist attacks
- Prepare: mitigate against its impact
- Protect: measures that can strengthen protection against terrorist attacks – anti-terrorism
- Prevent: stop people becoming terrorists

According to the following distinction between anti-terrorism and counter-terrorism, each of the above strands can find themselves subject to ideas related to both:

- anti-terrorism – defensive measures taken to reduce vulnerability to acts of terrorism
- counter-terrorism – offensive measures taken to prevent, deter and respond to terrorism.

The Prevent aspect of CONTEST itself had five key areas of work:

- challenging the violent extremist ideology and supporting mainstream voices;
- disrupting those who promote violent extremism and supporting the institutions where they are active;
- supporting individuals who are being targeted and recruited to the cause of violent extremism;
- increasing the resilience of communities to violent extremism;
- addressing the grievances that ideologies are exploiting (Khan, 2009, p 6).

This strategy has received criticism and critique (Khan, 2009; Kundnani, 2009; Choudhury and Fenwick, 2011; Husband and Alam, 2011). The coalition government has revisited the Prevent strand and the revised Prevent strategy 2011 cites the previous strategy as flawed on account of overlaps between:

> ... government policy to promote integration with government policy to prevent terrorism. It failed to confront the extremist ideology at the heart of the threat we face; and in trying to reach those at risk of radicalisation, funding sometimes even reached the very extremist organisations that Prevent should have been confronting. (HM Government, 2011b, p 1)

While criticising the operational impact of Prevent, the Foreword then goes on to emphasise the 'success' of the controversial Channel programme that sought to 'identify and provide support to those at risk of radicalisation'. The new Prevent strategy (2011), under its objective 3.21, has a specific focus on what could be termed as the five I's:

- *Ideology (and ideas)*: responding to the ideological challenge posed by terrorism. The document seems to suggest that this is a struggle about narrative (3.26), that community resistance or distrust is the result of poor communication of government security and foreign policy (3.27) and to 'rebut claims about them'.
- *Interventions*: advice and support that can prevent people from being drawn into terrorism. It is likely that the Channel programme will be particularly useful here.
- *Institutions*: work with institutions and sectors where there are risks of radicalisation (3.21). Strategies or language of collaboration, capacity building, partnership, community policing are all used here.

The rest of the Strategy document suggests that two further I's could be added:

- **Identity**: as this document is essentially about Muslim political identity and the 'Muslim imagination'.
- **Information**: with a particular focus on the role of the internet in radicalisation and in the maintenance of networks that facilitate the ideology that is being sought to be challenged.

The role of communities and community organisations in counter-terrorism is particularly important (3.25). The Prevent strategy 2011 suggests that the previous strategy failed to use the reach and influence of communities, and this had serious implications for individuals and organisations working with Muslim young people in particular, as young people, according to the 2011 strategy, were much more likely to support violent extremism.

The picture at the cover of this book has a number of labels that have been used to describe Muslim young people – fundamentalist, terrorist, radicalised, inbred. The Prevent strategy 2011 names two further categories, apologists and propagandists (3.28), who contribute to the narrative that informs terrorist ideology or the facilitation of radical sentiment. It is not clear whether this support is through sympathy, criticism of government foreign policy or the refusal to be co-opted into the counter-terrorism agenda or the view of the world that it proposes and the rules of belonging it conjures in the public imagination.

Jeffs and Smith's (1999) evocative chapter title, 'Dirty hands and tainted money', provides a helpful insight into the relationship between sources of money or funding and the moral integrity of the youth worker. Youth work specifically, whether based in the statutory or the voluntary sector, and non-governmental organisations (NGOs) generally, have struggled with generating funding without notions of 'strings attached' or charges of 'dirty money' to maintain the integrity of their relationships with communities, conscious that there is a price to be paid in legitimacy and trust.

While there has been consistent condemnation of the use of lottery funding by Muslim clergy due to it being seen as 'gambling money', there seems to be comparative silence in relation to PVE funding. In the struggle for hearts and minds that defined Prevent from the outset (Kundnani, 2009), the ability, capacity and often willingness of the *masjids* to convey or respond to this agenda or to be in a position to do so has been an important government aim, and the new Prevent strategy goes further in demarcating moderates from apologists, apologists from radicals, free radicals from terrorists. The whole community profiling based on the 'indefinable terrorist' means that all sit on this trajectory and therefore all are suspect.

The manner in which the Prevent discourse has saturated Muslim space and the role of some *imams* and *masjids* in particular in this process was powerfully demonstrated at the funeral of three young men killed in Birmingham during the summer riots of 2011 – Shahzad Ali (30), Abdul Musavir (31) and Haroon Jahan (21). It is customary that as people gather and await the funeral prayer, the *imam* delivers a sermon, which is normally to do with the fleeting nature of life, aspects of life after death and so on, but on this occasion the local *imam* used the funeral as an opportunity to talk about and to condemn terrorism and terrorists, using the Urdu term for terrorist, *dehshad garz*, which can only mean terrorism in the meanings generated by the war against terror. This act demonstrated the level of saturation of this discourse in 'Muslim spaces' without regard to context or appropriateness. The sermon was instructive in demonstrating a reason why many young Muslims do not confide in *imams* – they may turn to *imams* for judgements, but not for confessions.

This CONTEST narrative and the provisions within the variety of legislation passed by the New Labour administration in the war against terrorism, such as the Terrorism Act 2000, the Regulation of Investigatory Powers Act 2000, the Anti-Terrorism Crime and Security Act 2001, the Prevention of Terrorism Act 2005 and the Terrorism Act 2006, do seem to have a relationship with the way Community Cohesion pathologises and Prevent accuses – cumulatively they are an intervention in place, conversation and imagination, and this has particular implications for those using person-centred approaches to work with young people, such as youth workers. They collectively problematise a physical place, conversation and the imaginary as locales that host, ferment and conceal.

The intervention in 'place' is as much about the *feeling* of being watched as it is about *being* watched. The powers to make interceptions of communication in the Regulation of Investigatory powers Act 2000, the concentration of surveillance through projects such as Project Champion in Birmingham in which 169 cameras were mounted in two relatively small areas area of Birmingham, as well as the stop and search under Section 44 (without reasonable ground) of the Terrorism Act 2000, community mapping exercises, research activity targeted at neighbourhoods and communities – these have all generated a powerful sense of surveillance and experience of the state gaze. Under Section

44 of the Terrorism Act 2000, 101,248 stops and searches were made in 2009/10, according to Home Office figures; while one in every 200 led to an arrest, none were terror-related (reported in *The Guardian*, 17 June 2010). A total of 23,822 stops and searches were recorded in the year ending 2010 as the use of stop and search powers were scaled back. Up to June 2011 there were 675. In January 2010 the European Court of Human Rights ruled Section 44 illegal in contravention of Article 8 (respect for private and family life). This has been replaced by Section 47a that gives a senior police officer authorisation to stop and search if the officer '… reasonably suspects that an act of terrorism will take place'. This is marginally different from Section 44 in that there must now be reasonable suspicion that an act of terrorism will take place; previously no reasonable grounds were required. Anecdotal evidence suggests that stop and search is still being deployed as a preventative measure against terrorism, despite the fact that no stop and search detentions under Section 44 resulted in any terrorist prosecutions.

The numbers of Muslims held for 59 minutes or fewer under schedule 7 powers of the Terrorism Act 2000 (which affords police broad powers to detain and interrogate individuals at ports and airports in the UK in order to ascertain their support for or involvement in terrorist acts) is not even recorded but its use has a sense of something commonplace, as personal experience testifies.

There is a connection between this 'state gaze' which is not an 'innocent gaze' as discussed in the research chapter (Chapter Five), but is informed by a confident Islamaphobia that leaves leaves little doubt as to the virtue of the self in passing judgment on the virtue of the other. One in five of 15- to 18-year-old children and young people in custody are Muslims; this continued increase in the incarceration of young Muslims (from the 13% to 16% to 20%) runs contrary to a 13% drop in numbers of young people taken into youth custody during 2011-12 (HM Inspector of Prisons/Youth Justice Board, 2012).

The impact of terrorism legislation on civil liberties and communities has been documented by Choudhury and Fenwick (2011), Peirce (2010) and Muslim Voice UK (2007) as well as individuals such as the solicitor Imran Khan. The cumulative impact of these strategies and legislative provision is considered in the context of key youth work principles or values, namely, participation, relationships and conversation, and their practice impact (see below). All three are interconnected – each is dependent on the other and therefore the integrity of the three in practice is important.

Participation, relationships and conversation

In youth work the principles of participation are to ensure that young people have a voice and an opportunity to have an impact on the decisions that are made about them (Sapin, 2009). It is, as Davies (2010) described, a process that tips the balance of power towards young people. Ledwith and Spingett (2010) describe participation as a transformative concept that educates and empowers through acts of practice; genuine participatory practice cultivates a symbiotic relationship between belonging, doing and knowledge through which insight and learning emerge; it is therefore both practical and political.

Participatory practice in the context of informal education or social pedagogy is therefore deeply political (Freire, 1972); the act of transformation and challenge through doing (Horton and Freire, 1990) does not ask for belief or oaths of allegiance; rather, it asks people to think, and it employs Gramsci's notion of hegemony to critique everyday assumptions, given truths and notions of common sense. Ledwith and Springett describe Gramsci's notion of hegemony as follows:

> Gramsci's concept of hegemony in particular helped us to understand the subtle nature of power, and the way that dominant ideas of society infiltrate our minds through the diverse range of institutions in civil society – family, school and all the formal and informal groups – to persuade us that the interests of the powerful are the natural order of things. (Ledwith and Springett, 2010, p 19)

This approach suggests a more challenging and less romantic relationship with civil society and its institutions, whether family, religion, schools, law and order, and this is echoed by Soni (2011), who found the theory fundamental to understand inequality and relations of power. It is a concept that is frequently employed by informal educators to question given assumptions and ideas of common sense, but also to not forget individual intellectual capacity, irrespective of role in society.

Notions of participation, and their impact on self and collective empowerment, have historically often found themselves associated with the language of radicalism, for example, radical pedagogue, radical thought, radical youth work, radical feminism, but the association of radicalism with Islam has been firmly associated with terrorism rather than to legitimate the challenge to a dominant world view. The association of radicalism is with extremism and fundamentalism rather than with politics. The struggle for the meaning of these words and their associations has been fixed by the war against terror to Muslims, it seems. The creation of 'apologist' and 'propagandist' in the Prevent strategy 2011 only adds to this perception by Muslims that what is being denied to Muslims is 'politics', in which the state is something that demands consent rather than something that conveys rights. For young people growing up in a cultural milieu in which the testing of sensibilities and sensitivities as an artistic and political practice is a rite of passage that is emblematic of 'our culture'. This becomes a hazardous rite of passage, found to her cost by the 'lyrical terrorist' who was the first woman to be charged under Section 58 of the Terrorism Act 2000, which many human rights groups have stated is like prosecuting someone for thought crime. She was found guilty in 2007 and on appeal a suspended sentence was given.[5]

'Growing up' in youth work in the 1980s and early 1990s, participation or participatory practice seemed to be a concept peculiar to youth work, but the language of participation has been adopted across a range of institutions including government, NGOs and even The World Bank. For New Labour, participation or consultation became less about evidence-based policy as it was about managing the meanings and outcomes of the consultation through Whitehall. Participation seemed to move from an act of claiming voice, and act of politics, to a process that manipulated voice and expression.

Roger Hart's 'ladder of children's participation' (1992) has been commonly applied in youth and community work as it is instructive and useful in identifying the types of participatory practice engaged with in the case of children and young people, providing an eight-step range from participation as manipulation by the adult concerned to participation in which the activity is young person–initiated, with shared decisions with adults. However, in the case of the 'Muslim experience', Jules Pretty's (1995) model seems to have greater resonance, capturing the types of participatory engagement from the state with Muslim organisations and individuals. The meaning and interpretation have been adapted using Pretty's typology (see Table 8.1).

The cumulative impact of Community Cohesion and PVE have generated an experience of participation that seems to sit in the first five strands of Pretty's typology; however, it is the ability to inform the meaning about what you are doing that constitutes genuine participatory practice. The belief that one can inform change within a democratic system is important; the implications of these participatory

---

[5] Her conviction was overturned in 2008.

approaches has been that for many, this belief has been eroded, and the implications of this are much wider than the Prevent strategy as it introduces a level of antipathy, suspicion, cynicism and aggression to any consultative process that seeks to inform policy and practice.

The need to generate engagement or participation with the Muslim community has had a profound impact on Muslims working in the education and social welfare fields. Three distinct experiences emerge in terms of organisational practice and worker response among others.

The first is the 'ghettoisation' of Muslim workers channelled into Prevent or Community Cohesion posts and briefs. For some this was welcomed as an opportunity to work within the Muslim community on the basis of its 'Muslimness' rather than its ethnicity or a clearly defined issue, their professional identity acknowledging this 'expertise' to their role. The issues it raises are dependent on organisation and role, whether central government, the police, local services or NGOs. For those in positions of influence it culminated in individuals themselves becoming gatekeepers to 'opportunity' and 'funding', their personal religious identity privileged by both employer and community as compared to their professional identity.

At the level of interface with the community and young people there is a real angst, with issues of legitimacy among peers and/or young people being more of a concern than *masjids* and community leaders in many cases.

The second point is linked with the first, with the blurring of the boundaries between personal and professional identities encouraged by employers and used reluctantly or proactively by Muslim workers – this blurring of roles, blurring purpose and with it, the presence of Prevent as an agenda present in the relationship. The trading on identity seemed to be encouraged to take agendas and information into Muslim communities and to mitigate against the impact of the counter-narrative. This was consciously and unconsciously employed by Muslim workers and found its most crass manifestation in the Muslim 'family support officers' employed by the police following arrests on the grounds of terrorism to offer 'support' to their families.

The third experience involves a similar blurring of boundaries through the locating of Prevent in some local authorities alongside Community Cohesion within equalities functions – the latter two being problematic. On the one hand, the strategy brought individuals or groups practically and politically interested in agendas of equality within the remit of PVE agendas. On the other hand, the strategy may have excluded individuals and groups interested in issues of equality but

Table 8.1: Pretty's typology of participation

		Meaning	Interpretation
1	Manipulation	Pretence, tokenism	Through unelected representation or membership but with no power – the co-opted leader, member of the board Consultation processes in which the edit right remains with the state
2	Passive participation	Decisions already made, announcements made without listening to responses	Impact on those working within statutory organisations. The participation, however, is not always passive; there can be resistance to embodying this agenda in practice The invocation of belonging as a demand to follow the narrative of the state
3	Participation by consultation	Participation by being consulted, but problem or issue already defined	The Young Muslim Advisory Group (YMAG) can be an example of this approach. Organisations such as the Quilliam Foundation seem to reify the meaning and seek to inform its impact
4	Participation by material incentives	Funding necessitates acceptance of the issue being addressed	Here a line appears between organisations that have applied for PVE funding successfully or unsuccessfully, and those that have refused to use this source and in so doing refuse to reify the ideas that inform Prevent Youth workers may incentivise participation through using, for example, cost-free residential programmes to attract participants to discuss, for example, radicalisation or community cohesion
5	Functional participation	Shared decision making; the aims are already set but the local detail is jointly worked out	The purpose becomes the way it is used, often interpreted in ways that serve the agendas of the local authority and the NGO. PVE will not even be mentioned and euphemisms will be used such as 'community safety', 'community engagement' and even notions of interfaith applied.
6	Interactive participation	Joint analysis of issues, problems, participation seen as a right, ability to inform meaning of issue problem	The 2005 PET seemed to embody this idea
7	Self-mobilisation	Meaning and objectives established independently of institutions	Pure politics, non-governed spaces, defining and setting own objectives Development of Muslim perspectives Control of use and management of resources

not PVE because it problematised people and communities rather than addressing issues of inequality inspired by policy, process and prejudice.

The involvement of young people in such a politically charged agenda has its own dilemmas for youth workers and those working with young Muslims; for central government in particular it makes support and cooperation from the Muslim community visible. To this end it is important that a level of consent or engagement is manufactured to give legitimacy to the narrative that informs Prevent, and this has serious ethical dimensions for education practice.

However, the naming of Muslims has ensured that funding is targeted at young Muslims, and those with and without reservations of either the politics of PVE or its impact on community relations have sought to use it to support a variety of activities and capacity-building projects. The absence and therefore building of capacity and infrastructure became a necessary activity to create the vehicles that could deliver the message of Prevent; equally, for those working for NGOs and local government, it became an opportunity to develop youth activity, voice and participation while fielding a sense of unease towards a policy agenda problematising a community, and as Spalek, referencing to Jutla (2006), suggests, responding with rules and frameworks that exist outside what might be termed normal politics (Spalek, 2011, p 192).

Censoring conversation – 'talking shit'

The act of being measured has been a defining feature of a young person's relationship with the state, most powerfully in education. Therefore comparatively 'unmeasurable' educational practice, based on relationships and conversations, has been always been treated as educationally suspect by educators, civil servants and politicians generally, but seems to have found value in the world of the war against terror as youth workers have become important in counter-terrorism agendas due to their locale of practice and the depth of their relationships with young people. This relationship between security and education is played out in the way that issues to do with 'race' and now religion have always sat in the Home Office alongside remits of law and order and immigration rather than education – a huge leap of imagination is not required to understand the reasoning and perception for this. The Department for Communities and Local Government may have sought conceptually to make this distinction by introducing a third dimension of engagement, 'communities', but the PVE remit it carried meant that it seemed to be an addendum of the Home Office.

The word 'conversation' finds its roots in two Latin words, meaning 'to turn' and 'with' (Wolfe, 2005). Informal education practitioners in the West see themselves as inheritors of an education tradition that can trace its origin to Socrates, in which learning, insight, knowledge and the ability to reason is something that is brought forth from the individual through conversation or dialogue. Jeffs and Smith (2005) suggest a number of conditions that make conversation pedagogically valuable:

- *Being there:* it is a social activity that requires reciprocity
- *Shared:* they find something that they both can talk about
- *Immediacy:* conversations involve an exchange that is immediate
- *Culturally contingent:* be aware of the culturally contingent nature of conversation
- *Open mind:* trust and openness to the views of others
- *Interpretation:* we often put two and two together and get five because of assumptions, prejudices and leaps of imagination
- *Ego:* conversation is a complex and sophisticated art, it is not a battle of wills, it is not about belittling or putting someone in their place, it is at the heart of listening and realising what Powell (1999), in his five stages of conversation, suggests as deep insight.

Many of the above are necessary for 'entry' into relationships. The metaphor of a space craft having the force to get through the earth's outer atmosphere without being broken to bits is useful in picturing the degree to which young people test youth workers through challenging sensibilities, affronting belief and bravado, testing limits of patience and endurance in order to test their belief in them or their vocation, of seeing whether they can 'fly with them'. Much of this testing can be put in the realms of 'talking shit' and can lead to a sense of resignation, to a conviction that you cannot work with them (be there), have little in common, and most significantly in the case of counter-terrorism, misinterpret. The space of 'talking shit' can be interpreted as part of the process, a rite of passage for youth workers and young people in establishing relationships, or it could be seen purely through its content, problematised and now criminalised.

'Talking shit' is often a suspension of reality and testing of 'what ifs' for young people, the content contingent on a mix of context, identity and issues or interest occupying thought or time. It is a space that can serve a therapeutic purpose and a leisure purpose – of 'having a laugh' without costing anything financially. Its danger comes from how this conversation can be interpreted – of over interpretation whether as process or as content, but once past this stage there is a danger that radicalism, turning to 'pure politics' or turning to Islam, can be understood as radicalisation. This is, in essence, denial of politics and politicisation. I have mentioned the danger of the two new classifications of apologist and propagandist in the Prevent strategy 2011; this, in practice, is a subjective exercise. Schools up until February 2012 had still not been issued guidelines or training, and yet were expected to be one of the key counter-terrorism fronts, identifying 'potential radicals' for re-education. There are too many stories of this misinterpretation, whether in prisons if somebody finds religion, or in school if a young person starts to pray or 'displays' their Islam. Young people's interest in global events affecting Muslims can be a particular issue, especially in relation to views on Israel and Palestine, with Muslim students 'referred' to the government's Channel programme for assessment and, if necessary, de-radicalisation, if making anti-Israeli statements. This is a new dimension to the schooling of British Muslim young people. It is an example of the 'War on Terror' forcing a Muslim 'apoliticalness', a need to be in the middle, the cultivation of a 'moderate Muslim' that is a prerequisite to any official engagement with Muslims, Muslim workers or organisations by the 'political state'. However, this precondition is not relevant for the 'security state'. It asks of an alchemical process that transforms a sense of injustice, the experience of inequality and prejudice into an unquestioning and peaceful acceptance of the 'War on Terror' narrative and the status quo.

The Terrorism Act 2006 has received criticism from bodies such as Liberty who have argued that offences such as encouragement of terrorism and dissemination of terrorist publications are too broadly drafted and *do not require any intention to incite* others to commit criminal acts to be found guilty. This Act has moved liability from the realm of actions to the realm of ideas and associations. It is aimed at disrupting the nature of community and the ties and relations of recognition, solidarity and exchange that bind. It particularly seeks to break 'overly cohesive' communities that Cantle argues are a threat to community cohesion. These measures confront communities that organise informally with an inherent distrust of organisations and organising. It is sometimes difficult to follow the trail of good intentions when supporting causes or in responding to humanitarian emergencies.

It in its own way it criminalises a way of being. It leaves professionals working with young people such as youth workers in a precarious position. Youth workers require the trust and confidence of young people to establish associations and relationships for meaningful conversations. These conversations may serve the purpose of letting off steam, testing boundaries; they may be just about counselling and support; but as Banks (1999) states, young people will only have these conversations if they are confident that the worker is not going to report them to the police, their parents or their school.

However, youth workers are expected to notify the police, and can be charged under this legislation if they do not inform of young people who are demonstrating 'extremist views' or who are in danger of being radicalised. Yet, as many youth workers state, being extreme is not the same as extremism; for young people it is a rite of passage, a means to resist, and young Muslims have clearly worked out that this will shock the sensibilities of those they may feel most aggrieved by … it is their version of punk; according to Aki Nawaz, 'Islam is more punk than punk' (Open Democracy, 2004; Saini, 2006).

Anecdotal evidence suggests that youth workers employed by the Youth Offending Service Youth Inclusion Programmes are particularly prone to pressure from the police to reveal names of young people they are working with. These are often young people with offending history termed as NEET (not in education, employment or training). It is the mono perception of Muslim communities and 'Muslimness' that allows random connections between a young offender with a conviction for theft to being regarded as a potential terrorist, when the terrorism offender profile, according to leading criminal law advocates, suggests otherwise. The government has sought to 'mainstream' the 'War against Terror' through the national performance directive for local authorities and other key service providers – National Indicator (NI) 35 'Building resilience to violent extremism'. This is to see how effective local services are to building resilience to violent extremism and has been part of the drive to equip the 'home front' in the war against terror. Organisations such as An-Nisa and the Muslim Youthwork Foundation have already pointed out the danger of misjudgement from staff due to the lack of experience and knowledge of Muslims in a context where expressions of Islamophobia are made with ever increasing confidence by staff more readily able to internalise anti-Islamic sentiments presented through the association of values with professional approaches – those working in the service sector are particularly prone to this in their desire to make a difference.

Questioning 'Responding to lives not events'

'Responding to lives not events' was a slogan that was devised by the Muslim Youthwork Foundation to challenge policy and strategy, defined by global or local events and political imperative in relation to the Muslim community in general and young Muslims in particular in 2006, but it is a slogan whose applicability I have continually questioned. Was it a slogan that emerged out of naivety that one could inform government policy and strategy in relation to work with young Muslims? That maybe the confidence with which government names Muslims in CONTEST, the same confidence could have been applied to name young Muslims to secure the *Every Child Matters* five outcomes under the New Labour government or the Positive for Youth strategy of the coalition administration (HM Government, 2011a). It is by naming groups and naming need that one can challenge the discretionary powers of middle managers to navigate resources and interpret objectives to meet the continuing needs of existing professional commitments and relationships already hard pushed by limited resources.

That policy responses to issues affecting young Muslim should be based on the detail of their lives rather than as political imperatives emerging out of events was idealistically and practically understandable, but it was, in hindsight, politically naive when dealing with a system with a long history, institutional infrastructure and a conceptual language for managing dynamics of 'race', ethnicity and faith. Government strategies, experience suggests, rarely see their own faults or, for that matter, opportunity unless something *forcibly* makes them do so – but even then detail is rarely tolerated unless it provides the words to the mood music emerging out of Whitehall, and without internal champions, external bodies can do very little to challenge, change or transform. Events provide a temporary cognitive shock that generates a political will to temporarily look beyond the in-house strategy and established relationships.

The development of 'community-friendly' Prevent or the belief in the role of communities in counter-terrorism stands in sharp contrast to the force of state to find guilty those who find themselves in the wrong place, the wrong conversation or using the wrong language or who search for the wrong things on the computer or 'piss people off' the wrong way. The political imperative behind the 'War on Terror' and keeping people 'alive' to threat now also has the maintenance of the organisational infrastructure that has appeared through regional counter-terrorism units to think about, and this needs reasons for continued existence.

Any resistance, challenge or refusal to work on PVE agendas is leading Muslim youth workers to being seen as 'radicalisers' rather than 'de-radicalisers'. It is a repeat of the pattern established by the Runnymede definition of Islamophobia and the approach of the Bush administration supported by the British government in the 'War on Terror' – with us or against us. It is an example of how global struggles find themselves in the everyday practice of those working with Muslim young people.

The relationship between Community Cohesion and the PVE agendas is a symbiotic relationship that has saturated the Muslim community, denying politics and politicisation. There is a sense of living in a parallel world where you can see individuals operating on a level of trust with society that you can no longer take for granted.

NINE

Nothing to conclude ...

All intentions tainted
All certainties a haze
What now to bring
Where now your gaze?
So close the door
Turn away
There is nothing to bring
There is nothing to say.

All intentions tainted
All certainties a haze.

M.G. Khan

The new alchemists

Poetry is a beautiful way to simultaneously hide and reveal, an alchemical process through which anger, frustration, feelings of brutalisation, marginalisation, of being unheard, finds form. It asks of alchemists, individuals who can experience the aforementioned and yet engage with society, absent of any semblance of their effect. This is the alchemy asked of any marginalised group or individual, and it is a real *jihad*.

It is no surprise that music, and with it, poetry, has been an important vehicle of expression for young Muslims. Rappers refer to Islam as the unofficial religion of hip hop; as Samy Alim (2005) documents, seminal hip hop groups and figures have drawn inspiration, for the last two decades at least, from Islam and/or the experience of being Muslim, such as Ice Cube, Busta Rhymes, Mos Def, the Wu-Tang Clan, Public Enemy and Fun-Da-Mental, with its 'nice' counterweight appearing through *nasheed* artists in recent years (*nasheed* songs are those that praise Allah or the Prophet Muhammad, pbuh). Hishaam Aidi (2012), in his article for Al Jazeera 'Opinions', differentiates between poetry or lyrics that make no political demand, and those that do make a political demand, that name a condition, challenge or critique, and to this you could add a category that includes poets or musicians who celebrate religion or who exhort an individual spirit. While much of *nasheed* appears to make little political demand, providing 'halal soft pop' with clean-cut individuals and groups that make Justin Bieber or JLS look like the devil's spawn by comparison, the hip-hop field is much more of a site of struggle in terms of whose message reaches the ears of young people with increasing state intervention in using hip-hop to showcase and give credibility to its messages.

The following poem is, in some ways, the first part of the poem given at the start of this chapter, the chronological 'now' followed by 'then', the past, what used to be:

> Leave the door open for me
> I don't want to come empty handed
> At times I have wandered far from you
> And there are many I have offended
> Leave the door open for me
> I don't want to come empty handed.

M.G. Khan

Together they capture two states of being, a journey from a semblance of hope to one of resignation. In the first part there is something to offer, a willingness to hang on to a relationship that is challenged and challenging, something for which one would take risks to the point of causing offence, or hurt consciously or unconsciously, and for which one would persevere through the difficulties faced. The second state (given at the beginning of this chapter) is when there is nothing left to offer, nor any hope in the relationship, symbolised by the act of turning away, of exhausting what one has to say. The poem therefore captures both the spirit of Muslims who at least seek to continue to engage with government, and those who have given up, turned away, those who have, through experience, resigned themselves from engagement with the government as an act of making change possible for young Muslims, communities and the country to which they belong.

The need to be known, to reveal, seems to be a divine act, in which, for Muslims, the Qur'an is both an expression and a guide through the notion of *ayats* (signs). Discussed earlier in this book, *ayats* are signs that point to something hidden, the taken-for-granted, or as pointers to the esoteric. This act, of providing signs rather than acts of self-revelation, also seem part of the human condition, to draw those to us who comprehend and value what is being conveyed by the sign and to keep those who don't understand at a safe distance. We can argue that we are the creators of our *ayats*, of our signs, in the need or desire to be known or understood, whether this is done consciously or unconsciously – whether the *ayat* is the *hijab*, the cut of a beard, a tattoo, a scar on an arm or the colour of our clothes. The desire to mark our bodies is both ancient and present. It is how we do 'signs' – they are our *ayats*, our communications systems.

The relationships between signs and texts is significant in the Muslim world; the importance of text was particularly driven home to me on visiting a Byzantine church in Istanbul. The small church had a mosaic of Jesus (pbuh) and his companions. On looking at the mosaic for a while, I began to notice how the degree to which the qualities of love, patience and justice were greatly accentuated by the artist into the face of Jesus (pbuh) as compared to his companions. This was the means by which the artist was signalling the 'divine figure', and it was in the painting of these qualities that the artist was conveying the difference between Jesus (pbuh) and his companions. Here the act of knowing, differentiating and meditating on the divine was a pictorial act, whereas in the Muslim tradition, the textual is very important, through the written attributes (names) of God, while the visual dimension points out into creation to the world to 'know' something of the creator, in its beauty, its design; it is not a 'fallen world' as such, but a place through which its creator can be known.

As informal educators working with young people it is important that we understand signs – what do they point to? What do they mean? And what is asking to be known or understood? This is not possible by the mentally anaesthetising statements of 'I treat everybody the same irrespective of…'. As we become increasingly concealed by the market's desire to mark our bodies and worlds with its symbols, who *we are* in terms of our values and principles can shift quite dramatically in terms of where we look for certainties, self-value, and in which relationships we invest in and how, in terms of the relationships model presented earlier.

The resistance to this 'marking' is found in the creation and appropriation of symbols that challenge, that begin life uncommodified, and that reflect back what one sees and experiences of the world, whether acceptance, love, attraction or disdain, anger or disrespect, at how much of the self is unrecognised, unrealised and concealed, and yet this denial of potential, the magical, the significant within, finds itself profoundly and powerfully in J.K. Rowling's Harry Potter books and Phillip Pullman's *His dark materials*, two of the best-selling 'children's' books in recent memory, another example of the role of fiction to reveal the human condition or desire when there is such resistance to it as non-fiction.

Henry Giroux's (2009) use of the word 'war' to describe the intensity of the attack on the agency of young people is descriptively appropriate if it means an act that seeks to both deny and appropriate, but the appropriation has to be a 'voluntary' act, as it is, primed by the hegemony of global capitalism. Giroux's descriptor is not simply aimed at the experience of young Muslims at the hands of, for example, education, aspects of the criminal justice system and the markets; it is towards all young people.

Muslim young people are in an interesting position paradoxically, where religion is both a site of resistance against global capitalism and a site of commodification for the development of an Islam that is about lifestyle choices, through the processes of 'halalification', for example, halal, insurance, halal banking, halal foods, halal holidays, halal music, halal cosmetics, and anything else on which the halal label can be placed. This is creating an industry that is informing a Muslim identity that is experienced through acts of consumption, mitigated by arguments that claim this economy as an act of reclamation, of developing an alternative market that aims to synthesise the ethical and permissible in terms of consumption, but it can also be a place of exploitation in which the 'halal badge' is used to give legitimacy to products. And yet, it appears, at times, to be still an offer that is about an identity that is still consumption-related, that a key element of being a 'practising Muslim' is through the marketplace one privileges, and which mark or symbol one appropriates and displays as part of their 'Islamic lifestyle'.

The relationships model presented here as a 'theory for Muslim youth work' is not solely applicable to Muslim youth work; it is what I understand to be the purpose of the informal educator, whatever role s/he may find themselves in, for example, youth worker, community worker, detached worker, mentor, care worker, working in youth offending services, formal teaching environments or the factory floor. It has two key dimensions – that it is person-centred and about making tangible all these relationships by the principles that should act as our professional and personal compass – most succinctly expressed as the four cornerstones, that is, that our relationships with young people should be participative, educative, empowering, and there is equality of opportunity. It should not be about relationships that are a means to an end, whether that end is defined by the worker or by policy or politics.

There is an illuminating tension between belief and principle that is due to the interwoven nature of values, beliefs, principles and ethics, that finds itself in professional practice contexts. Should a doctor, due to his or her religious beliefs, refuse to treat a patient who is gay, or should a youth worker encourage a young woman not to abort and see through a pregnancy, be allowed to practice, should their 'religious principles' be privileged? Do we work with young people on the basis of beliefs that we hold, or the principles or professional values that we have adopted and which we should not forget have been sourced from a set of beliefs? The Muslim Youthwork Foundation in its inception first identified a set of principles to direct its engagement with young people and those working with young people; for some they were derived from their religious beliefs, for others their political beliefs, for myself the principles provided no contradiction to my religious beliefs, they were inspired by them – they were a challenge to the inhumanity that can be present in unreflective religious and political orthodoxy.

Freire's notion of the 'death of the educator' has powerful Christian symbolism; it is dramatic and it is final, and I can appreciate the power and meaning of this intent. However, more appealing to me is the idea of educators or mentors who realise they have nothing more to give to somebody, and point them in the direction of somebody else; it is less dramatic, less final and it means that roles can be reversed as to who 'guides' who. Muslim history is replete with such examples where a 'symbolic death' was not the answer.

Due to racism and Islamophobia, Black young people and Muslim young people have little choice but to make sense of their experience as Black young people and/or as Muslims, and many activists seeking to make a difference have been attracted to this field by a radical pedagogy informed by the work of individuals such as bell hooks, Paulo Freire, Steve Biko, Henry Giroux, Idries Shah, Malcolm X and other individuals, that have revealed a condition that has named the 'oppressed and the oppressor' and also sought to make sense of a pedagogy to respond.

The challenge to institutional practices and beliefs from Muslim communities on the basis of securing rights and opportunities, to challenge Islamophobic attitudes and practices, is a challenge to the orthodoxy of the norms, practices, narratives and people in situ, and the resistance is fierce, with the nervous and the scared appropriated by the desire of Islamophobes to preserve against an alien 'them', that brings to life Werbner's Islamophobia tropes of the plotting, deceptive 'witch', or the agendas of *Islamofication* presented by the 'grand inquisitor' trope. The education sector, both formal and informal, as guardians of the transmission of narratives is, as suggested earlier, particularly prone to this behaviour, as I have too often observed and experienced.

Returning to Giroux's notion of the 'war on youth', in Britain at least this claim cannot easily be made by a Muslim in the same way that it seems that no Black person of any significance can dare to claim the application of a White agenda, as Diane Abbott (2012) found to her cost by her comments of 'white people loving to play divide and rule'; it appears that Black people can say that racism can be an issue but not that we live in a racist society. It seems that street racism can be named, but societal racism cannot, or even that working-class racism can be named but middle-class racism cannot. It is more difficult now than ever to challenge this, and is one of the downsides of the struggle for justice for Stephen Lawrence which brought to the surface the strength and confidence of white victimhood as observed by Alana Lentin and Gavan Titley (2011), whereby a resurgent neoliberalist-inspired racism in denoucing multi-culturalims is really denouncing a 'lived multi-culture'.

The process of establishing group contracts is a useful insight into how everybody will want the fact that they are not racist or sexist accepted as a given; to suggest otherwise would be an insult to them and to their intelligence. It is fascinating to see how respect for one another will be highlighted, but disrespect will begin almost immediately. In a similar way Muslims can give the example of the power of the state gaze trained on them, but cannot use language that can describe the intensity of this lens, such as the notion of the police state, as Abu Bakr and Faraz Ahmad found to their cost with the furore it created[1] – this experience cannot be named, as Giroux has so forthrightly, as a 'war on youth', without it deemed to be an example of Muslim 'radicalisation or ungratefulness'. For Muslims this denial of politics, of the language of and concepts for challenge, is part of a process that is about a discursive and political marginalisation.

It feels that there is no conclusion to write about, as no journey here is complete; what there is to say has been said – questions about what next for Muslim youth work in a Britain seeking to reprise services and activity on the shoulders of sentiment, facilitated by the mainly uniformed Christian voluntary sector, requires research as does the pedagogy, values and capacity issues emerging in the Muslim voluntary sector. Each of the chapters is an experiential stream for many Muslims, which has its own shape and form, and the speed of change can leave anything one writes as a retrospective, out of date. But looking back, it becomes clear how young Muslims continue be at the interstices of where the 'war on youth' that Giroux names is being fought at its fiercest, but this would be the claim of anyone, one being the focus of such a sustained attack on identity and ways of being.

There is much that has not been written about and should have been, but it is time to call an end, for now.

---

[1] http://news.bbc.co.uk/1/hi/uk_politics/6342277.stm

Bibliography

Abbas, T. (2006) *Muslim Britain: Communities under pressure*, London: Zed Books.

Abou El Fadl, K. (2001) *Conference of the books: The search for beauty in Islam*, Oxford: University of America.

Abou El Fadl, K. (2003) *Speaking in God's name: Islamic law, authority and women*, Oxford: Oneworld Publications.

Aidi, H. (2012) 'Don't panic! Islam and Europe's "hip hop wars"', Al-jazeera Opinions, www.aljazeera.com/indepth/opinion/2012/06/20126310151835171.html.

Alam, M.Y. (2002) *Kilo*, Pontefract: Routes Publishing.

Alam, M.Y. and Husband, C. (2006) *Knowing our place*, Bradford: University of Bradford.

Alexander, C. (2000) *The Asian gang: Ethnicity, identity, masculinity*, London: Berg Publishers.

Al-Faruqi, I. (1978) 'Islamic renaissance in contemporary society', *Al-Ittihad*, vol 15, pp 15-23.

Al-Ghazali, A. (translated by R.J. McCarthy) (1980) *Deliverance from error: Five key texts including His spiritual autobiography, al-Munqidh min al-Dalal*, Louisville, KY: Fons Vitae.

Al-Ghazali, A. (translated by D.B. Burrell and N. Daher) (1992) *Al-Ghazali on the ninety-nine beautiful names of God*, Cambridge: Islamic Texts Society.

Ali, A.A. (2000) *The Holy Qur'an: Arabic text with English translation*, New Delhi: Kitab Bhavan.

Ali, A. (2005) *Muslim youth in Britain: A ticking time bomb?*, London: British Muslim Research Centre.

Ali, H.A.A. (1977) *The family structure in Islam*, Beltsville, MD: International Graphics Printing Service.

Ali, N., Kalra, V.S. and Sayyid, S. (2006) *A postcolonial people. South Asians in Britain*, London: Hurst & Company.

Ali, Y. (1992) 'Muslim women and the politics of ethnicity and culture in Northern England', in G. Sahgal and A.N. Yuval Davies (eds) *Refusing holy orders*, London: Virago Press, pp 106-30.

Alibhai-Brown, Y. (1997) *Community flashpoints*, London: Institute for Public Policy Research.

Allen, C. (2010) *Challenging Islamophobia: Ten years on*, Postgraduate Seminar Series, Birmingham: Theology Department, University of Birmingham.

Alsayyad, N. and Castells, M. (2002) *Muslim Europe or Euro-Islam: Politics, culture and citizenship in the age of globalisation*, Lanham, MD: Lexington Books.

Andreski, S. (1983) *Max Weber on capitalism, bureaucracy and religion: A selection of texts*, London: George Allen & Unwin Publishers Ltd.

Ansari, D.M.F.U.R. (1977) *The Qur'anic foundations and structure of Muslim society*, Karachi: Trade and Industry Publications Ltd.

Ansari, F. (2005) *British anti-terrorism: A modern day witch hunt*, London: Islamic Human Rights Commission.

Ansari, H. (2004) *The infidel within*, London: Hurst & Co.

Anthias, F. and Yuval-Davies, N. (1993) *Racialised boundaries*, London: Routledge.

Anwar, M. (1979) *The myth of return*, London: Heinemann.

Anwar, M. (1998) *Between cultures*, London: Routledge.

Apple, M.W. (1990) *Ideology and curriculum*, London: Routledge.

Armstrong, K. (2000) *The battle for God: Fundamentalism in Judaism, Christianity and Islam*, London: HarperCollins Publishers.

Arneil, B. (2007) 'The meaning and utility of "social" in "social capital"' in R. Edwards, J. Franklin and J. Holland (eds) *Assessing Social Capital: Concept, policy and practice,* Newcastle: Cambridge Scholars Press, pp 29-53.

Asad, T. (1973) *Anthropology and the colonial encounter*, New York: Humanity Books.

Ashcroft, B. and Ahluwalia, P. (2001) *Edward Said*, London: Routledge.

Back, L. (1996) *New ethnicities and urban culture: Racisms and multi-culture in young lives*, London: UCL Press Ltd.

Bakhtiar, L. (1994) *Moral healer's handbook: The psychology of spiritual chivalry*, Chicago, IL: Kazi Publications.

Baratz, S. (1970) 'Early childhood intervention: the social science base of institutional racism', *Harvard Educational Review*, vol 40, pp 29-50.

Barker, M. (1981) *The new racism*, London: Junction Books.

Barlas, A. (2002) *Believing women in Islam: Unreading patriarchal interpretations of the Qur'an,* Austin, TX: University of Texas Press.

Barndt, J (2011) *Becoming an anti-racist church*, Minneapolis, MN: Fortress Press.

Barnes, H. (2006) *Born in the UK: Young Muslims in Britain*, London: The Foreign Policy Centre.

Batmanghelidjh, C. (2006) *Shattered lives: Children who live with courage and dignity.* London: Jessica Kingsley Publishers.

Batsleer, J. (2008) *Informal learning in youth work*, London: Sage Publications.

Batsleer, J. and Davies, B. (2010) *What is youth work?*, Exeter: Learning Matters

Baudrillard, J. (1994) *Simulacra and simulation,* Michigan: University of Michigan Press.

Beckett, C. and Macey, M. (2001) 'Race, gender and sexuality: the oppression of multiculturalism', *Women's Studies International Forum*, vol 24, pp 309-19.

Beckford, R. (2004) *God and the gangs*, London: Darton, Longman and Todd.

Bell, M. (1983) *Multicultural education and the youth service*, London: National Council for Voluntary Youth Services.

Belton, B. and Hamid, S. (2011) *Youth work and Islam: A leap of faith for young people*, Rotterdam: Sense Publishers.

Berger, P.L. (1967) *The sacred canopy: Elements of a sociological theory of religion*, New York: Doubleday & Company Inc.

Berger, P.L. and Neuhaus, R.J. (1996) *To empower people*, Washington, DC: The AEI Press.

Berger, P. (2008) *Ways of Seeing.* London: Penguin

Berjak, R. (2006) 'Zalama' in O. Leaman *The Qur'an: An encyclopaedia*, London: Routledge.

Bhattacharya, G. (1998) *Tales of dark skinned women: Race, gender and global politics*, London: UCL Press.

Bhattacharya, G. and Gabriel, J. (1997) 'Formulations of youth in late twentieth century England', in U.S.T. Roche (ed) *Youth in society*, London: Sage Publications.

Billis, D. (1989) *A theory of the voluntary sector: Implications for policy and practice*, London: Centre for Voluntary Organisation, London School of Economics and Political Science.

Billis, D. (1993) *Organising public and voluntary agencies*, London: Routledge.

Billis, D. and Harris, M. (1996) *Voluntary agencies: Challenges of organisation and management*, London: Macmillan Press Ltd.

Billis, D. (ed) (2010) *Hybrid organisations and the third sector: Challenges for practice, theory and policy.* Basingstoke: Palgrave Macmillan

Birt, J. (2006) 'Lobbying and marching: British Muslims and the state', in T. Abbas (ed) *Muslim Britain: Communities under pressure*, London: Zed Books, pp 92-106.

Blacker, H. (2010) 'Relationships, friendships and youth work', in T. Jeffs and M.K. Smith, *Youth work practice,* Basingstoke: Palgrave Macmillan

Board of Education (1939) *In the service of youth*, Circular 1486, London: HMSO.

Bochner, A.P. (1997) 'It's about time: narrative and the divided self', *Qualitative Inquiry*, pp 418-38.

Bodi, F. (2002) 'Muslims got Cantle. What they needed was Scarman', *The Guardian*, 1 July.

Bowlby, J. (1969) *Attachment and loss, Volume 1: Attachment,* New York: Basic Books.

Brah, A.K. (1978) *Working with Asian young people*, Leicester: National Association for Asian Youth.

Brah, A.K. (1996) *Cartographies of diaspora*, London: Routledge.

Bright, M. (2006) *When progressives treat with reactionaries*, London: Policy Exchange.

Bronfenbrenner, U. (1979) *The ecology of human development,* Cambridge, MA: Harvard University Press.

Buchman, D. (1998) *Al-Ghazali: The niche of lights,* Provo Utah: Brigham Young University Press.

Bunt, S. (1990) *Years and years of youth*, Rochdale: RAP Limited.

Butters, S. and Newell, S. (1978) *Realities of training*, Leicester: National Youth Bureau.

Campbell, H. (1985) *Rasta and resistance: From Marcus Garvey to Walter Rodney*, London: Hansib Publications.

Cantle, T. (2001) *Community cohesion: A report of the Independent Review Team*, London: Home Office.

Carby, H.V. (1999) *Cultures in Babylon*, London: Verso.

Cashmore, E. (1979) *Rastaman: The Rastafarian movement in England*, London: Unwin.

Castells, M. (1996) *The power of identity*, Oxford: Blackwell Publishers.

Cesari, J. (1998) 'Islam in France: Social challenge or challenge of secularism', in S. Vertovec & A. Rogers (eds) *Muslim European youth: Reproducing ethnicity, religion and culture,* Aldershot: Ashgate.

Chauhan, V. (1989) *Beyond steel 'n' bands and samosas: Black young people in the youth service*, Leicester: National Youth Bureau.

Chazan, B. (2003) 'The philosophy of informal Jewish education', [online] infed: the encyclopedia of informal education, www.infed.org/informaljewisheducation/informal_jewish_education.htm.

Christian, C. (1999) 'Spirituality in the context of multi-cultural youth work', *Youth & Policy,* vol 65, no 1.

Chittick, W.C. (2000) *The Sufi path of knowledge*, Lahore: The Suhail Academy.

Choudhury, T. and Fenwick, H. (2011) *The impact of counter-terrorism measures on Muslim communities*, Manchester: Equalities and Human Rights Commission.

Clark, E.M. (1990) *Heuristic research*, Berkeley, CA: Sage Publications.

Clark, J. (2004) *Islam charity and activism*, Bloomington, IN: Indiana University Press.

Clarke, H. (1993) 'Sites of resistance: place, "race" and gender as sources of empowerment', in P. Jackson and J. Penrose (ed) *Construction of race, place and nation*, London: UCL Press Ltd, pp 121-42.

Coard, B. (1971) *How the West Indian child is made educationally subnormal in the British school system*, London: New Beacon Books.

Cohen, L. (1993) *Stranger music*, London: Jonathan Cape.

Cohen, P. (1988) 'Perspectives on the present', In P. Cohen and H.S. Bains (eds) *Multi-racist Britain*, London: Macmillan Press Ltd.

Cohen, S. (2005) *Folk devils and moral panics*, London: Routledge.

Coles, M. (2008) *Every Muslim child matters: Practical guide for schools and children's services*, Stoke on Trent: Trentham Books.

Colley, H. and Hodkinson, P. (2001) 'Problems with "bridging the gap": the reversal of structure and agency in addressing social exclusion', *Critical Social Policy*, vol 2, no 3, pp 335-59.

Cottle, T. (2002) 'On narratives and the sense of self', *Qualitative Inquiry*, vol 8, pp 535-49.

Couss, F., Verschelden, Van de Walle, T., Medlinska, M. and Williamson, H. (eds) (2010) 'The history of European youth work and its relevance for youth policy today', in *The history of youth work in Europe*, Vol 2, Strasbourg: Council of Europe.

Cowan, J. (1997) *Rumi's Divan of Shems of Tabriz: A new interpretation*, Salisbury: Element Books.

CRE (Commission for Racial Equality) (1995) *Standard for racial equality for services working with young people*, London: CRE.

Cressey, G. (2007) *The ultimate separatist cage? Youth work with Muslim young women*, Leicester: National Youth Agency.

Cross, M. (1982) 'The manufacture of marginality', in E. Cashmore and B. Troyna (ed) *Black youth in crisis*, London: George Allen & Unwin, pp 35-52.

Crotty, M. (1998) *The foundations of social research*, London: Sage Publications.

Crowe, B (2008) *People don't grow by being measured: Recollections and reflections of a dyslexic grandmother*, Leicester: Matador.

David, C. (1989) *Community education: Towards a framework for the future*, Birmingham: Westhill College.

Davies, B. (1999a) *From voluntaryism to welfare state: A history of the youth service in England, vol 1*, Leicester: Youth Work Press.

Davies, B. (1999b) *From Thatcherism to New Labour: A history of the youth service in England, vol 2*, Leicester: National Youth Agency.

Davies, B. (2010) 'What do we mean by youth work?', in J. Batsleer and B. Davies (2010) *What is youth work?*, Exeter: Learning Matters.

Davies, B.D. and Gibson, A. (1967) *The social education of the adolescent*, London: University of London Press.

DCSF (Department for Children, Schools and Families) (2007) *Aiming high for young people: A ten year strategy for positive activities*, London: HM Treasury.

Deakin, N. (2001) 'Public policy, social policy and voluntary organisations', in M. Harris and C. Rochester (eds) *Voluntary organisations and social policy in Britain*, Basingstoke: Palgrave, pp 21-36.

Department of Education and Science (1982) *Experience and participation. Report of the Review Group on the youth service in England: The Thompson Report*, London: HMSO.

DES (Department for Education and Skills) (1969) *Youth and community work in the 1970s* (The Fairbairn–Milson Report), London: HMSO.

Dewey, J. (1991) *How we think*, New York: Prometheus Books.

Dewey, J. (1997) *Experience and education*, New York: Touchstone Books.

DfEE (Department for Education and Employment) (2001) *Transforming youth work: Developing youth work for young people*, Nottingham: DfEE Publications.

DfES (Department for Education and Skills) (2002) *Transforming Youth Work: Resourcing excellent youth services*, London: DfES/Connexions.

DfES (Department for Education and Skills) (2003) *Every child matters*, London: The Stationery Office.

Diani, D.D.P.A.M. (1999) *Social movements: An introduction*, Oxford: Blackwell Publishers.

Dorling, D. (2011) *Injustice: Why social inequality persists*, Bristol: The Policy Press.

Dummett, M.A.A. (1984) 'The role of government in Britain's racial crisis', in C. Husband (ed) *Race in Britain: Continuity and change*, London: Hutchinson, pp 111-41.

Dungate, M. (1984) *A multi racial society: The role of the voluntary sector*, London: National Council for Voluntary Organisations.

Dyke, A.H. (2009) *Mosques made in Britain*, London: Quilliam Foundation.

El Guindi, F. (2008) *By noon prayer: The rhythm of Islam*, New York: Berg.

Elsdon, K.T., Reynolds, J. and Stewart, S. (1995) *Voluntary organisations, citizenship, learning and change*, Leicester: NIACE.

Esack, F. (1997) *Qur'an liberation and pluralism: An Islamic perspective of interreligious solidarity against oppression*, Oxford: Oneworld Publications.

Esack, F. (2005) *The Qur'an: A user's guide*, Oxford: Oneworld Publications.

Esposito, J.L. (1999) *The Islamic threat: Myth or reality?*, Oxford: Oxford University Press.

Etzioni, A. (1964) *Modern organisations*, Englewood Cliffs, NJ: Prentice Hall.

Fanon, F. (1994) 'The fact of blackness', in J. Donald and A. Rattansi (eds) *'Race', culture and difference*, London: Sage Publications, pp 220-40.

FCO (Foreign Commonwealth Office) and Home Office (2004) *Report on young Muslims and extremism*, London: Home Office.

Feinstein, L., Bynner, J. and Duckworth, K. (2005) *Leisure contexts in adolescence and their effects on adult outcomes*, London: Institute of Education.

Fekete, L. (2009) *A suitable enemy: Racism, migration and Islamophobia in Europe*, London: Pluto Press.

Fenton, S. (1999) *Ethnicity, racism, class and culture*, London: Macmillan.

Fetzer, J.S. and Soper, J.C. (2005) *Muslims and the state in Britain, France and Germany*, Cambridge: Cambridge University Press.

Field, C. (2011) 'Young British Muslims since 9/11: a composite attitudinal profile', *Race, State and Society*, vol 39, nos, 2/3, pp 159-73.

Field, J. (2003) *Social Capital*, London: Routledge

Finch, J. (1986) *Research and policy: The uses of qualitative methods in social and educational research*, London: The Falmer Press.

Fisher, G. and Joshua, H. (1982) 'Social policy and Black youth', in E. Cashmore and B. Troyna (ed) *Black youth in crisis*, London: George Allen & Unwin, pp 129-42.

Freire, P. (1974) *Education for critical consciousness*, London: Continuum.

Freire, P. (2010) *Pedagogy of the oppressed*, London: Continuum.

Fryer, P. (1984) *Staying power: The history of black people in Britain*, London: Pluto Press.

Fryer, P. (1988) *Black people in the British Empire*, London: Pluto Press.

Gerth, H. and Wright Mills, C. (1964) *From Max Weber: Essays in sociology*, London: Routledge & Kegan Paul.

Giddens, A (1994) *Beyond left and right: The future of radical politics*, Cambridge: Polity.

Gilchrist, R., Jeffs, T. and Spence, J. (2001) *Drawing on the past*, Leicester: National Youth Agency.

Gilroy, P. (1993) *The black Atlantic: Modernity and double consciousness*, Cambridge, MA: Harvard University Press.

Giroux, H. (2009) *Youth in a suspect society,* Basingstoke: Macmillan

Green, M. (2006) *A journey of discovery: Spirituality and spiritual development in youth work*, Leicester: National Youth Agency.

Green, S. (2010) 'The I in oppression', unpublished, Oxford: Ruskin College.

Hall, G.S. (1904) *Adolescence*, New York; Appleton.

Hall, S. (1987) 'Minimal selves', in *The real me: Postmodernism and the question of identity*, ICA documents 6, London: ICA.

Hall, S. (1990) 'Cultural identity and diaspora identity', in J. Rutherford (ed) *Community, culture, difference*, London: Lawrence & Wishart, pp 222-37.

Hall, S. (1992) 'The question of cultural of cultural identity', in S. Hall, D. Held and T. McGrew (eds) *Modernity and its futures*, Cambridge: Polity Press, pp 273-326.

Hall, S. and McGrew, T. (1992) *Modernity and its futures*, Cambridge: Polity Press.

Halliday, F. (1995) 'Islam is in danger: authority, Rushdie and the struggle for the migrant soul', in J. Hippler and A. Lueg (eds) *The next threat: Western perceptions of Islam*, London: Pluto Press, pp 71-81.

Halliday, F. (1996) *Islam and the myth of confrontation*, London: I.B. Taurus.

Halliday, F. (2006) *A transnational umma: Reality or myth?*, London: Open Democracy.

Halliday, F. (2011) *Shocked and awed: How the war on terror and Jihad have changed the English language*, London: I.B. Tauris.

Harris, M. (1998) *Organising God's work: Challenges for churches and synagogues*, London: Macmillan Press Ltd.

Harris, M. (2001b) 'Voluntary organisations in a changing social policy environment', in M. Harris and C. Rochester (eds) *Voluntary organisations and social policy in Britain*, Basingstoke: Palgrave, pp 213-28.

Hart, R.A. (1992) *Children's participation: From tokenism to citizenship*, Florence: UNICEF Innocenti Child Development Centre.

Hartley, B. (1971) *The final report of a three-year experimental project on coloured teenagers in Britain*, London: National Association of Youth Clubs.

Haykal, M.H. (1976) *The life of Muhammad*, Oak Brook, IL: American Trust Publications.

Helminski, C. (2004) *The book of character: Writings on character and virtue from Islamic and other sources*, Bristol: The Book Foundation.

Hesse, B. and Sayyid, S. (2006) 'Narrating the post-colonial political and the immigrant imaginary', in N. Ali, V.S. Kalpra and S. Sayyid (eds) *A postcolonial people*, London: C. Hurst & Co, pp 13-31.

Hitti, P.K. (1970) *History of the Arabs*, London: Macmillan Press.

Hiizb Ut –Tahrir. *Radicalisation, extremism and Islamism: Realities and myths in the 'War on Terror'*.

HM (Her Majesty's) Government (2008) *The Prevent strategy: A guide for local partners in England*, London: The Stationery Office.

HM Government (2009) *Pursue, prevent, protect, prepare: The United Kingdom's strategy for countering international terrorism*, Cm 7547, London: Stationery Office.

HM Government (2010) *Channel: Supporting individuals vulnerable to recruitment by violent extremists*, London: Home Office.

HM Government (2011a) *Positive for youth: A new approach to cross-government policy for young people aged 13-19* (www.education.gov.uk/positiveforyouth).

HM Government (2011b) *Prevent strategy*, London: Cabinet Office.

HM Inspector of Prisons/Youth Justice Board (2011) *Children and young people in custody 2010-11. An analysis of the experiences of 15-18 year olds in prison*, London: The Stationery Office.

HM Inspectorate (1990) *Youth work with black young people*, Stanmore: Department of Education and Science.

Home Office (1985) *The Brixton disorders 10-12 April 1981 (The Scarman Report)*, London: HMSO.

Home Office (2001) *Building cohesive communities: A report of the Ministerial Group on public disorder (The Denham Report)*, London: Home Office.

Home Office Task Force (2005) *Working together to prevent extremism*, London: Home Office, Cohesion and Faith Unit.

Hood, R. (1994) *Begrimed and black: Christian traditions on blacks and blackness*, Minneapolis, MN: Fortress Press.

hooks, b. (1994) *Outlaw culture*, London: Routledge.

hooks, b. (2003a) *Teaching community: A pedagogy of hope*, London: Routledge.

hooks, b. (2003b) *Rock my soul. Black people and self-esteem*, London: Atria Books.

Horton, M. and Freire, P. (1990) *We make the road by walking: Conversations on education and social change*, Philadelphia, PA: Temple University Press.

House of Commons Education Committee (2012) *Services for young people: Third report of Session 2010-2012, Vol 1*, London: The Stationery Office.

Humphrey, D. (1972) *Police, power and black people*, London: Panther.

Huntington, S.P. (1998) *The clash of civilisations and the remaking of the world order*, London: Touchstone.

Husain, S.S. and Ashraf, S.A. (1979) *Crisis in Muslim education*, Jeddah: King Abdulaziz University/Hodder and Stoughton.

Hussain, T. (2006) 'Working Islamically with young people or working with Muslim youth?', *Youth and Policy*, vol 92, pp 107–18.

Hussain, D., Malik, N. and Seddon, M.S. (2004) *British Muslim identity: British Muslims between assimilation and integration – historical, legal and social realities*, Markfield: The Islamic Foundation.

Husband, C. (ed) (1985) *Race in Britain: Continuity and change*, Melbourne: Hutchinson.

Husband, C. (2001) *Young people's entry into the labour market in a multi-ethnic city*, Bradford: University of Bradford.

Husband, C. (2005) 'Doing good by stealth, whilst flirting with racism. Some contradictory dynamics of British multiculturalism', in W. Boswick and C. Husband (eds) *Comparative European research in migration, diversity and identities*, Bilbao: University of Deusto, pp 191-206.

Husband, C. and Alam, Y. (2011) *Social cohesion and counter-terrorism: A policy contradiction*, Bristol: The Policy Press.

Ifekwunigwe, J. (1999) *Scattered belongings: Cultural paradoxes of race, nation and gender*, London: Routledge.

Iqbal, M. (translated by A.J. Arberry) (1953) *The Mysteries of the Self: A philosophical poem*, London; John Murray.

Imam, U.F. (1995) 'Youth workers as mediators and interpretors: ethical issues in work with black young people', in Banks, S. *Ethical issues in youth work,* London: Routledge.

Isiorho, D. (1998) *Deep Anglicanism: A sociological and political analysis of the mode of involvement of Black Christians in the C of E with special reference to English ethnicity*, Social and Economic Studies, Bradford: University of Bradford.

Iqbal, M. (translated by A.J. Arberry) (1953) *The Mysteries of the self: A philosophical poem translated with introduction and notes,* London: John Murray

Izetbegovic, A.A. (1993) *Islam between east and west*, Plainfield, IN: American Trust Publications.

Jacobson, J. (1997) 'Religion and ethnicity: dual and alternative sources of identity among British young Pakistanis', *Ethnic and Racial Studies*, vol 20, pp 238-56.

Jaques, R.K. (2010) *Belief in Jamal J. Elias: Key themes for the study of Islam*, Oxford: Oneworld Publications.

Jeffs, T. (2004) 'Curriculum debate: a letter to John Ord', *Youth & Policy*, no 84, pp 55-62.

Jeffs, T. and Smith, M. (1987) *Youth work*, Basingstoke: Macmillan Press.

Jeffs, T and Smith, M (1999) 'Resourcing youth work: Dirty hands and tainted money', in S. Banks, *Ethical issues in youth work*, London: Routledge.

Jeffs, T. and Smith, M. (2005) *Informal education: Conversation, democracy and learning*, Nottingham: Education Heretics Press.

Jeffs, T. and Smith M.K. (1989) *Young people, inequality and youth work*, Basingstoke: Palgrave Macmillan

Jeffs, T. and Smith, M.K. (2010) *Youth work practice*, Basingstoke: Palgrave Macmillan

Jenkins, M.P. (1995) *Children of Islam*, London: Trentham Books.

Jochum, V., Pratten, B. and Wilding, K. (2007) *Faith and voluntary action: An overview of current evidence and debates*, London: NCVO.

John, G. (1981) *In the service of black youth*, Leicester: National Association of Youth Clubs.

Joly, D. (1995) *Britannia's crescent: Making a place for Muslims in British society*, Aldershot: Avebury.

Jones, G. (2005) *The thinking and behaviour of young adults (aged 16-25)*, London: Social Exclusion Unit, Office of the Deputy Prime Minister.

Jones, S. (1988) *Black culture, white youth*, London: Macmillan Education.

Jordan, W.D. (1974) *The white man's burden*, Oxford: Oxford University Press.

Kabanni, R. (1986) *Europe's myths of Orient*, London: Macmillan Press Ltd.

Kahteran, N. (2006) 'Fitra' in O. Leaman *The Qur'an: An encyclopaedia*, London: Routledge

Kay, R. (1996) 'What kind of leadership do voluntary agencies need?', in D. Billis and M. Harris (eds) *Voluntary agencies: Challenges of organisation and management*, London: Macmillan Press, pp 130-48.

Khan, I.A. (2005) *Reflections on the Qur'an: Understanding Surah's Al-Fatihan and Al-Baqarah*, Leicester: Islamic Foundation.

Khan, K. (2009) *Preventing violent extremism (PVE) and PREVENT*, London: An-Nisa Society.

Khan, M.G. (2006) *Towards a national strategy for Muslim youth work*, Birmingham and Leicester: University of Birmingham and National Youth Agency.

Khan, M.G. (2012) 'Turning to my religion' in F. Ahmad and M.S. Seddon (eds) *Muslim youth, challenges, opportunities and expectations*, London: Continuum.

Khan, V.S. (ed) (1985) *The role of the culture of dominance in structuring the experience of ethnic minorities*, Melbourne: Hutchinson.

King, J. (1977) 'Tablighi Jamaat and Deobandi mosques', in S.V.A.C. Peach (ed) *Islam in Europe*, Basingstoke: Macmillan Press.

King, J. (1994) *Three Asian associations in Britain*, Monographs in Ethnic Relations, Coventry: Centre for Research in Ethnic Relations, University of Warwick.

Knapp, M. (1996) 'Are voluntary agencies really more effective?', in D. Billis and M. Harris (ed) *Voluntary agencies: Challenges and organisation and management*, London: Macmillan Press, pp 166-86.

Knight, B. (1993) *Voluntary action*, Newcastle upon Tyne: Centris.

Knight, M.M. (2007) *Taqwacores,* London: Telegram Books.

Knott, K. (1992) *The changing character of the religions of the ethnic minorities of Asian origin in Britain: Final report of Leverhulme Project*, Leeds: University of Leeds.

Kubler-Ross, E. (1970) *On death and dying*, London: Routledge.

Kugle, S.S.H. (2010) *Homosexuality in Islam*, Oxford: Oneworld Publications.

Kundnani, A. (2009) *Spooked: How not to prevent violent extremism*, London: Institute of Race Relations.

Ladinsky, D. (1999) *The gift: Poems by Hafiz the great Sufi master*, New York: Penguin Compass.

Ladinsky, D. (2002) *Love poems from God*, London: Penguin.

Ladkin, D. (2005) 'The enigma of subjectivity', *Action Research*, vol 3, no 1, pp 108-26.

Lapidus, I.P. (1988.) *A history of Islamic societies*, Cambridge: Cambridge University Press.

Lave, J. and Wenger, E. (1991) *Situated learning: Legitimate peripheral participation*, Cambridge: Cambridge University Press.

Leaman, O. (2006) *The Qur'an: An encyclopaedia*, London: Routledge.

Leat, D. (1996) 'Are voluntary organisations accountable', in D. Billis (ed) *Voluntary agencies: Challenges of organisation and management*, London: Macmillan Press, pp 61-79.

Leavitt, H.J., Leavitt, D.W. R. and Eyring, H.B. (1973) *The organisational world*, New York: Harcourt Brace Jovanovich, Inc.

Ledwith, M. and Springett, J. (2010) *Participatory practice: Community-based action for transformative change*, Bristol: The Policy Press.

Lee, R.M. (1993) *Doing research on sensitive topics*, London: Sage Publications.

Lentin, A. and Titley, G. (2011) *The crises of multiculturalism: Racism in a neoliberal age*, London: Zed Books.

Lesser, E. and Storck, J. (2001) 'Communities of practice and organisational performance', *IBM Systems Journal*, vol 40, pp 831 -41.

Lewis, P. (1997) 'The Bradford Council for Mosques', in S. Vertovec and C. Peach (eds) *Islam in Europe*, Basingstoke: Macmillan Press, pp 103-28.

Lewis, P. (2002) *Religion, politics and identity among British Muslims*, London: I.B. Tauris & Co.

Lings, M. (1983) *Muhammad: His life based on the earliest sources*, Cambridge: Islamic Texts Society.

Lings, M. (1991) *Symbol and archetype: A study of the meaning of existence*, Cambridge: Quinta Essentia.

Littlejohn, H.T. (2011) *Al-Ghazali on patience and thankfulness. Kitab al-sabr wa'l-shukr. Book XXXII of the revival of religious sciences Ihya: 'ulum al-din*, Cambridge: Islamic Texts Society.

Lorde, A. (2007) *Sister outsider*, Berkeley, CA: Crossing Press.

McLaren, P. (2003) 'Critical pedagogy: A look at the major concepts', in A. Darder, M. Baltodano and R.D. Torres, *The critical pedagogy reader*, London: Routledge, pp 69-96.

McLoughlin, S (2005) 'Mosques and the public space: conflict and cooperation in Bradford', *Journal of Ethnic and Migration Studies*, vol 31, no 6, November, pp 1045-66.

McRoy, A. (2005) *From Rushdie to 7/7: The radicalisation of Islam in Britain*, London: Social Affairs Unit.

Mac An Ghaill (2005) *Young Bangladeshi people's experience of transition to adulthood*, York: Joseph Rowntree Foundation.

MacDonald, I. (1989) *Murder in the playground: The Burnage Report*, London: Longsight Press.

Macpherson, W., Cook, T., Sentamu, J. and Stone, R. (1999) *The Stephen Lawrence Inquiry: Report of an inquiry by Sir William Macpherson of Cluny* (the Macpherson Report), Norwich: The Stationery Office

Maddern, K. (2010) 'Schools defy government on counter-terrorism', *The Times Education Supplement*, Friday 16 April.

Mahmood, S. (2005) *The politics of piety: The Islamic revival and the feminist subject*, Princeton, NJ: Princeton University Press.

Majeed, J. (2009) *Muhammad Iqbal, Islam, aesthetics and postcolonialism*, London: Routledge.

Marshall, G. (1998) *Oxford dictionary of sociology*, Oxford: Oxford University Press.

Marshall, T.F. (1996) 'Can we define the voluntary sector?', in D. Billis and M. Harris (eds) *Voluntary sector: Challenges of management and organisation*, London: Macmillan Press Ltd, pp 45-60.

Maslow, A.H. (1982) *Towards a psychology of being*, New York: Van Nostrand Reinhold International.

Mason, J. (1997) *Qualitative researching*, London: Sage Publications.

Masood, E. (2006) *British Muslims: Media guide*, London: British Council.

Mayer, T. (2005) *Al-Ghazali letter to a disciple Ayyuha'l-Walad. Bilingual English-Arabic edition*, Cambridge: Islamic Texts Society.

Mazrui, A. (1990) *Cultural forces in the political world*, London: James Currey.

Mernisi, F. (1987) *Women and Islam. An historical and theological enquiry.* Oxford: Blackwell.

Ministerial Conferences Steering Committee (1990) *Towards a core curriculum: The next step*, Report of responses to the Ministerial Conferences Steering Committee Consultation Document, Leicester: National Youth Bureau.

Ministry of Education (1944) *Education Act*, London: HMSO.

Ministry of Education (1960) *The youth service in England and Wales (The Albemarle Report)*, Cmnd 6458, London: HMSO.

Mir, M. (2006) *Iqbal*, London and New York: I.B. Tauris.

Modood, T. (1977) *Debating cultural hybridity*, London: Zed Books.

Modood, T. (1992) 'British Asian Muslims and the Rushdie affair', in J. Donald and A. Rattansi (ed) *'Race', culture and difference*, London: Sage Publications, pp 260-77.

Modood, T. (2005) *Multicultural politics: Racism, ethnicity and Muslims in Britain*, Edinburgh: Edinburgh University Press.

Mohamed, Y. (1996) *Fitra: The Islamic concept of human nature*, London: Ta-ha Publishers.

Mohamed, Y. (2006) 'Morality' in O. Leaman (2006) *The Qur'an: An encyclopaedia.* London: Routledge.

Morrell, G., Scott, S., McNeish, D. and Webster, S. (2011) *The August riots in England: Understanding involvement of young people*, London: National Centre for Social Research (NatCen).

Moustakas, C. (1990) *Heuristic research: Design methodology and application*, London; Sage.

Murata, S (1992) *The Tao of Islam,* Albany: State University of New York Press.

Murdock, G. and McCron, R. (1976) 'Consciousness of class and consciousness of generation', in S. Halls and T. Jefferson (eds) *Resistance through rituals: Youth subcultures in post-war Britain*, London: Hutchinson, pp 192-207.

Muslim Voice UK (2007) Submission on the proposed anti-terrorism laws.

Muslim World League (1992) *A guide to Islamic organisations*, Muslim World League.

Muslim Youth Helpline (2010) *Young British Muslims and relationships*, London: Muslim Youth Helpline.

Nairn, A. (2011) *Children's well-being in the UK, Sweden and Spain: The role of inequality and materialism*, London: Ipsos MORI.

Nasr, S.H. (1993) *The need for a sacred science*, Albany, NY: State University of New York Press.

Nasr, S.H. (1997) *Man and nature: The spiritual crisis in modern man.* Chicago: Kazi Publications.

Nasr, S.H. (1999) *Sufi essays*, Chicago, IL: Kazi Publications.

Nasr, S.H. (2010) *Islam in the modern world: Challenged by the West, threatened by fundamentalism, keeping faith with tradition,* New York: Harper Collins.

National Youth Bureau (1990) *Danger or opportunity? Towards a core curriculum*, Leicester: National Youth Bureau.

Neumann, S.M.A.P. (ed) (2006) *The year after the London bombings: An assessment*, London: Centre for Defence Studies, International Policy Institute, King's College.

Newby, G.D. (2002) *A concise encyclopaedia of Islam*, Oxford: Oneworld Publications.

Nicholls, D. (2012) *For youth workers and youth work: Speaking out for a better future*, Bristol: The Policy Press.

Nielsen, J. (1997) 'Muslims in Europe', in S. Vertovec and C. Peach (eds) *Islam in Europe: The politics of religion and community*, London: Macmillan Press Ltd.

Nielson, W.A. (1979) *The endangered sector*, New York: Columbia University Press.

Nolan, P.C. (ed) (2003) *Twenty years of youth and policy*, Leicester: National Youth Agency.

Nyman, A.-S. (2005) *Intolerance and discrimination against Muslims in the EU*, Vienna: International Helsinki Federation for Human Rights.

Office for Standards in Education (2003) *National voluntary youth organisations grants*, London: Ofsted Publications Centre.

Ord, J. (2004) 'The youth work curriculum and the transforming youth work agenda', *Youth & Policy*, no 83.

Osbourne, S.P. (1996) 'What kind of training does the voluntary sector need', in D. Billis and M. Harris (eds) *Voluntary agencies: Challenges of organisation and management*, London: Macmillan Press, pp 200-21.

Ouseley, H. (2001) *Community pride not prejudice: Making diversity work for Bradford*, Bradford: Bradford Vision.

Pamuk, O. (2005) *Snow*, London: Faber and Faber.

Pamuk, O. (2006) *Istanbul: Memories of a city*, London: Faber and Faber.

Parekh, B. (1983) 'Educational opportunity in multiethnic Britain', in N. Glazer and K. Young (eds) *Ethnic pluralism and public policy*, London: Heinemann, pp 108-23.

Parekh, B. (1992) 'Between holy text and moral void', in S. Hall, D. Held and T. McGrew (eds) *Modernity and its futures*, Cambridge: Polity Press (in association with Blackwell Publishers and The Open University).

Parekh, B. (1997) *When religion meets politics*, London: Demos.

Parekh, B. (2000) *Rethinking multiculturalism: Cultural diversity and political theory*, London: Macmillan Press Ltd.

Parkin, F. (1982) *Max Weber*, London: Tavistock.

Parsons, T. (1960) *Structure and process in modern societies*, Glencoe, IL: Free Press.

Parvez, Z. (2000) *Building a new society: An Islamic approach to social change*, Leicester: Revival Publications.

Patel, P. and Chauhan, V. (1998) *Guidelines for developing work with black young people*, Leicester: National Youth Agency.

Paton, R. (1996) 'How are values handled in voluntary agencies?', in D. Billis and M. Harris (eds) *Voluntary agencies: Challenges of organisation and management*, London: Macmillan Press Ltd, pp 29-44.

Peirce, G. (2010) *Dispatches from the dark side: On torture and the death of justice*, London: Verso.

Peperzak, A.T., Critchley, S. and Bernaconi, R. (1996) *Emmanuel Levinas: Basic philosophical writings*, Bloomington, IN: Indiana University Press.

Phillips, M. (2006) *Londonistan: How Britain is creating a terror state within*, London: Encounter Books.

Phizacklea, A. and Miles, R. (1980) *Labour and racism*, London: Routledge & Kegan Paul.

Poole, E. (2002) *Reporting Islam: Media representations of British Muslims*, London: I.B. Taurus.

Powell, J. (1999) *Why am I afraid to tell you who I am?*, London: Fount.

Pretty, J.N. (1995) *Regenerating agriculture: Policies and practice for sustainability and self-reliance*, London: Earthscan.

Ramadan, T. (2004) *Western Muslims and the future of Islam*, Oxford: Oxford University Press.

Ramadan, T. (2009) *Radical reform: Islamic ethics and liberation*, Oxford: Oxford University Press.

Rampton, A. (1981) *West Indian children in our schools: Interim report of the Committee of Inquiry into the education of children from ethnic minority groups*, London: Department of Education and Science.

Ranjan, G. and Clegg, S.R. (1997) 'An inside story: tales from the field – doing organisational research in a state of insecurity', *Organisation Studies*, vol 18, pp 1015-23.

Raudvere, C. (2002) *The book and the roses: Sufi women, visibility and Zikr in contemporary Istanbul*, London: I.B. Taurus.

Redman, P. and Kapasi, R. (1994) *Asian good and kicking: Anti-racism, cultural studies and HIV prevention*, Birmingham: East Birmingham Health Promotion Service.

Rex, J. (1982) 'West Indian and Asian youth', in E. Cashmore and B. Troyna (ed) *Black youth in crisis*, London: Goerge Allen & Unwin, pp 53–71.

Rifaat, A. (1987) *Distant views of a minaret*, Portsmouth: N.H. Heinemann,

Rochester, C. (2010–11) 'Re-thinking voluntary action', Notes for a series of seminars held at Roehampton University, Unpublished.

Rodinson, M. (1988) *Europe and the mystique of Islam*, London: I.B. Taurus.

Rogers, C. (1961) *On becoming a person: A therapist's view of psychotheraphy*, Boston: Houghton Mifflin.

Rogers, C. (1980) *A way of being*, Boston: Houghton Mifflin.

Runnymede Trust (1977) *Islamophobia: A challenge for us all*, London: Runnymede Trust.

Runnymede Trust on Anti-Semitism (1994) *A very light sleeper: The persistence and dangers of anti-Semitism*, London: Runnymede Trust.

Ruthven, M. (1991) *A Satanic affair: Salman Rushdie and the wrath of Islam*, London: Hogarth Press.

Safak, E. (2010) *The forty rules of love*, London: Viking Penguin.

Safran, W. (1991) 'Diasporas in modern societies', *Diaspora*, vol 1, pp 83–99.

Sahgal, G. and Yuval Davies, N. (1992) *Refusing holy orders*, London: Virago Press.

Said, E. (1978) *Orientalism*, Harmondsworth: Penguin.

Said, E. (1981) *Covering Islam*, London: RKP.

Said, E. (1993) *Culture and imperialism*. London: Chatto and Windus

Saini, A. (2006) '"Islam for me was more punk than punk", Nawaz interviewed', *openDemocracy*.

Salecl, R. (2011) *The tyranny of choice*, London: Profile Books.

Sallah, M. and Howson, C. (2007) *Working with black young people*, Lyme Regis: Russell House Publishing.

Samad, Y. (1996) 'The politics of Islamic identity among Bangladeshis and Pakistanis in Britain', in T. Ranger, Y. Samad and O. Stuart (eds) *Culture, identity and politics*, Aldershot: Avebury.

Samsudin, M.Z. (2005) 'Psychology of motivation from an Islamic perspective', Paper presented at the 3rd International Seminar on Learning and Motivation, Faculty of Cognitive Sciences and Education, Universiti Utara Malaysia, Sintok.

Samy Alim, H. (2005) 'Exploring the transglobal hip hop umma', in M. Cooke and B.B. Lawrence (eds) *Muslim networks: From hajj to hip hop*, Chapel Hill: University of North Carolina Press.

Sapin, K. (2009) *Essential skills for youth work practice*, London: Sage.

Sardar, Z. (1985) *Islamic futures: The shape of ideas to come*, London: Mansell Publishing Ltd.

Sardar, Z. (2004) *Desperately seeking paradise: Journeys of a sceptical Muslim*, London: Granta Books.

Sardar, Z. (2011) *Reading the Qur'an*, London: Hurst & Company.

Sayer, A. (2005) *The moral significance of class*, Cambridge: Cambridge University Press.

Sayyid, S. (1997) *A fundamental fear*, London: Zed Books.

Sayyid, S. and Vakil, A. (2010) *Thinking through Islamaphobia: Global perspectives*, London: C. Hurst & Co Ltd.

Schimmel, A. (1994) *Deciphering the signs of God: A phenomenological approach to Islam*, Albany, NY: State University of New York Press.

Scott, R.W. (2003) *Organisations: Rational, natural and open systems*, Upper Saddle River, NJ: Prentice Hall.

Seddon, M.S., Hussain, D. and Malik, N. (2004) *British Muslims between assimilation and segregation*, Markfield: Islamic Foundation.

Seierstad, A. (2003) *The Bookseller of Kabul*. London: Virago

Select Committee on Race Relations and Immigration (1969) *The problems of coloured school leavers*, London: HMSO.

Sells, M. (1999) *Approaching the Qur'an: The early revelations*, Ashland, OR: White Cloud Press.

Selznick, P. (1957) *Leadership in administration*, New York: Harper & Row.

Shah, I. (1978) *Learning how to learn*, London: Octagon Press.

Sha-Kazemi, R. (2011) *Justice and remembrance: Introducing the spirituality of Imam Ali*, London: I.B. Taurus.

Shaikh, F. (1992) *Islam and Islamic groups: A worldwide reference guide*, London: Longman.

Shukra, K. (2008) 'From anti-oppressive practice to community cohesion', *Youth & Policy*, no 100, pp 231-40.

Siddiqui, A. (1998) 'Muslim youth: between tradition and modernity in Britain', Eighth International Conference of WAMY, Amman, Jordan, 20-23 October.

Singerman, D. (2004) 'The networked world of Islamist social movements', in Q. Wiktorowicz (ed) *Islamic activism: A social movement theory approach*, Bloomington, IN: University of Indiana Press, pp 143-63.

Sivanandan, A. (1982) *Writing on Black resistance*, London: Pluto.

Small, S.V. (1994) *From arts to welfare*, London: Sia.

Snow, D. and Benford, R.D. (1988) 'Ideology, frame resonance and participant mobilisation', in B. Klandermass (ed) *From structure to action: Comparing movement participation across cultures: International social movement research*, Greenwich, CT: JAI Press.

Solomos, J. (1988) *Black youth, racism and the state*, Cambridge: Cambridge University Press.

Soni, S. (2011) *Working with diversity*, Exeter: Learning Matters.

Sorhaindo, A. and Feinstein, L. (2007) *The role of youth clubs in integrated provision for young people: An assessment of a model of practice*, London: Institute of Education, University of London.

Soroush, A. (2000) *Reason, freedom and democracy in Islam*, Oxford: Oxford University Press.

Spalek, B. (2011) '"New terrorism" and crime prevention initiatives involving Muslim young people in the UK: research and policy contexts', *Religion, State and Society*, vol 39, nos 2/3, pp 191-207.

Spence, J. (2006) 'Working with girls and young women: A broken history', in R. Gilchrist, T. Jeffs and J. Spence (eds) *Drawing on the past: Essays in the history of community and youth work*, Leicester: NYA.

Sultan, S. (2004) *The Koran for dummies*, Hoboken, NJ: Wiley Publishing.

Sunier, T. (1998) 'Islam and interest struggle: religious collective action among Turkish Muslims in the Netherlands', in S. Vertovec and R. Rogers (eds) *Muslim European youth: Reproducing ethnicity, religion and culture*, Aldershot: Ashgate, pp 39-58.

Sunier, T. and Van Kuijeren, M. (2002) 'Islam in the Netherlands', in Yazbeck Haddad, Y. (ed) *Muslims in the West: From sojourners to citizens*. New York: Oxford University Press, 144-157.

Tajfel, H. (1982) *Social identity and intergroup relations*, Cambridge: Cambridge University Press.

Taylor, C. (1992) 'The politics of recognition', in A. Gutmann (ed) *Multiculturalism and the politics of recognition*, Princeton, NJ: Princeton University Press.

Taylor, M. (1996) 'What are the key influences on the voluntary sector?', in D. Billis and M. Harris (eds) *Voluntary agencies: Challenges of organisation and management*, London: Macmillan Press, pp 13-28.

Thompson, A. (1982) *Experience and participation: Report of the Review Group on the youth service in England*, London: HMSO.

Thompson, N. (2006) *Anti-discriminatory practice*, Basingstoke: Palgrave Macmillan.

Thompson, S. and Betts, J. (2003) 'Youth work and anti-racism', in P.C. Nolan (ed) *Twenty years of youth and policy*, Leicester: National Youth Agency.

Treacher, A. (2006) 'Something in the air: otherness, recognition and ethics', *Journal of Social Work Practice*, vol 20, no 1, pp 27-37.

Trimingham, J.S. (1998) *The Sufi orders in Islam*, Oxford: Oxford University Press.

Troyna, B. and Williams, J. (1986) *Racism, education and the state*, London: Croom Helm.

UK Action Committee on Islamic Affairs (1993) *Muslims and the law in multi-faith Britain*, London: UK Action Committee on Islamic Affairs.

Ul Hassan, M.S. (1992) *A guide to Islamic organisations and institutions*, Makkah al- Mukarramah: Muslim World League.

Unison (2011) 'New figures reveal £200m of youth service cuts', Press release 26 October (www.unison.org.uk/asppresspack/pressrelease_view.asp?id=2503).

Vertovec, S. and Peach, C. (1997) *Islam in Europe: The politics of religion and community*, Basingstoke: Macmillan Press.

Vickers, M. (2002) 'Researchers as storytellers: writing on the edge and without a safety net', *Qualitative Inquiry*, vol 8, pp 608-21.

Ward, L. (2005) 'Youth clubs can be bad for you, says report', *The Guardian*, 20 January.

Watson, J. (1977) *Between two cultures*, Oxford: Blackwell.

Watt, W.M. (1953) *Muhammad at Mecca*, Oxford: Oxford University Press.

Weber, M. (1964) *Essays in sociology*, London: Routledge.

Wenger, E. (1998) *Communities of practice*, Cambridge: Cambridge University Press.

Werbner, P. (2002) *Imagined diasporas among Manchester Muslims*, Oxford: James Currey.

Werbner, P. (2003) *Pilgrims of love: The anthropology of a Sufi cult*, London: Hurst & Company.

Werbner, P. (2005) 'Islamophobia, incitement to religious hatred – legislating for a new fear', *Anthropology Today*, vol 21, pp 5-9.

Westwood, S. (1995) 'Gendering diaspora: space, politics and South Asian masculinities in Britain', in P. van der Veer (ed) *Nation and migration: The politics of space in the South Asian diaspora*, Philadelphia, PA: University of Pennsylvania Press.

Wiktorowicz, Q. (2004) *Islamic activism: A social movement theory approach*, Bloomington, IN: Indiana University Press.

Wiktorowicz, Q. (2005) *Radical Islam rising: Muslim extremism in the West*, Lanham, MD: Rowman & Littlefield Publishing, Inc.

Williams, B. (2001) 'Global youth work is good youth work', in Factor, F., Chauhan, V. and Pitts, J. *The RHP Companion to Working with Young People*. Lyme Regis: Russel House Publishing.

Winter, R. (1987) *Action-research and the nature of social inquiry*, Aldershot: Gower Publishing Company.

Winter, T. (2003) 'Muslim loyalty and belonging: some reflections on the psychological background', in M.S. Seddon, D. Hussain and N. Malik, *British Muslims: Loyalty and belonging*, Markfield: The Islamic Foundation.

Winter, T.J. (2005) *Al-Ghazali on disciplining the soul: Kitab Riyadat al-Nafs and on breaking the two desires. Kitab kasr al-shawatayn. Books XXII and XXIII of the revival of the religious sciences Ihya' 'ulum al-din*, Cambridge: Islamic Texts Society.

Wolfe, M. (2005) 'Conversation' in L. Deer Richardson and M. Wolfe, *Principles and practice of informal education: Learning through life*, Abingdon: Routledge Falmer.

Wolfenden Committee (1978) *The future of voluntary organisations*, London: Croom Helm.

Yavuz, H. (2004a) 'Is there a Turkish Islam? The emergence of convergence and consensus', *Journal of Muslim Minority Affairs*, vol 24, pp 213-51.

Yavuz, H. (2004b) 'Opportunity spaces, identity, and Islamic meaning in Turkey', in R. Yin, *Case study Research* (2nd edn), London: Sage Publications.

Yavuz, H.M. and Esposito, J.L. (eds) (2003) *Turkish Islam and the secular state.* New York: Syracuse University Press

Young, K. (1999) *The art of youth work*, Lyme Regis: Russell House Publishing.

Youth Service Development Council (1967) *Immigrants and the youth service (The Hunt Report)*, London: HMSO.

Yusuf, H. (2004) *Purification of the heart: Signs, symptoms, and cures of the spiritual diseases of the heart – Translation and commentary of Imam al-Mawlud's matharat al-Qulub*, Bridgeview, IL: Starlatch Press.

Yusuf, H. (2010) *The prayer of the oppressed*, Sandala Publications.

Yuval-Davis, N. and Silverman, M. (1988*) Racialised discourses on Jews and Arabs in Britain and France*, Greenwich: University of Greenwich.

Zizek, S. (2002) *Welcome to the desert of the real*, London: Verso.

Zizek, S. (2011) *Living in the end of times*, London: Verso.

Index

A

Abbott, Diane 180
Abdullah, Sufi 137
Abou El Fadl, K. 43
accountability to God 60
action, and knowledge 36
activism, Muslim 112, 117–18, 126–7, 136, 146
adl (justice) 50
Ahmad, Faraz 180–1
aid agencies, Muslim 113, 149
Aidi, Hishaam 176
Aisha (wife of Muhammad) 86
Alam, Yunis 96, 152, 155
Alexander, Claire 152
Ali, Yasmin 116
Ali, Yusuf 41, 64
alienation 48–9
  in Islam 50–1, 55–6, 64, 69–70
  of young Muslims 145
Allen, C. 154, 155
Ansari, D.M.F.U.R. 138
anthropological research *see* social science research
anti-immigration sentiments 154
anti-Muslimism 155
  see also Islamophobia
anti-oppressive practices 80, 81–2, 90–1
anti-racism approaches 79
anti-Semitism 155
anti-terrorism legislation/policies 152, 153, 157–8, 159–60, 162–3
  impact of 115, 116, 134–5, 163, 165, 166, 168, 170, 180–1
  see also CONTEST Strategy; PVE programme
Apple, M.W. 38
Asad, Talal 98
Ashraf, S.A. 58
The Asian gang (Alexander) 152
attributes 58–9
authenticity 132
  of youth workers 23–4
authority, types of 128
ayats (signs) 34–5, 177

B

bad, and good 61–2
Baden-Powell, Robert 12
Bakhtiar, L. 52, 55
Bakr, Abu 180–1
Banks, S. 171
Barelvi *masjids* 144
Batmangelidjh, Camila 84
Baudrillard, J. 2
beards 147
Belton, B. 110
Benford, R.D. 145
Berger, P.L. 48, 119, 131
Berjak, Rafik 87
'Big Society' 2–3, 116
Billis, David 111–13, 118, 120, 121, 129, 132–3, 139, 144, 145
Birmingham 135, 137, 140, 162
Blacker, H. 22–3
Blacks
  empowerment of 31
  youth work for 4, 5, 8, 17, 102, 179–80
Blair, Tony 78
Blunkett, David 156
BNP (British National Party) 154
The bookseller of Kabul (Seierstad) 100
Bousted, Mary 103
Boys' Brigade 12, 13
Bradford 146
Bridging the Gap programme 15, 17
British Empire 12, 143–4
British Muslim Forum 141
Bronfenbrenner, U. 38
Buchman, D. 28
bureaucracies 120, 124
Butters, S. 32

C

Cameron, David 15, 156
Cantle Report (Home Office, 2001) 15, 153, 170
Castells, M. 17, 40
charismatic leadership 127–8
  in Muslim organisations 137–8, 141, 142